Atticus Greene Haygood, George F. Pierce

Bishop Pierce's Sermons and Addresses

With a few special discourses by Dr. Pierce

Atticus Greene Haygood, George F. Pierce

Bishop Pierce's Sermons and Addresses
With a few special discourses by Dr. Pierce

ISBN/EAN: 9783337266042

Printed in Europe, USA, Canada, Australia, Japan

Cover: Foto ©Lupo / pixelio.de

More available books at **www.hansebooks.com**

BISHOP PIERCE'S
Sermons and Addresses.

WITH A FEW

SPECIAL DISCOURSES BY DR. PIERCE.

EDITED BY
REV. ATTICUS G. HAYGOOD, D.D., LL.D.

NASHVILLE, TENN.
Southern Methodist Publishing House.
1886.

Entered, according to Act of Congress, in the year 1886,
BY THE BOOK AGENTS OF THE METHODIST EPISCOPAL CHURCH, SOUTH,
in the Office of the Librarian of Congress, at Washington.

INTRODUCTION.

THREE characteristic sermons of Dr. Lovick Pierce are included in this volume. It is to be regretted that no sermons of his early ministry could be found. Dr. Pierce began to write in the latter part of his seventy-five years' ministry; it is doubtful if he wrote a dozen sermons during the first fifty years of his itinerant life. I have not found any that belong to the first forty years; there are only a few unclothed and imperfect skeletons that bear evidence of having been "put together" after preaching. For example: I find among some old scraps of papers three or four pages of notes of a discourse delivered at the funeral of the Rev. Hope Hull—a man he greatly honored and loved. One familiar with Dr. Pierce's preaching would conclude from the size and shape of these few "bones" that this funeral-sermon was one of his two hours' masterful discourses.

Dr. Pierce never wrote many sermons; it is almost certain that he never delivered a sermon from manuscript. It would have been very awkward to him, and partly because he thought it "wrong" for a Methodist preacher to read sermons. I never saw him with a "scrap of paper" in the pulpit, except, now and then, a copy of the numbers of the hymns he had given to the choir leader.

His method of preparation for the pulpit was to him so simple that he thought any man of "good natural parts" could practice it if he would, though most men who have any conception of what thorough work is could neither wear nor use the armor of this preaching king. He did not write, he did not make notes, he did not think out his sermons in detail; his mind was saturated with the Scriptures, he was always thinking, he brooded over his themes, he was always full of topics, and, as a rule, could preach as well with thirty minutes' as thirty days' notice. The topic, say, was conformity to the world. He had thought it through in a general way, some instances were brought to his attention, an opportunity to preach came to him, and at once a fit text rose up in his thoughts. He never went "fishing for texts," and as to other men's "Skeletons of Sermons" it was a humiliation to him that any preacher ever used them. All he wanted was five minutes to "put the text on its basis," as he expressed it to me once, and he was ready to begin. He knew the road he wished to travel, and entered it without first counting the mile-posts; and he would as unhesitatingly clear a road where he had "blazed a few trees" as he would take the beaten highway.

I do not believe that he ever arranged two sentences before beginning to preach; the sermons in this volume were written after delivery. How many thousands of sermons he preached he never knew himself; it is doubtful if any preacher ever handled as many different texts.

Most of this volume is taken up with sermons and speeches by Bishop Pierce. He wrote little; writing was very irksome to him—chiefly, I think, because he wrote slowly and thought very rapidly. He shared his father's opinion—I had almost said prejudice—against writing sermons. Most of the few sermons that Bishop Pierce wrote were put on paper after preaching, with this difference as compared with his father: some of the sermons the Bishop wrote after preaching he would preach again. I do not believe that the "Old Doctor" ever preached what he had written—partly because the occasion had passed, and partly because he did not like to be inconsistent with his view of the best preparation for the pulpit. I have evidence that some of the "Conference sermons" in this collection were first preached in Sparta, in his home church—"blocked out" as the Bishop once expressed it to me—then preached at some Conference, then written out, and afterward preached repeatedly. There was this among other differences between the two great preachers: the son could repeat a sermon, and often did; the father did not, and, except as to substance of thought and general form, could not. This also as to preparation: the son could think a sermon through, exegesis, arguments, enlargement, illustrations, and the very words, and deliver it as accurately as if he had written and memorized it. Knowing this peculiar gift of his tenacious memory for words as well as thoughts, I once ventured to say to him that his condemnation of those who could not do like him and must needs write on paper in order to memorize was hardly fair. To me he seemed unconscious of any peculiar gift of the sort here mentioned.

Most of Bishop Pierce's sermons and speeches that were written out in full by him are in this volume. A few have been published in pamphlet form before, and one in the Smithson collection of sermons. They are included in this collection to give them permanent form, and because they fairly represent their author in some of his best moods. In selecting them I have been guided by two principles: first, to publish those that most characteristically express the great preacher at different periods of his ministry and on different occasions; second, to publish those he attached most importance to, because he thought them most likely to do good.

Bishop Pierce often disappointed his admirers by choosing for some state occasion the plainest and most practical of themes. He abhorred being made a show of. The country churches in Hancock county, where his former neighbors worshiped, heard from his lips not only as good but as eloquent preaching as he ever did. He was more apt to give them a brilliant, electrifying sermon than to splendid congregations in the great city churches; not because he tried to preach so to them, but because he was "off guard" in the midst of his plain neighbors, and did not try not to please the ear and tickle the fancy of the curious.

I have on my desk, while writing this brief Introduction, a sort of "log-book" used by Bishop Pierce for thirty years. It is a plain blank-book, and the first entry is as follows: "1. Heb. iv. 16—Greensboro, Ga., Jan. 31, 1836." The last on the last page is as follows: "6,382—2 Cor. viii. 12—Culverton, Ga., Dec. 16, 1866."

After this he grew tired of keeping the account; the little book was full to the last page, and I find no further memoranda of texts, places, and times. All who care to know his manner of life will be sorry to learn that this little book of dates, texts, and places is all in the shape of diary that exists. He only noted what in his view was the important thing in his life—his preaching. In the whole record there is nothing but what is here given—not a note as to the "occasion," the "effect on the congregation," the "comments of the press." I think he never cut out and pasted in a scrapbook any newspaper notice of any thing he ever did.

If there is any difference in the indications of these brief memoranda of his preaching, it is that after he became Bishop he was more intensely practical and evangelical in his ministry.

One month during the thirty years he seems to have been silent. It was in 1859. He had started to California by the overland route. I find the record thus: "New Orleans, April 25; Shreveport, May 1; Rusk, May 4; San Marcos, May 14, 15; Stringtown, May 15 (three sermons that Sunday); San Antonio, May 19; Uvalde, May 21; San Francisco, June 19—morning and evening." October 10 he preached at Los Angeles—between San Francisco and Los Angeles preaching fifty times.

The record is not complete—being most imperfect in 1860 and 1861. The storm was gathering and breaking, and his long habit of jotting down his texts, places, and times for awhile lost its hold upon him. There are only eight sermons noted in 1861, and they were all preached in Hancock county. For 1862 the record appears to be nearly complete.

It would be hard to say which preacher—the father or the son—most rejoiced in preaching. It was to each a perpetual delight. They were unhappy if silent two successive Sundays; they preached every opportunity that offered, and would make opportunity if it was slow coming. Both did their best preaching in the midst of revivals, and for their best efforts were consciously dependent on the presence and power of God. They responded promptly to evidences of interest and emotion in their hearers, and deprecated to their dying-day the growing fashion of suppressing feeling.

It is not the language of exaggeration to say that not many greater preachers have appeared in Methodist history. Possibly future times may develop as great or greater preachers, but two such men will appear no more; the conditions of life that made them what they were are gone forever.

It should be said in conclusion that these sermons and addresses have been "edited" only in the sense that they have been prepared for the printer. It was not my place to harmonize—if there were need of it—expressions in sermons and speeches delivered years apart and under different surroundings. Nor would it have been fair to the honored dead to have toned down language here and there that may displease the fastidious. These preachers, while yet among us, did not study to please, but to do good. What is in this volume, as far as it goes, expresses what these men believed to be the very truth. Let it go forth to continue the ministry which was so long a joy and blessing to the Church.

ATTICUS G. HAYGOOD.

OXFORD, GA., March 1, 1886.

Contents.

SERMONS.

	PAGE
Devotedness to Christ	63
Why Women Should be Well Educated	90
Paul's Commission to Preach. By Dr. Lovick Pierce	110
The Word of God a Nation's Life	137
Make Full Proof of Thy Ministry	158
The Office and Work of a Bishop. By Dr. Lovick Pierce	179
Christ and Him Crucified	218
Paul's Charge to the Elders in Ephesus	232
Bishop James Osgood Andrew	249
The Moral Power of a Good Woman. By Dr. Lovick Pierce	267
Mary's Love	291
The Inadequacy of Secular Learning	307
Friendship with the World Enmity with God	318
Moral Principles the Only Safeguard	335
Character and Work of a Gospel Minister	353

ADDRESSES.

Learning and Religion	9
Church Colleges	38
Public Opinion	203
The Portrait of a Friend and Helper	330
Revival Needed. Addressed to the Church through the Press	367

(8)

SERMONS AND ADDRESSES.

Learning and Religion.*

YOUNG gentlemen, summoned by your kindness, I appear before you, not only as an act of reciprocal courtesy, but in obedience to a higher impulse—the desire to be useful.

Custom has appropriated occasions like this to the discussion of questions connected with literature, science, and elocution so exclusively that a change may strike you not only with the disagreeableness of surprise, but disappoint you of your anticipated entertainment. The subjects to which I have referred are rich, various, and elevated; yet every inch of ground within the length and breadth of their range has been occupied and cultivated, and now every division of the land is called by some mighty name. If I had no other reason for change of topic, the simple fact that Boaz and his reapers had been before me would justify me in seeking another field—one that has neither been mowed nor gleaned.

---

*This address was delivered before the Few and Phi Gamma Societies of Emory College, Oxford, Georgia, at the Commencement, July 19, 1842. A considerable portion of it was introduced into an address delivered at the anniversary of the American Bible Society, in New York, during the session of the General Conference of 1844. The most careful search failed to find the speech as delivered in New York. The address, as it appears here, was published by request of the two literary societies soon after its delivery in 1842. By request of the same societies it was republished in 1852.—EDITOR.

But why should religious subjects be denied a prominent place in the literature of the country? Why should this, the largest territory over which the mind of man has ever expatiated, be excluded from the republic of letters? By whose authority, by what enactment, has it been ordained that these themes should be restricted to the Sabbath and to the temple of God, and that the introduction of them on other occasions should be regarded as a trespass on taste and an infringement of propriety? It is high time that the class of men who arrogate to themselves the right of building up or pulling down, of recommendation to fame or consignment to obscurity—who assume to be the guardians of learning and the standards of judgment—proscribing this and adopting that, should learn that wisdom will live long after they are dead. These self-constituted judges pronounce upon style without regard to doctrine, and give a certificate of character to a book that it may make its way in the world, though it deals death at every step, and leaves desolation throughout its progress. The eloquence of the language redeems the corruption of the sentiments, and the skill of the swordsman disguises the agonies of the victim.

I am aware that the conventional signification of the term "literature" restricts the application of it to essays, novels, poetry, periodicals, and kindred works, with all their diversity of characters, incidents, and themes; but in all these there is no inculcation of religious truth of set design. An occasional moral reflection—the making of the catastrophe of a tale speak upon the side of virtue, satirizing an unfashionable vice—can never invest a book with a moral character or neutralize the evil of its tendency. The subtle poison, though diluted and spiced, will infect with disease, which, however modified in its development, is the pledge and precursor of death.

Works confessedly designed for entertainment rather than

the communication of useful knowledge must needs be accommodated to popular sentiment and prevailing taste; and these demand, as the food of their gratification, what is an element of destruction to the nobler powers of the understanding and the better interests of human society. And those who in the chase of honor or the lust of gold cater to the morbid cravings of a fastidious, dainty, vitiated appetite, in the very extravagance of accommodation, corrupt in order to indulge, and kill for the sake of pleasing. Books are made to order; and authors, shifting all responsibility from themselves to the applicant, coolly delude into error, if not vice, by removing the way-marks of virtue, and fritter away the distinctions of right and wrong by reducing the standard of obligation and erecting upon the substratum of what are called the honorable principles of human nature the filigree temple of a morality in which no God is recognized but fashion, and no creed but licentiousness. These magicians so invest sensual pleasure with the enchantments of genius that the unholy theme well-nigh beguiles the imagination of the purest. Nature's solitudes are peopled with their fairy creations, and all her echoes held mute by their minstrelsy. The flowers of the garden, the herbs of the field and the forest, the everlasting rocks, from their summits in the clouds to their deep foundations in the earth, all have their worshipers, riding upon the ocean, wayfaring in the desert, making pilgrimage to every region of nature for offerings to their patron muses. The noble sentiments of the heart, domestic joys, sorrows radiant with virtue's light, or dark with the gloom of guilt, all have their priests and sacrifices and devotees. All these have been wrought into the song of love, the voluptuous poem, the dramatic tale, the romantic story, and have been mingled with scenes and characters and opinions disgusting, abominable, and impious. Those that are too graceful to offend, too chaste to be reproved, yet minister no good, exist and operate in utter separation from the true interests, the high destinies of man, whether regarded as a useful citizen of the country or a responsible subject of the divine government.

This light literature, made up as it is of fine words and false sentiments, oftentimes, like the seed borne upon the winds, has fallen, vegetated, matured into harvest far beyond the fields from whence it sprung. Now, when we remember that reading is the food of thought, and thought the cause of action, who that thinks can but feel the necessity of impregnating literature with religious truth, and imbuing the now discordant mass with the leaven of salvation? Ministers and servants of God, stepping beyond the limits of pulpit theology, must throw into all their effusions, whether from the press or the rostrum, an admixture of pious thought and devotional feeling; must secure passage for the Bible upon every vehicle—history, science, politics, poetry, sentiment—and give it circulation round the world; for if, like its author, it were permitted "to go about," like him, it would "do good."

The age in which we live is remarkable in its aspects, literary, political, and religious. The causes which have operated to produce these appearances are as various as their effects; and the developments of character that have been molded by them all indicate the presence and dominion of feelings and opinions malign and corrupting. To analyze them is not my purpose. The futility of the attempt would rebuke the trespass upon your patience. Nevertheless, it is worthy of remark that the agencies which for the last few years have been at work upon the human mind demonstrate the identity of their design by uniformity of evil, whatever the diversity of results. Whatever the shape, it has been Proteus still. The rush of energy which has marked the movements of society, in the fury of its progress and the recklessness of its demands, has proscribed all soberness of judgment, and swept the multitude along by the force of an impulse too capricious for examination and too headlong for reflection. Men and books and opinions have all partaken of the same qualities. Strong, rapid, intense, these have been their characteristics. The only antagonistic principle in the mechanism of motives that could have preserved an equilibrium has been wanting; and the human mind, wrought up well-nigh to frenzy by the perpetual application of stimulants, has grown vagrant and vicious, frothy and frivolous, seeking rest and finding none; the sport of every freak of fancy and of passion, and careless at last of its foul disfigurement, is glad to find forgetfulness of its miseries in the turbid excitement of the worst opinions and the vilest crimes.

Adaptation to such a mental state is the desideratum in every thing, without which no moral property can secure it currency, and with which no perilous effect will prevent embracement. The consequence has been and is that truth, without the gold ring and the goodly apparel, without the parade of paradox or the pretension of novelty, has been despised; while falsehood, with letters of credit, has been lifted to pride of place and power of position because of the boldness of its diction and the effrontery of its air. Sentiments which ought to have been denounced for their impiety have been tolerated for the daring of their independence. Actions which ought to have stigmatized the perpetrator as a felon, and have consigned him to the gibbet or the prison, have been admired for the vigor of their conception and the hardihood of their execution. That famous line,

> One murder makes a villain; millions, a hero,

contains at once the rule of judgment and the principle of action. Sin—corruption on a small scale—has been construed to betray a littleness of soul beyond redemption, to define a straggler upon the trail where mind has marched, too feeble to follow, too worthless to be carried, and fit only for contempt. A bolder crime, though a more decided expression of the same depravity, has been mitigated of its horror by the facetiousness of its name, or even invested with a charm by the splendor of its title. In the one case the criminal has been arraigned, condemned, sent out upon the earth a vagabond, with the law's penal brand upon him; the other has been pitied as an archangel fallen, lionized as a man capable of glorious virtue, though stained with foulest crime.

But a little while ago the rabid lust of gold luxuriated in the abundance of its treasures, taxed winds and waves and forest to minister to its cravings, climbed mountains, crossed seas, visited islands, reaped and gleaned and garnered, pulled down its old barns and built greater, ate the lambs of the flock, lay down upon beds of ivory, invented instruments of music like David, and in the extravagance of its folly and the carnival of its delight polluted the very vessels of the sanctuary with the wine of its intoxication. But now, stripped, bereaved, forlorn, it mourns in stupid grief, or raves in wild insanity, the barrenness of its fields, the spoliations of its commerce, and the bankruptcy of all its resources, and even the futurity of its hopes is shrouded in cheerless, palpable gloom.*

The convulsions of the monetary world seem to have produced or developed a depravity unparalleled, to have loosened all the habits of business honesty, to have stirred the foundations of character with the upheaving, disruptive energy of an earthquake. Over society at large degeneracy has gone like a wave of ruin. Law is weak in its

---

*This speech was delivered when the country was in deep financial depression.—EDITOR.

strongest arm; morality is prostrate; politics, disjoined from patriotism, has become a mere strife of tongues; the legislature, Congress, the country, alike one unvaried scene of change, licentiousness, and tumult. The storm-spirit is upon the waters, and the elements, roused and raging, dash in eternal collisions the interests and passions of men. The world, exhausted and bewildered, is powerless to do or to plan. The necessity to do something, pressing alike upon every department of society, has produced words without knowledge, commotion without action, restlessness without progress, and enterprise without achievement. Where is the remedy to be found? Must we await the action of natural causes? invoke the aid of legislation, and hope against hope for a brighter, better day? Society never works off its own evils by fermentation unless there is the importation of a foreign ingredient. There is no self-purifying process, and the evils that afflict humanity are too subtle and intangible oftentimes to be subjected to any of the modes of correction known to the laws of the land. The best that fleshly wisdom can do is, by a modification of existing and intolerable corruption, to substitute a less for a greater. And perhaps yet oftener, when once the turbid, violent effervescence of public passion has subsided, and the raging fires that flamed beneath the mighty caldron have expired in ashes, it is found that the elements of evil have only been boiled down to consistency and substance. Agitated or at rest, there is death in the mixture, unless the meal, the leaven of Christianity, be cast into the vessel.

A formidable obstruction to any salutary change is to be found in the fact that the simplest truths are those which the human mind is the slowest to learn. Too often obscurity is the proof of wisdom, and involved and tortuous arrangement presumptive evidence of genius and adaptation for great results. This is true in philosophy; it is so in the business of civil government, and especially so in education and religion. A doctrine too true for controversy, an opinion too trite and obvious for explication or argument when expressed at large, is the very point which the perversity of the human mind evades. If unperceived before, it is rejected in compliment to that pride of heart which spurns the idea of dependence, and disdains the confession of ignorance; if perceived, because simplicity is regarded as incompatible with efficiency. There must be a complex mechanism of means and motives, an imposing array of plans and reasons, a recognition of the philosophy of mind —falsely so called—before public confidence can be fixed or expectation created. Man must weave the net if incense is to be offered to it.

Those who have aspired to the control of society have accommodated their policy to the flattery of this innate pride, these self-conceited prejudices, and have become purveyors to passions that ought to have been starved instead of being pampered. No lesson of history, no disappointment of experience, no abortion of effort, no calamity of result, has been able to dethrone that overweening confidence in ourselves which presides over the decisions of the understanding and assumes to control the feelings of the heart. Compelled to see, and desirous of meliorating, the moral woes of the world, we yet obstinately rely upon earthly schemes, almost excluding, or at best but partially adopting, the only remedial agent which, in the judgment of the great I Am, is competent to effectuate the desired end.

While I yield to none in my admiration of the zeal that has distinguished the last few years of our country's history for the diffusion of knowledge, the promotion of learning, I have looked with some apprehension upon the probable results, simply because the Bible—the great conservative power of the world's happiness and prosperity—has not been recognized with sufficient distinctness, nor incorporated so intimately with the course of instruction as duty and interest conspire to demand.

Knowledge, learning, reputation, are not ultimate ends; and those systems which look not beyond these, though perhaps temporarily expedient, politically wise, are nevertheless radically defective. There is a carnal policy, honest and judicious as to this world, considering man apart from his eternal relations, but ruinous to him as a creature responsible to God. There may be an undue appreciation of scholarship, valuable as it is; there *are* mistaken views of interest lying at the foundation of popular opinions on this subject. The infidel sentiment that the youthful mind should be left free; that no direct, undisguised effort should be made to lead it to religion and to God; that to teach repentance, the love of Christ, the duty of prayer, is a sectarianism, offensive and intolerable, has obtained footing in the Church, and, with all our advances to a better state of things, yet lingers among us an incubus and a shame. There has been a timorousness and a caution which seemed to indicate a secret conviction of at least the doubtfulness of our movements and a willingness to conform to popular sentiment upon the first murmur of dissent. We have become the abettors of a popular evil for the sake of patronage by a partial performance of a duty that ought to have been considered by a Christian people as inviolable as one of the laws of nature. As if ashamed of the word of God, or suspicious of the political expediency of its influences, we have substituted some human writer on its evidences for Moses and the prophets, Christ and the apostles. We have walked round about Zion and gazed from the mole-hills of science upon the towers thereof as they rise in the grandeur of their strength and the awfulness of their elevation, but we have not gone in to furnish the rising generation with weapons from her armory for the defense of virtue and the destruction of her foes.

We admit the capital doctrine of Divine Agency, and believe Christianity to be the medium through which God's blessing comes to the world, and recognize that the vital force of any instrumentality, however intelligent, depends upon association with the power of this divine economy; and yet we pay more attention to other truths than to these. We rely upon proximate and visible means, and render undue homage to the ordinary appliances of instruction. I insist that, while we believe the perpetuity of a free government to hang upon Heaven's protection, all proper and legitimate means should be used to conform the people to his will. If the nation's safety consists in the nation's purity, sanctify the sources of thought and feeling by Biblical knowledge. If correct opinions, sound morals, real happiness are the fruits of revealed religion, connect religious instruction—not nominally and partially, but really and thoroughly—with the course of education. Strange to tell, however, with the popular system of instruction there has been no necessary moral influence, the cultivation of no individual virtue, the correction of no evil in society. Regarding man as a creature of time, a citizen of the country, a social being, he has been taught to compute, to examine, to speculate, to write, to speak, as if these were all the furniture of life and the preparation for its duties. The meager morality which asks no better Bible than the enactments of human legislatures, or the conventional codes of fashionable society, has been the safeguard of character and the guardian of general interest.

What are the results? Public sentiment corrupt, principles sapped, passions uncontrolled, vice triumphant. The wall of defense has been whitened, but the coloring cannot conceal its weakness. The sepulcher has been painted, but within its beautiful exterior the worm has lived and battened. The mind, cultivated, expanded, strengthened, has been surrendered to the stimulus of passion bent on the work of destruction. The torpid serpent has been warmed and nourished in the spirit of mistaken kindness, and without the extraction of a fang or the subjugation of a passion has been turned loose for the work of a keener rapine and a more sanguinary desolation. Who more vicious than many of our graduates? Who more dissolute than the distinguished, the great, the prominent men of the country? Who have contributed so much to the deterioration of sentiments and of manners as those who, by an ill-judged education, have been empowered to redeem the corruptions of private life by the public display of imposing talent? O when will the world, when will the *Church*, learn wisdom from the past? Heaven knows we have had enough of philosophy without religion, of reason without conscience, and of education without God's Bible at the bottom of it.

For one, I have no idea of erecting the bumps of craniology into oracles of wisdom, of unveiling the source of the world's evils by phrenological disclosures, or of gathering the secret of their cure from the transcendental nonsense of one of your mesmeric sleepers. Let Saul consult with the witch of Endor, if he will, and invoke the ghosts of a mystic philosophy for the revelations of truth, but never will the mephitic vapors that now infest the atmosphere with the poison of death sink to the caverns and sepulchers from whence they sprung until the Church, the legitimate patron of learning, set free from the leading-strings of fleshly wisdom, recognizes and acts upon the truth that the Bible, the only book of the soul, is also the best book for the intellect. The times are propitious for a change. Now that every earthly scheme has failed, now that derangement and defeat and dismay have subdued the world into something like humility, let the Urim and Thummim proclaim the will of God and the duty of the people. Now that Pharaoh and his hosts are ingulfed in the sea, let the armies of Israel seize the weapons that have been thrown upon the beach by the returning waters, and go forth to guard the rising generation from every foe, and locate them in a land illustrious with virtue's light and rich in honor's rewards.

Theorists have said that knowledge and virtue are essential to the perpetuity of freedom and the prosperity of the nation; but they have connected with it the false, delusive assumption that knowledge and virtue are inseparable. Hence, a spirit of enthusiasm has gone forth on the subject of learning. Legislators, statesmen, editors, preachers have rivaled each other in their panegyrics on schools and literary institutions. A distinguished foreigner has said, "The school-master is abroad," and like the midnight watchman's cry, "All's well!" the sound has been caught and prolonged till well-nigh all the echoes of the earth have waked to give the world assurance of safety and the liberty of repose.

But for the purposes of restraint knowledge is nugatory. There is no moral quality in intellect; there is no moral power in science. While I would scout with indignation the doctrine that "ignorance is the mother of devotion," I am far from believing that learning is favorable to piety, unless the process by which it is acquired is *strictly, literally religious education.* To develop the resources of mere mind is but to furnish incitements to pride, incense to vanity, facilities to wickedness; it is to train soldiers for battle and provide ammunition for the war which error wages with truth; man's rough nature may be softened into humanity, and the uncouthness of his manners polished into grace;

the cannibal may become a man; the moral brute a reasoning slave, but the same vices and the same depravity, modified and civilized perhaps, which belong to a more rude and savage state will still nestle in his heart, and leave the venom of their nature on every thing their snakish teeth do touch.

It is true knowledge opens numerous sources of enjoyment, diminishes the dependence on the sensitive appetites, and invests human nature with a glory well adapted to disguise the fact that there is after all no renovation of that nature, and that the only change is from coarse to refined, from loathsome wickedness to polite transgression. I hold that blasphemy is blasphemy, whether it drops from vulgar lips in negro dialect or comes in polished sentiments and graceful style from the tongue of the accomplished transgressor; corruption is corruption, whether found in the rags and tatters of an ignorant and degraded poverty, reveling in the filth of a hovel, or amid the embellishments of higher life, where taste lounges in splendid parlors, with carpets, curtains, and sofas to match; crime is crime, whether submerged in the ditch or washed in snow-water, whether drunk in the gutter or sober at the card-table.

Who does not know that in this land of ours evils have circulation and character because of their association with taste, talents, and refinement? The most groveling passions have been brought out from the seclusion of the dark retreats to which their odious character had consigned them, and brushed and painted and refined, have been introduced to society as harmless things, hitherto maligned by a sour godliness or exiled by a fastidious morality. Who does not know that after all the marchings of mind and the multiplication of colleges, crimes have multiplied and law grown weak? Deeds which but a few years ago would have blasted character and proscribed the perpetrator forever only furnish material for editorial wit and evidence of increasing wickedness. In the modern vocabulary, by the legerdemain of genius, names are no longer things, either substantially or ostensibly; breach of trust is the misfortune of speculation; stealing, abstraction; and the plunder of the Government one of the rights of the people. It is not to be denied that there is an increasing laxity of moral feeling and restraint in the country, and that, too, chiefly among those whom intellect and education have elevated to station and influence in society. Assuming a sort of independence by virtue of superior acquirements, they assert exemption from vulgar bonds; and to the corruption of an example rapid enough in its propagation they add the momentum of authority, and so accelerate the ruin of the land. The work of degeneracy never proceeds from the lower to the higher classes—if I may use these words in this republican country—but the reverse. The poor, the ignorant, the vulgar, never affect the rich, the learned, the elegant. It is the last who give tone to society. Exalted high, living upon the mountain's top, these are they who loosen the avalanche and hurl the rushing ruin upon the vale below.

History—ancient and modern—attests that the profoundest moral degradation may coëxist with the highest intellectual culture. Painting, sculpture, poetry, oratory, may obtain their ultimatum of excellence, and their authors and admirers be imbruted in the bondage of the flesh, and enslaved by the dominion of the senses. A man may be a scholar and a drunkard; a poet and yet a ruffian in society; a naturalist, brooding in rapture over minerals and plants, and be without household feeling; an astronomer without devotion or the knowledge of God; a mathematician without having numbered his days or applied his heart unto wisdom. What is true of individuals is true of nations. Egypt, with her philosophers, her libraries, and her monuments, some of which yet remain to mock with their grandeur the littleness of modern works, was one vast "chamber of imagery," where iniquity wrought its abominations. Greece—the land of the Muses, the birthplace of eloquence, of poetry, of Demosthenes and Homer, of sages whom the moderns yet quote, with reverence acknowledging their pre-eminence—with all her academies, groves, and Olympic entertainments, was superstitious, fickle, and corrupt. Rome, with her empire, though the depository of the learning of the world—learning which she enlarged, enriched, diffused—was, even in the Augustan age, but refined in her barbarism, and abandoned to voluptuousness and crime. Society may be roused from the night and sleep of ages, and all the restless faculties of the human mind released from their confinement may stand erect and commune with nature's visible things, and roam in freedom earth, air, and sky; accumulate, diffuse, invent, discover, apply, and yet "mind earthly things" and "glory in their shame."

While, therefore, I would not affirm that knowledge corrupts, it certainly does not purify; and in its action generates temptations, for resistance to which it provides no adequate motive, and rears up full and impassable in the way no opposing authority to stop the tide destined to sweep down the outworks of morality. Whatever the field of its operations, the remark is true; and in the absence of a controlling, counteracting moral power, all that it does to stimulate art, agriculture, commerce, is only providing fuel for the fire that is consuming us. As rivers are affected by the character of soil over which they run, so knowledge partakes in its progress of the qualities of the nature on which it operates, and, inseparably commingled, flows on, the vehicle of its own pollutions.

The source of all the evils that afflict humanity lies far beyond the reach of all legislative or educational remedies.

Indeed, these remedies multiply, aggravate, compound those calamities unless they acknowledge this fact and conform themselves as subordinate means to the superior instrumentalities of a divine economy. Reason, in its natural or cultivated state, is impotent to restrain or to guide, to declare the character of God, to develop the sanctions of his government, or even to preserve a revelation of his will. Modern history exhibits a demonstrative experiment of its blindness and its perversity. The reign of reason was the reign of terror, torment, and wickedness, so far exceeding all other modes of torture and of crime that in its stead popery was welcomed as a blessing, and a military despotism adopted as a refuge from its enormities. Philosophy, with its scholastic theories, and deep speculations, and subtle metaphysics, has no power to bind the strong man, no authority to enforce her opinions; and, if she have a heart to mourn at all, is doomed to the anguish of one who, standing upon the shore, gazes, incapable of affording relief, upon a distant shipwreck.

The prevalent system of education, the most popular books, even if they admit, do not insist upon, the Bible doctrine of depravity as a fact in the moral constitution of man. They take the youthful mind according to Locke's famous idea of its being "a blank page," not remembering that however destitute of ideas or ignorant of words, according to the word of God it is fearfully blurred and blotted; that whatever the character of the education, the moral truths communicated will have to wrestle with a nature that loves to err. That the intellect is allied with a leprous heart—"a heart deceitful above all things, and desperately wicked"—appears in every stage of life and every condition of society. Yet, the books that are used in our institutions—the mental and the moral philosophies—deal with man as if ignorance of science, of government, and of his own intellectual capacities, were the only evil of his nature, and school instruction the only salvation that he needed. The obligations of morality as inculcated are presumed to arise from civil relations—from the artificial and changing modes and aspects of society—and are enforced by mere prudential reasons of business, economy, and character. Hence, virtue is made to vary in the elevation of its standard and the amount of its exactions with latitude and longitude, with city or country, with the comparative wealth or poverty, station or obscurity of the people. From such a course, variable in its nature, inadequate in motive, and limited in range, what nobleness of mind, what purity of heart, what reward of usefulness, can be expected?

If the Christianity of the Bible be the basis of every excellence, the subsistence of every virtue; if it follow man into the domestic circle, the fellowship of the Church, the community of the country, the citizenship of the world, why not at once initiate the young mind into its doctrines, mysteries, and duties? If foolishness be bound up in the heart of a child, if it go astray from the womb speaking lies, if the elements of all corruption are to be found in every bosom, and if the experiment made for five thousand years demonstrates the incapacity of all merely human means to purify, restrain, or renew, why pertinaciously adhere to the system as if wisdom and obstinacy were synonymous, and experience a lying oracle? Why rely upon the nostrums of an intellectual empiricism when we have a sovereign panacea? Why deal with man in one view of his nature, and that the most important, one day in seven, and then expend the care and labor of six on subordinate interests, which derive all their significance and value from their relations to the first?

We were not sent into the world to draw diagrams and to prove that any two sides of a triangle are greater than a third side, nor to find the roots of verbs, nor to walk in admiring wonder through botanic gardens, nor to classify the minerals of the earth, nor to count and name the stars of heaven. Important as these may be—and far be it from me to undervalue them—a man may be saved as well without as with them. Nor do they make men temperate or honest or kind; nor are they indispensable qualifications for the necessary duties of life. They are relative and subordinate, and in the absence of moral principles and religious knowledge minister to individual pride and social corruption quite as often as to purity and virtue.

It is true—and this consideration serves to obscure the facts I am stating—that those evils which connect themselves with the intellect are not so alarming or odious as those that belong to the flesh. In the one case the mode of operation is understood by all—the results are seen, felt, deplored; in the other, insidious and fatal, because unseen and unsuspected. As the subtle and noxious vapors of the morass mingle with the atmosphere, are inhaled along with the vital air, and are detected only by their perilous effects on health and life, so error and impurity blend with the feelings and sentiments of mankind, and often indicate their existence only by the obstructions they offer to truth and righteousness. If, then, these sources of action are left to the corruption of active but invisible agencies, no marvel if in after days, like the lightning of heaven, they flash into revelation only to scathe and to kill. The temptations that attend the ascent to mental illumination, to intellectual power—operating upon the feebleness of a nature round which no guard has been stationed, and whose weakness no reënforcements of principle have forfeited—will be sure to push the battle beyond the gates, and quarter their attendant troops of evil for life.

If education be worth its time and its expense—and who

doubts it—why not make it yield in kind as well as quantity according to its capacity? If the garden be worth cultivation, why not inclose it? To plow, to sow without a fence, is but to jeopard the maturity of the crop or to rear a harvest for waste and destruction. To impart knowledge, to refine taste, to rouse the imagination, to stimulate ambition, without directing all by the authority and influence of Christianity to the great moral end of our creation, is but to furnish tools for the devil and kindle a fire for him to work by; it is to give him a Paixhan gun to fight with, while morality is doomed to depend upon an Indian bow and arrow. It is an affront to reason as well as to theology to assume that there can be any other foundation to virtue than the fear and the love of God. The education, therefore, which does not inculcate these of design, habitually and earnestly, leaves the pupil to the choice of immoralities, to be determined by temperament and circumstances. The love of reputation, respect to parental authority, an honorable ambition, may all combine to modify the expression of depravity, but they leave that depravity unsubdued to work its perilous effects in the safe lodgment of an unenlightened and carnal heart. All the considerations that earth can furnish to incline man to morality, unless subordinate to the higher reasons set forth in revelation, operate disastrously, whether they succeed or fail. In their success they graft upon the native stock of human pride a self-complacent delusion, fatal to right convictions of sin, and therefore excluding "the highest style of man;" in their failure they surrender man to the ambuscade of corruption without warning and without defense.

To occupy the right ground upon this subject is the more important because there is a natural tendency in us—one, too, promoted and justified, as the world supposes, by apparent reasons—to believe that in the progress of society, of science, of government, there must be a corresponding change in our nature itself. Hence we hear so much of illumination and freedom as the great conservative elements of character. It is argued that a free people must be happy, that an enlightened people must be virtuous. There is partial, comparative truth in these propositions, and upon the credit of what cannot be denied they have passed into republican axioms. Schools and colleges are regarded as the bulwarks of our land, the pledge of the perpetuity of our political institutions, and the guard against any encroachment of "the powers that be." All this may be, and yet the very wisdom of legislation, as it respects the diffusion of intelligence and the development of the nation's resources, will promote other evils and accelerate ruin in the absence of the restraints of religion and that moral balance of power that is to be found only in the belief of the inspired records. Why is not the voice of history regarded on this subject? Our mechanical improvements, our works of art, our discoveries of science, may all survive our political institutions, for these depend upon the private virtue of the citizens, upon the prevalence of right sentiments as it re-relates to God and the Bible. There are no elements of perpetuity, no imperishable principles of virtue, apart from revealed religion. The sacred Scriptures are the only rule of faith and practice. All other standards are defective, variable, and doubtful. To neglect the Scriptures, then, to refuse them precedence in the order of time, to separate and cull, is to diminish conviction of their value, and to give countenance and prominence to antagonistic principles injurious at best, and fatal when allowed to occupy the vantage-ground.

There has been a change for the better in the last few years. Denominational colleges constitute an era in literature and religion, and were it not that they are yet modified in their internal policy by respect to prejudices the most foolish and absurd, they would have exhibited such ocular and palpable proofs in attestation of the value of the Bible as a book of instruction that they would have converted the doubts of the skeptical into faith and the fears of the timid into rejoicing. As it is, though not so decidedly religious in all respects as they might and ought to be, they have greatly diminished the dangers attendant upon a collegiate career. The fact that an institution is under the patronage and control of an ecclesiastical body, that its trustees are pious men, its president a minister of the gospel, and its professors members of the Church, does not, whatever facilities for it these circumstances and agencies afford, necessarily secure a thoroughly religious education.

If our duty is to be determined by the value of religion and the absolute wants of the human mind, if the results of partial experiments are allowed to indicate the adaptation of Christianity to promote whatever is desirable in order, character, and destiny, then does it seem to me as plain as daylight that Sabbath-school instruction, as now understood, should be incorporated with all our common schools as an integral part of education. The Catechism and the Bible ought to be among the first books put into the pupil's hands. The first in importance, let them occupy the same rank in the order of instruction, and not by criminal delay obliquely insinuate that other things are entitled to preference. The truths that are left to be gathered up incidentally are not likely to impress with such vividness and permanency as when received through a deliberate and serious communication. Reading, writing, and arithmetic can never impress upon the moral powers the right direction, nor fortify the heart against the assaults of temptation or the seduction of ungodly example. The government of the family, the regulation of the academy, ought all to be based upon this fundamental fact: that the saving knowledge of God is emphatically "the one thing needful." Carry out the plan; graduate the instruction by the progress, the age, the circumstances of the scholar; take it up from the primary department to the college, the university, and let the whole course from the spelling-book to a diploma be sanctified "by the word of God and prayer." Let the Bible be the nucleus of knowledge, the central point, radiating its own blessed light over the whole range of learning and of literature. The youth of the land should be taught its history, its chronology, its geography, its evidences, its doctrines, and its ethics. It is folly to call that religious education which has no fact to justify the appellation other than morning and evening prayers. The other exercises on which reliance is placed belong to them, not in the character of students, but as citizens, and lack that distinctness of aim, that personality of direction as to class, for which we plead and on which we insist as the only legitimate and authenticated instrument of successful operation. It will never do to leave the necessary knowledge of the religion of Christ to the presumptuous hope of a providential interposition while we forego the appropriate means of communication, to the probabilities of a revival in the community where the college is located, or to the resurrection of the impression casually made in the scholastic career. The foundation must be laid by lesson upon lesson, seriously given and affectionately enforced.

It has been the policy to repose the hopes of society, as far as they were connected with the plastic influences of education, upon the inculcation of morality. But this does not meet the exigencies of the case, even though the Christian code itself be adopted. The efficiency of revealed religion resides not in its *morals*, as some vainly suppose, but in its *doctrines* and *motives*. Pure, divine as the precepts of the Bible are, they are powerless when dissevered from "the mount that burned with fire" and the cross that streamed with blood. Associated with these and with the terrors of that conflagration that shall veil even yonder sun with the intensity of its glare, and the revelation of that doom that hangs upon the lips of eternal judgment, then they come with an authority so imposing, venerable, and awful as wellnigh to compel reverence and homage. The duties of religion derive their force from no worldly consideration, no prudential policy; and they who rest them upon these, consign them to neglect, if not contempt. If we believe Christianity to be what our creeds maintain and our professions affirm, let us see to it that we spurn that policy of compromise and exclusion which gratifies its hostility to the peculiar verities of revelation under cover of a just abhorrence of an intriguing sectarianism. How long shall an ungodly world prescribe to a Christian community the measure of their duty and the character of their efforts? How long shall conscience be reconciled to a partial and defective arrangement for meeting our whole responsibility by alleging in justification the prejudices of those whom we are under no obligation to consult? The characteristics of freedom, vigor, activity will scarce ever broadly attach to an experience of grace itself unless it is based upon an intelligent apprehension of the remedial economy of our holy religion.

This is important, if not essential, to give tone, strength, elevation, stability to experience, and to redeem the profession of it from the reproach of being the mere enthusiasm of ignorant impulses. But there may be high attainments in philosophy; intimate knowledge of letters, of law, of human nature, of the principles of government, and yet the mind remain intensely dark on the great and leading doctrines of revelation. The doctrinal terms of theology and the pulpit shall convey to such a mind either no distinct ideas or ideas so perverse as utterly to neutralize the truth. To one who has not given special observation to this subject, the ignorance of many enlightened men, if disclosed, would be perfectly astounding, and constitutes, in my humble opinion, one among the many reasons—and that not the least—of their indifference and lethargy. To neglect the legitimate means of information is not only to fail of our duty, but to create a palpable obstruction to future conversion.

By what sort of reasoning has it been found out that one class of men demand a particularity of instruction upon the entire system of religion, and that the disclosure and enforcement of all often fail to reform or redeem, and yet that we are authorized to hope for better results from a partial course; that the weight which has resisted the lever and the pulley can be lifted by the finger? Are not those who frequent our college-halls personally responsible to God, and as such legitimate subjects on whom to operate by the whole apparatus of gospel means and motives? Is it not an intolerant interference with the rights, liberties, and interests of this class of society for any authority, whether of person, prejudice, or opinion, to consign them for a term of years to a sort of compulsory neutrality, which the Christian teacher must not invade by the demonstration of argument or the excitement of a tender appeal?

The things that are revealed belong to us and our children by divine bequest; and to preclude them from the inheritance for any reason is an infraction of the Eternal Will. Not to teach them is infidelity to our trust as guardians on a plea of a minority that will not be recognized and sustained in the decisions of the last day. The time, the mode of teaching the truths of salvation should carry along with them the conviction of their title to precedence and the preeminence of their importance. Let doctrine be taught; it is no sectarianism. If it be, it is obedience to a divine behest; and let those who complain settle the controversy with the Almighty. It is no more denominational intrigue to press religion upon the college-boy than upon his worldly-minded sire. Nor would I limit the range of instruction to the points on which orthodox Churches agree, but would extend it over the whole field of theology as found in the sacred canon. It is as inadmissible for the professor's trump to give an uncertain sound as for the watchman's on the walls of Zion.

And if a Methodist interpretation of the Bible be adopted in a Methodist college, who ought to be surprised? There is no deception; the charter, the board of trust, the name, all proclaim the character of the institution. There need be no debate about the right of search; we ride upon the high seas, engage in lawful business, carry but one flag, and fling that to the wind and the sunshine. We neither impress nor proselyte, and if the officers can make abiding friends of the passengers by courtesy and usefulness, who dare reproach us with being selfish intriguants? Let us, then, teach the doctrine, apply the motives, and enforce the morals of the Inspired Volume, and the annual revolutions of time's wheel shall evolve from these literary retreats virtuous citizens if not pious saints. As the tree of knowledge was the original instrument of temptation, let us remember in all our aspirations after learning that, as the society of the world approximates nearer and nearer to that state when men are governed by opinion rather than by law, it becomes more and more necessary that the process of education should become a living organism, instinct with the spirit and power of our holy religion.

He who is best educated for the world to come is best educated for the world that now is. I would not displace any book necessary to be known, I would not substitute the

Bible for every thing else, but I would have it the groundwork and companion of the whole course. We talk of the expansive power of other studies, of their discipline, their scope, and their elevation; and true it is that the mind grows dwarfish or gigantic according to the subjects with which it is familiar. If, then, you would set to your seal and give the world assurance of a man, set him to span the disclosures of revelation, scale the altitudes of eternal truth, explore the depths of Infinite Wisdom, and soar amid the glories of immortality unveiled and spiritual, and then he shall descend, like Moses from the mount, radiant with the light of high communion. In the treasured volume lies not only the mystery of mysteries, but in it is the oldest history—history past, present, and to come—poetry alive, breathing, bounding; philosophy condensed but comprehensive, deep but clear, profound but intelligible. We wander with the geologist, book in hand, all delight; look upon the surface, dig through some few strata of the earth; enter some dark and curious caverns; scan the precipitous banks of some rushing torrent as it hastens to its ocean home; but this Book plants us amid the angel groups as they gaze upon the laying of the corner-stone of this material temple, and poises us over the heaving abyss where creative power is energizing, and wraps us in wonder and praise as the choral song of the morning-stars breaks upon the cradled slumbers of the new-born world. We talk of the illustrious discoveries of science, and disport among stars and suns and systems; stand upon the outposts of telescopic vision, awe-struck with the amplitude of our range; but *this Book* stretches infinitudes beyond the orbits of astronomy, and, leaving all calculation and measurement behind, dooms imagination itself to fold its wings in weariness; opens faith's interior eye; unrolls the scenery of judgment; sweeps off our terrestrial habitation, and the planetary glories that now bestud our sky; reörganizes the dust of the sepulcher; bids a new creation rise; redeemed man rejoice, heaven his home and eternity his life-time.

O tell me if a Book like that can be read and studied without a quickening impulse, without expansive views, without an upward, onward motion. As well might the flowers sleep when spring winds her merry horn to call them from their wintry bed. As well might the sunbeam lie folded in the curtains of night when "the king of day comes rejoicing in the east." As well might the exhalations of the ocean linger upon its bosom when the sun beckons them to the thunder's home. Away, away forever with the heresy that the Bible fetters intellect! It is the oracle of all intelligence, the charter of our rights, "the day-spring from on high." What was the reformation but the resurrection of the Bible? Cloistered in monastic seclusion, it lay for a thousand years hidden, silent, and degraded. The dense vapors that went up from the fens of papal corruption shrouded in deep eclipse the lore of the world, and men groped in the gloom of a long and awful night. Intellect, smitten from its pride of place, fell cowering in abject servility at the footstool of power. Superstition shackeled the multitude, and the spirit of liberty slept beneath its wizard spell. Opinion, panic-stricken by the thunders of the Vatican, hushed its trumpet-tones and left the empire of mind to darkness and to Rome. But lo! in the cycle of years a change. The genius of Luther evoked the Bible from its retreat to disenchant the nations. It came, and breathing upon the valley of vision, its dishonored relics lived. It looked upon the sleeping sea, and the ice-bound waters melted beneath its glance. When from her dungeon gloom imprisoned Europe cried, "Watchman, what of the night?" the watchman said, "The morning cometh." The ghosts of a mystic theology fled from the spreading day. The gloomy prejudices which had stagnated all the elements of enterprise let go their barbarian hold, and the powers which had rusted for ages in iron sleep, emancipated, rushed to the conflict, on the issue of which the destinies of the world were periled. Intellect, roused by the battle-shout, with new-found strength burst from its thralldom, forged its fetters into swords, and fought its way to freedom and to fame.

Yes, it was the Bible which presided over the revival of letters and unrolled the manuscripts of ancient wisdom for the perusal of the nations; it was the Bible that unlocked the prison-doors of knowledge and bid her go forth to teach the people their dignity and their rights; it was the Bible that wrenched from the reeking jaws of a ravenous usurpation the bleeding form of mangled liberty, and restored her to the earth, healed and sound, a blessing and a guardian. When in after years denied a home by the despotic monarchies of the Old World, these ancient companions braved the wide Atlantic's roar, and together sought a refuge in these Western wilds. Let the Bible keep alive the spirit of liberty among the people and the spirit of reverence for God, and the republic is safe. Let lawless violence, or reasons of State, or an intriguing infidelity sequester the Holy Volume, forbid it to walk upon the unquiet sea of human passions, and the last hope of patriots and the world is gone. This young republic, smitten in the greenness of her years, shall be stretched to the gaze of nations a livid corpse, the scorn of kings, and none so poor as to do her reverence.

Hear me, my country! hear me for your honor and your perpetuity! Have done with your idolatry of patriotism, of talent, of government—your dependence on men and wealth and power! Away with your jealousy of the Bible, its influences and its institutions! Christianity is the vital spirit of the republic, the richest treasure of a generous people, the salt of our learning, and the bond of our union. Send religion and education in indissoluble wedlock to traverse the land in its length and breadth; let the mother teach the Bible to her daughters, the father to his sons, the school-master to his pupils, the professor to his class, the preacher to his congregation. Let the people read it by the morning's dawn and at evening's holy hour. Let the light of it gleam from the sanctuary, the college, the academy, and the private dwelling, then will glory dwell in our midst, and the light of salvation overlay the land "as the morning spread upon the mountains."

Church Colleges.*

AS a Georgian, as a Methodist, as a friend of education, I rejoice in the enterprise which convenes us to-day. It is an atonement for the past and a prophecy of the future. Night—a long, dark night—from whose sky, amid careering clouds, hope let fall a dubious, trembling ray, has overhung the fortunes of Emory College. But the ceremonies of this occasion herald the morning—a morning whose ascending sun, streaming in full-orbed effulgence, shall know, I trust, in future years neither eclipse nor decline.

I rejoice too in the coincidence which unites this event with a day memorable and hallowed in the annals of our country—commemorative alike of the immortal Washington's infant wail and Buena Vista's battle thunder.

A Georgia audience—Americans all—will pardon me if I turn aside from the more direct and legitimate object of the occasion to pay a passing tribute to the illustrious Washington, "the father of his country"—a title which he more richly deserves than any man, living or dead, who ever wore the honor.

Since I came to years and learned to think for myself, I have been amazed at the prevalent opinion which regards Washington as a good rather than a great man. The popular idea that he was an intelligent farmer, a prudent general, and an incorruptible patriot, is praise—high praise—but

---

*This address was delivered in Oxford, Georgia, February 22, 1852, on the occasion of laying the corner-stone of a new college-building. The speaker was then president of the college.—EDITOR.

far below the merits of the man. It is well that the moral sense of the people compels them to do homage to virtue and goodness, and to award the meed of an unequaled fame to the chief who prayed to God while he fought the battles of his country, and who resisted the charms of power when a nation bowed before him in admiration of his achievements. But presiding over the moral excellences of the man, the patriotism of the soldier, the integrity of the civilian, there was an intellect vast, varied, and prophetic. His opinions were judicious, distinguished by their breadth, sagacity, and strength; his "letters weighty and powerful;" and his "Farewell Address" a treasury of wisdom, a political chart, a national amulet. Let the people read it; it is an antidote to the degeneracy of the times. Let the officers of government study it; it is a guide to duty amid the perils of party strife. Let our statesmen—North, South, East, and West—imbibe its spirit, and the sectionalism which threatens the unity of the republic will hide its Gorgon head, and its Babel tongue be heard no more in the councils of the nation. The time is coming when that document will be regarded as the offspring of a mind on which, while yet illumined by the lights of the past, the unrisen sun of a future century was beaming.

Appropriate on its first presentation, its value increases with the lapse of years and the progress of commerce and knowledge and liberty. Adherence to its doctrines will be the cement of the Union, and give perpetuity to republican government. It was a patriot's legacy to the American people; and let Washington's policy interpret Washington's opinion. Mount Vernon's sage needs not the Hungarian* expounder with his dulcet tongue to teach his countrymen

---

* Kossuth, the Hungarian patriot and revolutionist, visited the United States in 1851-52, and in many cities made addresses which were greatly applauded.—EDITOR.

their duty. He loved us well and taught us wisely. We understand him. I pray Heaven that our great men may not forsake the steady light of his oracular wisdom for the delusive glare of Kossuth's eloquence. Intoxicated by the adulation of England and the United States, the Magyar dreams of the eventful future, and his "counsel is foolishness," his policy madness. Enthroned in the admiration of the world, without a peer in the history of men, consecrated by death, Washington's words survive him, instinct with truth, a pillar of fire in the political firmament, the guardian of our freedom, and the index of our destiny. Let his monument rise; "we ne'er shall look upon his like again." Dig deep, lift it high; "call marble honor from its caverned bed;" bring granite, copper, brass, and gold; "grave with an iron pen and lead in the rock forever" his name, his deeds—his worthy deeds—and let the generations to come know *there was a man*, GEORGE WASHINGTON.

We have met to lay the corner-stone of Emory College—a Methodist institution, under the supervision of the Georgia Annual Conference of the Methodist Episcopal Church, South—created and sustained by the voluntary contributions of the Methodist people and the friends and adherents of the Methodist Church in Georgia.

Preliminary to the present state of the facts, however, there is a history, brief but interesting—interesting as it shows the state of the public mind twenty years ago, and indicates the progress of opinion and enterprise since that period.

In the winter of 1832 and 1833 the Georgia Annual Conference held its session in La Grange, Troup county. We were visited by the Rev. John Early, from Virginia, and the Rev. Wm. McMahon, from Tennessee—the first as agent for Randolph-Macon College, and the last as agent for La Grange College. Virginia proposed to Georgia to endow a professorship—price, twenty thousand dollars—in Randolph-Macon College. It was assumed and expected that patronage in the way of students would follow this investment. Tennessee proposed nothing very specific, but would be glad of our countenance and encouragement—perhaps would like permission to circulate an agent through our territory to levy contributions both of money and students. The rival agents each presented his case and its claims. Location, climate, the relation of the States, the comparative advantages of neighborhood and distance, were all duly discussed. I shall never forget how the grave and courtly old Virginian was annoyed by the raillery and humor of his competitor from the West. The discussion ended; the Conference adjourned. No positive promises were made, no specific pledges were given. But a *new idea* had been thrown into our midst. It was a living idea, capable of growth, expansion, and destined to a glorious development. Like the grain of mustard-seed in our Saviour's parable, there was in it a living principle, a vital element. It germinated, grew, waxed strong, became a great tree, and our children and children's children will feed on its fruits and be refreshed by its shadow. But I anticipate.

The Conference held its next session at Washington, Wilkes county. Bishop Emory—from whom the college takes its name—presided. We were visited by Dr. Olin, recently elected President of Randolph-Macon College. He came to renew the proposition of the Virginia brethren, to urge its acceptance upon the Conference, and to have an agent appointed to give it practical form and execution. The subject was introduced in open Conference, in the presence of numerous auditors. Olin, with his great mind—and there have been few, if any, of more colossal proportions in this great country—introduced the topic. He brought his mighty powers to bear with an intensity of zeal, an enthusiasm of interest, perfectly overwhelming. Conviction followed his reasonings, persuasion his appeals. When he concluded, and the Conference was ready to carry the proposal by acclamation—to vote him, with uplifted hands, every thing he asked, and even more—to the surprise of most and the merriment of some, a grave brother (the Rev. Allen Turner) rose in opposition. My old friend will pardon me if I say the general impression was there would be no fight, or at most a very unequal combat. But if he lacked any thing in the shape of mental power, he made it up in resolution. He squared himself for the conflict, and with an unblanched brow, and his lance in rest, bore down on his formidable opponent. "Long time," though not in even or doubtful "scale, the battle hung." The spell of a glorious intellect was upon every judgment. The victory was gained before the war began. Olin carried the day, but, as I now believe, Turner had the best of the argument. He took the ground that we ought not to go into this Randolph-Macon arrangement; that Georgia needed a college of her own—ought to have it, must have it, would have it; that the people were ready for it, and that we were injudiciously forestalling ourselves by collecting so large an amount from our people for a distant institution. Fortunately or unfortunately, these views did not prevail. It might be a question whether this preliminary movement, this discussion and agitation, were not necessary to arouse, deepen, and expand the conviction of the public mind as to the importance of denominational education. If so, the results are worth the twenty thousand dollars we paid in advance. If not, let Turner have the credit of his foresight and heroism.

Simultaneously with these movements the Manual Labor School was projected. It was proposed to raise fifty thousand dollars, and the Rev. John Howard was appointed agent. The manual labor system proved to be exceedingly popular. It was the very idea, harmonizing public sentiment in two very important particulars. It was to cheapen education and teach literary men to work. Polished minds in robust bodies, this was the doctrine. Orators rang the changes upon it. It was set to music, and the common ear drank in the balmy sound. A new era was about to dawn on society. The whole tribe of gentlemen loafers were to be superseded and substituted by a nobler genus, and the poor were to be elevated by bringing education within the reach of all who were willing to work to pay for their bread.

Coincident with these changes the deposits had been removed;* the "pet banks," as the politicians called them, were chosen; they were stimulated to expand their issues; the surplus revenue was distributed; the seasons were prosperous, money was plenty; the people were liberal, and it verily seemed as if "the golden age" and the age of letters had come together, a compound blessing upon the United States in general and the State of Georgia in particular. The Conference, emboldened by the prospect, commenced its arrangements for a college. A charter for "Emory College" was obtained, trustees appointed, an agent sent out, a faculty organized; lands were bought, houses built, stock and farming utensils provided, and we launched on the tide of what promised to be a successful experiment. The system was fine, the theory beautiful. Everybody believed in it, everybody admired—except the boys who were to do the labor—but somehow the scheme would not work. The farm failed in its products, expenses increased, debts accrued, embarrassments accumulated, and by and by, like mariners in a storm when they throw the cargo overboard

---

*The allusion is to what was known as the "bank war" during the second term of President Jackson's administration.—EDITOR.

to save the ship, the trustees were compelled to disencumber the experiment from its unnatural appendages to save it from violent, utter explosion.

And here began our troubles; nor did they come alone. A monetary crisis came on, the banks suspended, cotton fell, the commerce and prosperity of the country were prostrated, the oldest institutions of the land were shaken to their foundations, bankruptcy swept over the people, and amid the upheavals and convulsions of the times ruin threatened every enterprise. Many who had subscribed a thousand dollars to our beloved institution were dead, and their estates insolvent. Others had broken, and gathering the fragments together, like the prodigal son, had taken their journey into a far country. Yet others refused to pay because the manual labor feature was abandoned, alleging that their obligations were thereby annulled. A perfect caravan of misfortunes came up from the wilderness and encamped upon the garden of our hopes. Trampled, blasted, wasted, scarce a rose was left upon its stem to tell where once the garden stood. All was paralyzed, dead, except our debts. They were alive and clamorous for payment, principal and interest. The trustees had every thing to do and nothing to do with.

That the institution lived at all is just one of those problems in history which can be solved only by reference to the will of Heaven and the self-denial of those men who, in the days of its darkness and trial, generously, magnanimously bore its burdens. Emory College was not born to die. It is an amaranthine plant. There are seeds which, cast upon the ground or thrown upon the waters, soon rot and sink and disappear. It is so with many a worldly scheme. Springing from a solitary mind, men greet it coldly. It finds no fitting lodgment, no gentle nurture, no fostering kindness; it droops, grows old and obsolete. The thought dies. Oblivion claims its relics. No mourner visits the grave to commune with the departed. It is not so with the efforts of Christian philanthropy. Our Sunday-schools, missionary societies, and educational enterprises are not the lucky thoughts of a sagacious man, the well-meant purposes of fallible humanity. No; but the inspiration of God, the suggestion of the Eternal Spirit. And they are under the guidance of a wisdom infinite and infallible, and the protection of a power unwearied and exhaustless. We are but instruments, and in our labors there will always be enough of infirmity and weakness to conceal the effective hand and hide pride from man. But do the right deed; do it in faith; commit it by prayer to the care of Heaven, and fear no evil. Untoward circumstances may attend it, disaster come, defeat threaten. No matter. See yonder little ark of bulrushes on the banks of the Nile? Within, in innocence and beauty, sleeps a child—an infant of three months, but the victim of persecution. A mother's heart, trusting in God, has committed it to the unconscious waters—more pitiful than Pharaoh's bloody decree. Yet, there lay the future leader of the hosts of Israel, the King of Jeshurun, the Lawgiver of Christendom.

There are seeds which the Bible significantly calls bread—not because they are bread, but they contain that which in due time will make it. Thrown upon the waters—an uncongenial element—they may drift to and fro, now buried by the billow, anon floating upon the surface; at last stranded upon the shore, they find a generous soil; nourished by the sunbeam and the dew, the harvest waves in green and gold, and there are "seed for the sower, and bread for the eater." So when honest, God-fearing, truth-loving, philanthropic men combine and plan for the weal of the world, to dare is to do, to do is to succeed. Truth is eternal, and the thought which embodies or appropriates it will live forever.

The seed will grow; the plant will thrive; the fruit will ripen; the blade, the stem, the ear—bud, blossom, and maturity—all "in due season, if we faint not." If this enterprise had been projected for denominational aggrandizement, for the world's applause, "the honor that cometh to men," then verily it had died. No earth-born scheme could have found an Ararat in such a deluge of trouble. There was a time when the trustees had no coffer but prayer, no resource but faith, no encouragement but hope. Yet, Emory lives—lives and prospers.

And now, making all due allowance for mistakes in financial policy, for errors of judgment, for mismanagement if you please, for occasional misdemeanors among the students, I am bold here, in the presence of a community who know the history of the past as well as I, or better, to assert and maintain that Emory College has already fulfilled all the reasonable calculations of sober wisdom. Ay, all the rational, consistent hopes of sanguine piety. Let us refer to the records.

The first class graduated in July, 1841; the last, of course, in 1851—ten classes, averaging fifteen and a little over in numbers. *One hundred and fifty-five* young men have passed from these humble halls with the diplomas of the institution to take their places in the world's arena. Of the whole number *sixteen* are ministers of the gospel, *three of them missionaries on our Pacific coast* (a notable fact—let the Church mark it: our poor colleges supplying the missionary field); *forty* are engaged in teaching—some as professors in colleges, others as principals in institutes and academies, and yet others in the common schools of the land.* Some

---

*1885. The alumni number 743; the preachers, teachers, lawyers, and doctors are numbered by hundreds; the college has furnished five missionaries to China, one to Mexico, and scores to the West.—EDITOR.

have gone to agriculture, and thus add to the moral and intellectual force of a large class of our fellow-citizens. The professions of law and medicine have shared in the distribution; and but recently our alumni were to be found in your Senate-chamber and your House of Representatives; and to-day, when the country is depressed, the cry of "hard times" upon every lip, and the proof of it in every pocket, Emory numbers more than a hundred students—young men who will compare in mind, manners, and morals with any equal number gathered I care not where. Combine the facts; what more could have been expected? The institution has declared an ample dividend; paid usurious interest on every dollar invested by the Church and country in her resources. There is no ground for discouragement. Let no friend of education despond. And especially let our brethren ponder the question: If, without an endowment, with insufficient buildings, irregular, uncertain income, the college has effected so much for the various departments of society, what might she not do properly endowed, commodiously housed, and more extensively furnished?

Emory College originated in a popular necessity. It was demanded by the wants of the people. It was not a sectarian scheme to promote denominational interests, though justified by the mission of the Church, and imperiously necessary to the discharge of her high obligations. In these days of light and progress and achievement, the Christian community failing to occupy with her own instrumentalities that preliminary ground where opinions are formed and character molded, and over which it is the province of education to preside, must inevitably grow imbecile, effete, and disreputable. This result must follow, not only because the accessions to her number, strength, and influence are cut off by her suicidal neglect, but the work of alienation and enfeeblement will go on by the effect of agents without, either directly hostile or more *virtuously* active. Bigoted, ignorant, superstitious, such a Church would deserve her doom. The curse of Meroz is her legal inheritance.

But "blessed are they who sow beside all waters." "In the morning" let us "sow our seed, and in the evening withhold not" our "hand; for we know not whether shall prosper either this or that, or whether they both shall be alike good." While, therefore, we seek to do our duty, let us move understandingly, lest we "grow weary, and faint in our minds."

The self-same facts which authorized and now vindicate this enterprise at the same time operate to limit its resources and circumscribe its usefulness. Education *is* a public necessity. But everybody does not know it. Everybody does not feel it. Many do not believe the doctrine. The truth in the premises is to be taught. It will take time to propagate it. It is true that many apprehend and appreciate the value of knowledge, the importance of schools, and even the higher grades of scholarship. The mountain-tops are shining, but there is darkness in the vales below. There is ignorance to be enlightened, prejudices to be overcome, and proper views of parental duty and personal responsibility to be inculcated. The college, therefore, has not only to supply wants, but to correct faults; not only to furnish instruction to those who feel the need of it and come to get it, but to increase the demand by diffusing light among the people. As the farmer clears the forest that he may have ground to make his bread or to increase his income by the sale of its products, so education must repel darkness, correct error, disseminate knowledge, to multiply its friends and extend its patronage. This is a work of time. We shall fight and win full many a battle before we "conquer a peace." But every victory strengthens the right and weakens the wrong. We must "push the battle to the gate," storm the last fortress, nor rest till the banner of light and truth waves the emblem of universal empire.

Born and reared in this good old commonwealth, I love her soil, her institutions, and her people. Her progress delights me. Her growing cities, her improving agriculture, her thrift and intelligence, her buoyant steps in the pathway to aggrandizement and renown, as Samson said of the Philistine maid, "please me well." The ninth State in the Union in respect to population, the sixth in the area of her square miles, the third in the number and length of her railways, almost equal to any in her manufacturing enterprise, the first, foremost, best, ahead of all her sisters in the number and character of her seminaries of learning. But how came she so? Who put her into this proud position as to her literary institutions? It was not her legislation, not her politicians, not her mass-meetings or party conventions. No; but her Christian denominations. They began the work by projecting schools and colleges, circulating their agents among the people, answering objections, diffusing information, and rousing to action the long dormant energies of the land.

Previous to these movements there was general apathy. The State University languished, the town academies were occupied by imported teachers, and the common schools of the country cursed by the incumbency of a class of men who knew the taste of whisky better than they did orthography, and loved the shade of a house more than the progress of their pupils or the interest of their patrons. The first quickening impulse on the inert mass, the first breath of life upon "the valley of dry bones," the first bold, robust, expansive movement is to be traced to the leading Churches of Georgia, their Synods, Associations, and Conferences.

An impression—doubtless divine in its origin—seemed to pervade these religious communities that they could not fulfill their high vocation without occupying the entrance gates of life with the Bible in one hand and the text-books of education in the other, and thus train the rising generation to knowledge and virtue. The Methodists, true to the spirit and plans of their venerable founder, marched abreast with the foremost in this conservative enterprise. The Rev. Jesse Mercer—honored be his memory and efficacious his example!—by a munificent bequest endowed the Baptist University which bears his name. The Presbyterians, never behind where learning is concerned, bestirred themselves, and "Oglethorpe" rose from the ground. Nor were these schemes effected without opposition. The friends of the State College were alarmed, lest these rival institutions should drain its patronage and alienate the confidence of the country. Sectarianism, priestly intrigue, Church bigotry, were dreaded and denounced. Mistaken men! We but meant to do our duty and bless our country. Injure Franklin College! We never designed or wished it. Nor have we done it. Yet perhaps the groundless apprehension itself has been useful. Her exclusive friends have been rallied, their zeal renewed, and the result a comparative revival of the institution. The old eagle has molted and renewed her youth. She never thrived so well. Once, alone in her aerie beside the rolling Oconee, she drooped, solitary and sad. No kindred pinion fanned the air. But when Oglethorpe and Mercer and Emory spread their wings and began to soar, she saw, and competition waked her ancient ambition. Together let them rise, and blasted be the archer whose envious arrow plucks a feather from their glory!

The sensitiveness, the squeamish fear of some, in reference to the connection of the clergy and the Churches with our institutions of learning, is unnecessary and unwarranted by the facts of history. In every country converted by the gospel, the Church and the school-house have risen side by side, and the light of science has mingled with the light of revelation. It is a natural alliance; the affinity is divine. God hath joined them together. Augustine, the apostle of England, founded the famous school of Canterbury. Christian kings established her universities, Christian zeal endowed their fellowships. In our own country Christian charity created almost all our older seminaries. Christian minds toiled in them and for them. And every experiment in education which excludes religion and the teachers of religion, thank God, has been a failure. Jefferson tried it in Virginia, Girard in Pennsylvania. They are dead, and their plans are dead, and the surviving managers have been forced to open the doors of these magnificent structures for the Bible and prayer and religion to come in; for these are the basis of discipline, the bonds of restraint, the support of virtue. Without them, disorder reigns, corruption grows apace, and the temple of learning becomes a bedlam of passion, a sink of sin.

The Church is the natural guardian of the minds and morals of the people. To enlighten, to purify, is her mission. This is her business in the world. It is hers to teach, mold, and direct—not by the authority of law, but the persuasion of truth; not by the terrors of her anathema, but the revelation of her motives—motives august yet tender, future and eternal yet present and powerful.

With joy I say it, no State in this broad Union is more indebted to her Christian Churches and the zeal of individual Christians for the instrumentalities and agencies of education than Georgia. The Methodists started the Georgia Female College—now the Wesleyan—at Macon in 1839, and in 1852 there are twelve chartered female colleges in the State—Baptist, Presbyterian, Methodist, Episcopalian denominations all represented—besides the individual and local establishments, created to meet the necessities of particular communities. True, some of these are yet in embryo—buildings going up; not yet fully organized—but the most are in successful operation, crowded with pupils, and dispensing instruction to at least fifteen hundred young ladies year by year. The cry is, "Still they come!" Colleges rise, and pupils flock to their halls. It is marvelous; without a parallel. Whence come they? Why this disproportion? The male colleges do not altogether number more than four hundred. Why is this? They are well located, easy of access, involve less expense. What means this inequality? Is it merely the fashion of the times? a parental mania? female ambition? or have the young men of the day been seized with the love of pleasure or gold, and determined that money is better than knowledge, and pastime more to be desired than scholastic honors? Or, is it that parental authority is surrendered, and the beardless youths of the land, disliking the confinement and tedium of study, and longing for the freedom of the world, are allowed to choose for themselves? I am afraid the satirical remark of a shrewd and observing friend when he said he "*would give a thousand dollars to see a sixteen-year-old boy*" has in it more of truth than censoriousness. There are but too many Eli's in the land, whose sons make themselves independent and criminal, and they "restrain them not." Sons go to college if they like, quit if they please, change if they will, and many, very many, decline the pursuit of knowledge, and rush prematurely into the business and relations of active life. "Woe to thee, O land, when thy king is a child!"

But after all these institutions, male and female, are doing a mighty work. For the present it is vast; for the future incalculable. Well-nigh every county feels their influence and shares their benefits. They have brought education down from the upper walks of life to the humble and needy. This has been accomplished, not by depreciating the standard of scholarship, but by availing themselves of influences local, denominational, and patriotic. The interests of society are harmonized, prejudices accommodated, and the apprehensions of the pious forestalled by a guardianship of their own election. Antipathies, prejudices, peculiar notions obtain and prevail among all classes. They are natural; the result of infirmity, ignorance, and misapprehension. They are not necessarily criminal. And though when excessive or uncharitable they are to be deplored, it is wise, when it can be legitimately done, to make them co-operate in a good thing. Education is a public blessing and when these can be turned to good account in its promotion, society is improved, and these faults themselves assuaged and liberalized. In the apocalyptic vision "the earth helped the woman;" and the work of popular instruction has been greatly accelerated by Church pride—if you will, by local accommodation, and the generous rivalry of the various religious denominations. It is my deliberate conviction that in the last fifteen years more has been effected by these Church enterprises for the intellectual cultivation of the people than by all the plans of the State since the adoption of its constitution.

It is true the early fathers of the State made in the beginning large, liberal, munificent provision for general education. Every successive legislature has modified or remodeled the original arrangement, evincing at all times an intelligent conviction of the wants of the people and their duty as representatives to provide for them.

We have had an educational fund of millions. It has been appropriated, distributed, lost, till only a small part remains. At one time it was determined to endow academies, one at least in every county; and then the "Academic Fund" and the "General Education Fund" were amalgamated and set apart distinctively as a "Poor School Fund." Our legislation has been retrograde—"a step backward" with every modification—from a magnificent provision for general education down to a partial and inefficient plan for the instruction of the poor. This is history, the history. Every change has been a failure, every experiment an abortion. According to the recent census there are forty-one thousand seven hundred and eighty-six white persons over twenty-one years of age who cannot read or write; and these have grown to legal age under the provisions of a system which seems to be an idol with our law-makers. Willing, anxious, earnest as our people and their representatives are and have been to elevate the State and to wipe off this great reproach, I wonder at the pertinacity with which they cling to an ineffectual scheme. The law which gives the inferior courts authority to assess an extra tax equal to the wants of the counties respectively, on the recommendation of the grand juries, is in my judgment decidedly the best effort of the General Assembly to meet the necessities of the case. But this has not been tried, so far as I know and believe, in more than five counties out of the hundred which make up our territory. In those few it has worked well, done good, and is capable of more extensive application. The last enactment, I fear, will only encumber and enfeeble it, without substituting any more active element.

Let me be understood. I am not using the language of complaint or censure. I state the facts as I see and understand them. This is a grave subject, big with the interests of the future. It needs and deserves discussion. I speak as an unpretending citizen, a friend of education, a man who loves the land of his birth. There seems to me to be an unreflecting prejudice abroad in relation to what is called a "Common School System." There seems to be a charm in the name. It is popular—appeals to "the million," and implies a promise utterly beyond its capacity to redeem. It realizes the old heathen tradition, the mythological curse, of Tantalus in the stream dying of thirst but denied a draught. But then it sounds liberal, looks republican, is based on indisputable truth; and though it has failed and failed, and done little else but fail, still the conviction lingers that there must be virtue in it. A scheme so patriotic and benevolent must have capability, adaptation, and be the desideratum of the land. And here lies the error. Such a system employs but cannot produce. It has no innate vitality, no self-sustaining power; cannot move of itself; is inert; an idea, an abstraction. Its action is dependent upon a force without, and needs instruments which it never did and never can create. As a people, we have been mocked by one of those delusive theories which, involving much truth, contains an error fatal to its wisdom and its working.

A free people ought to be educated; it is the duty of government to aid this interest; knowledge and virtue are the guardians of liberty; ignorance promotes crime. These are maxims—democratic axioms. The rich can educate themselves, and the poor are to be the especial objects of legislative sympathy and care. There is some, much truth in this last proposition. But the rich have rights and wants and interests, and they must not be disregarded. Benevolence is not always wise, and there is a benevolence which says, "Be ye warmed and be ye filled," notwithstanding gives not those things which are needful. What doth it profit? Universal education is desirable, but it is not to be compassed by an exclusive provision for the poor, plausible as it might seem in view of the assumed fact that all the rest may help themselves if they will; and especially when the plan proposed is as a watch without a mainspring. If there were school-houses in every poor district of Georgia, and the children were collected, still there would be no school for the lack of books and teachers. If the money appropriated were distributed and applied to the purchase of books, still there would be no school, for there would be nothing left to pay the teachers. If the extra tax were raised and applied to the payment of teachers, still there would be no school, for the teachers are not here, nor would the insignificant remuneration command them.

But if the plan were well conceived, and the necessary funds were available, there are other and for the present insuperable difficulties. A scheme of education designed to act at once upon the masses implies, presupposes an amount of intelligence, public spirit, and enterprise among the people which does not exist. Our politicians flatter us "sovereigns" in their campaign speeches before our great elections. Their encomiums are too broad and universal. They exaggerate; the truth is eulogy enough for the present. There is more sober sense—practical, conservative wisdom—in Georgia than in any other State of this vast Confederacy. For uniformity, the absence of humbuggery, fanatical excitement, this is emphatically "the land of steady habits." But still there is ignorance, gross ignorance, in our midst. It is in every county, lives in the shadow of our court-houses, within sound of our college-bells—ay, sits upon the tripod and waves the imperial birch in all the pride of power, or struts in majesty the tyrant of the log-cabin, and the terror and the curse of the trembling school. Besides, there are many, very many parents who do not and will not send their children to school, however provided. They do not appreciate the blessing; have lived

and made their bread, enjoyed the right of suffrage without
it, and are content for their offspring to plod the same humble
path. In some cases these boys and girls constitute the
effective force of the little farm, and cannot be spared from
their daily labors. Again, the debasement of crime—drunkenness,
sloth, and sensuality, and almost all the paupers come
under this category—has so besotted a certain class, what
care they for education?

But rise a little higher; contemplate a class on the ascending
scale. They would gladly avail themselves of the
offered privilege, if the subject were brought home to their
understanding. But who will give the time, take the trouble,
encounter the expense? The judges may charge the juries,
and juries recommend taxation, and inferior courts assess it,
but who will hunt up the beneficiaries of the arrangement?
Talk ye of patriotism? Alas! on this subject it is an obsolete
virtue. The Church cannot find the men to officer
her Sunday-schools; teachers are wanting, and the children
cannot be gathered in many places; good neighborhoods
too—your better sort of people living there. And if men
will not give an hour to God on Sunday for the benefit of
the poor, will they explore a district in the week to the neglect
of their business? Preposterous inference!

Moreover, we are a hasty, impulsive people, jealous of
our rights; and a visible or imaginary injustice in the immediate
working of a legislative enactment—though a little
time would have corrected the evil—inflames all the revolutionary
blood of the land, and "Repeal" is the watch-word.
Now, no plan of education will work equally at once in
Georgia. Such are the inequalities of population and wealth
—and may I not add of intelligence?—such the industrial
pursuits and local habits of the people, such the distance
and inconvenience of families in some counties, that no system
of the Old or New World would fit the endless contra-

rieties of place, circumstances, and wants. If a general plan were now in full operation, five years would disarrange it. This result is not only incident to, but inseparable from, "our peculiar institutions." Slavery, by its natural increase and the product of its labor, repels white population. The master grows rich and buys the lands of his poor neighbors till he is alone in the midst of what was once a populous region. The very prosperity of the country breaks up the system, leaves the school-house to emptiness, and creates the necessity for a different agency. For the same reason church-houses are abandoned or removed, and it is with difficulty that a congregation can be gathered or a circuit maintained. What! Would you have no denominational organization? Yes; but I would have it in an element of expansion and adaptation which would survive change and follow emigration, while yet it met the local demand.

Schools originating in the felt wants, the active convictions of the people will sustain themselves by virtue of the circumstances which bring them into being. This is natural, the result of powerful causes now working energetically among us and producing their legitimate effects in every place. The process is slow, but healthful and sound, and in the lapse of time and events will bring about the consummation at which we aim. It cannot be greatly accelerated by any mechanical, arbitrary system without violating what Kossuth calls the "logical consequences of events" and producing a precocious state of society, full of mischief in tendency and in fact. There is a providence over mind and opinions as well as over the seasons, seed-time, and harvest; and we had as well attempt to fill the granary of the world in a time of comparative famine by the productions of a hot-house as to banish ignorance by the developements of a system in advance of the desires and voluntary coöperation of the benighted and the needy. In the one case, we must break the ground, prepare the seed, get ready for the time of buds and blossoms, sow and work, and trust the sun and the rains to mature the crop. In the other, we must talk, write, publish, demonstrate the utility of knowledge, invoke the parental instinct, rouse personal ambition, and form a public opinion which shall pioneer the progress of education and make its achievements easy and its conquests permanent. A more virtuous and dignified population will grow up under an economy which springs from and is expanded by natural causes, operating in natural channels, than under a system which invades—however kindly—and weakens the feeling of personal independence. A great public charity which provides indiscriminately for the poor is a social and political evil, exerts a debasing influence on the morals and habits of the people, and multiplies the claimants on the distributive fund. An established provision, under the authority of law, for the education of children corrupts the parents by diluting the sense of responsibility, and defrauds the child of a sympathy which none but a parent can feel. Far better leave this great interest to individual benevolence; then discrimination will do its work, and the modest, unobstrusive, deserving poor will find friends to aid them in such a way and to such extent as that charity shall not offer temptation to idleness or a premium to voluntary pauperism. The feeling of dependence cannot be engendered, for the spontaneous offerings of an individual or community cannot be counted on as the dividends of a thrifty fund set apart by legislative bounty alike for the unfortunate and the dissolute, the poverty of misfortune and the destitution of crime.

A system of education which looks primarily to the poor and dependent can never meet the wants of a diversified population, or realize the hopes of its projectors. By the blessing of Providence and the general thrift and industry of our people the poor constitute a very inconsiderable portion, a mere fraction, of the whole number. The proposed result can be effectually accomplished by a mode more in accordance with the relations of society and the laws which govern the world of mind. Christianity achieves her triumphs by beginning with "the least" and ascending to "the greatest." But there is a moral reason for this, and the success of it is attributable to the energy of an omniscient power. In human enterprises the order of nature must be followed. Streams run downward. Light comes from above. And we had as well attempt in a season of drought to replenish the failing streams by an engine and hose, or supersede the sun by setting candles "upon a thousand hills," as to enlighten and refine society by the instrumentality of a low grade of free schools while the higher institutions of learning are left to feebleness and want. Brew the clouds in the heavens and let them drop their fatness upon the land below. Set the sun in the firmament to rule the day and he will kindle "the lesser lights to rule the night." Build up your colleges; endow them; capacitate them to help the needy, and they will educate the people. Any other plan will degrade scholarship, lower the standard, and what we gain in extension we shall lose in elevation. Multiply the number in our college classes; increase the moral and intellectual force of society; throw into every county young men themselves exalted and refined by liberal education; incarnate, embody the advantages of knowledge; let the people see and know what instruction can do for a man, and every right-minded graduate will become a nucleus around which will gather in crystalline beauty influences radiant with light and suggestive of reform. Every educated man—unless he be dissolute or immoral—is a blessing to the country. Locate him in town or country, give him a learned profession, or set him to till the earth, and he will elevate those about him. But let him feel the obligations of patriotism, the responsibilities of an immortal agent, and give himself, as he ought and likely will, to usefulness, and the State will reap a harvest where she never sowed.

What will Georgia do with her schools without teachers? Where will she find them? She must look to her colleges. They have supplied her in part, and will yet do more. The common school system of New England has been highly, perhaps extravagantly, extolled. But where would she have found her instruments and agents but for Harvard and Yale, and Princeton and Middletown? These filled the land with educated men, enlightened public opinion, supplied her academies and schools with superintendents and teachers, and sent into every village and hamlet a man competent to direct the ignorant, to arouse the indifferent, and give form and energy to the common effort. This is what we need and must have. And we can have it; yet a little while and we will have it. Let the State foster her university, let the Christian denominations rally to their respective institutions, and these agents, with their annually increasing force, will cultivate the land, the wilderness become a garden, and "the Empire State of the South" set a Kohinoor in her queenly diadem.

I cannot conclude without stating a fact which illustrates and confirms the preceding thoughts. Emory College, though scanty in her resources, and mainly dependent on tuition and receipts to meet her necessary expenditures, is dispensing education to many who, but for her kindness, could never have known the benefits of knowledge. She educates without charge for instruction the sons of all the preachers of the Georgia and Florida Conferences, and receives many more on the pledge of payment when they shall have graduated and made the money by their own exertions.* Almost all this class—besides others—resort to teaching as a vocation at once useful, honorable, and lucrative. Here are the materials out of which society is to be furnished with its active, laborious, enterprising members. O what a field for usefulness is here! The privilege might be indefinitely extended if the college were but endowed. Where are the friends of education? the patriots? the Methodists? Unlock your coffers and invest for virtue, your Church, and country. Shake off your apathy! Awake to duty! Help us to supply the pulpit, occupy the school-house, enrich the country with the good, the gifted, and the wise.

Rejoicing in the evidences of public confidence and present prosperity, let us look forward to the future with hope. Emboldened by the history of the past, let us press on to nobler triumphs. Strong in the consciousness of a single desire to be useful, let us continue to invoke the blessing of Heaven, without which labor is but drudgery and success an impossibility. May the institution live, enduring as the granite on which this rising superstructure rests, and useful to the end, an honor to Methodism and a blessing to Georgia!

---

* Emory has done this for nearly fifty years; she gives (1885) this privilege to the "sons of pastors" in all Conferences and all Churches. Also two tuition scholarships to each presiding elder's district in Georgia and Florida.—EDITOR.

Devotedness to Christ.*

"For none of us liveth to himself, and no man dieth to himself. For whether we live, we live unto the Lord; and whether we die, we die unto the Lord; whether we live therefore, or die, we are the Lord's." (Romans xiv. 7, 8.)

THE spirit of Christianity is essentially a public spirit. It ignores all selfishness. It is benevolence embodied and alive, full of plans for the benefit of the world, and actively at work to make them effective. Catholic, generous, expansive, it repudiates all the boundaries, prescribed by names and sects and parties, and "stretches its line into the regions beyond," even to the uttermost parts of the earth. The world is its parish. Its wishes are commensurate with the moral wants of mankind, and the will of God, who gave his Son to die for us sinners and our salvation, is the authority for its labors and the pledge of its triumphs.

It is the policy of every form of infidelity and speculative unbelief, and of every false religion, to depreciate and undervalue the nature of man. They despoil him of his true glory by their chilling, preposterous theories, even while they affect to magnify him by fulsome eulogy of his intellect and its capacious powers. By false notions of personal independence, they isolate him from his kind, and the sensibilities, which Heaven intended should flow out free as the gushing spring, they contract and stagnate, till the heart grows rank and putrid with its own corruptions. But while

---

*Preached in McKendree Church, Nashville, Tennessee, April 15, 1855, in memory of William Capers, D.D., one of the Bishops of the M. E. Church, South.—EDITOR.

our holy religion exalts man as made in the image of God, the head and chief of the system to which he belongs, and thus invests the *individual* with dignity and value, vast and incalculable—far, far beyond "worlds on worlds arrayed"—it yet links him in closest fellowship with the kindred of his race. For him the ground yields its increase, the sun shines, the stars beam in beauty, the winds blow, the waters run. Earth, air, and ocean are all astir with agencies commissioned to do him good; but not for him alone. No matter what his rank, power, influence, he but shares the bounties which have been provided in the munificence of Heaven as the common inheritance of all his fellows. No matter what his personal rights and interests, he is but a part of a great whole. He belongs to a system. No choice of his own, no social caste, no civil distinctions, can detach him from it. Linked with the world around him by a law of his nature and the decree of his Maker, every plan of isolation is abortive; and the very effort at separation and exclusiveness brands him as a miser, a misanthrope, a selfish, heartless wretch, without natural affection or any redeeming principle. A brute in human form, a demon, with the lineaments of man, he is under the outlawry of a world itself, alas! but too ignorant of the law of love and the noble aims and ends of this mortal life.

Bound together, as we are, by the ties of common nature and of mutual dependence, every man is a fountain of influence, good or bad, conservative or destructive. Whether he will or not, he is an example. His language, spirit, actions, habits, his very manners, all tell—forming the taste, molding the character, and shaping the course of others, to the end of time. *No man liveth to himself.* He cannot. Apparently he may, but really he does not. His plans and his aspirations may all revolve around himself as a common center, but within and without their orbits will be concentric circles, inclosing other agents and other interests. He may rear walls around his possessions, call his lands by his own name, and his inward thought may be, as the world phrases it, to take care of himself and his dependents, but he can neither limit the effect of his plans nor forecast the inheritance of his estate. Another enters even into his labors. Disruptive changes abolish his best concerted schemes, and scatter to the winds all the securities by which he sought to fence and individualize his own peculiar interests.

But while all this is true, and constitutes the basis of a fearful responsibility, it is not exactly the idea in our text. In the declaration before us the apostle does not affirm a principle as predicable of our nature and its social relations, nor merely state a fact as resulting from an immutable law of our being, but he presents a moral rule, and erects it into a standard for the adjudication of character. He defines the rights of Jesus Christ our Lord, and the obligations of those who claim to be his disciples and representatives.

A dispute had arisen in the Church concerning meats and days—what was allowable and consistent in the one case, and what was required and binding upon the other. It was a question of privilege—of Christian liberty. Assuming that the parties were equally sincere, the apostle did not seek to quell the agitation by a temporary expedient, a dubious, unreliable compromise, but took occasion to declare a principle of universal authority and application. He lays down a rule by which we are to judge others as well as to measure ourselves. What one may regard as a ceremony and a superstition is not to be charged upon another whose opinion is different as proof that his profession is a mask or his piety insincere. Nor is the latter to denounce the former as a time-server, a man-pleaser, turning the grace of God into licentiousness. "He that regardeth the day, regardeth it unto the Lord; and he that regardeth not the day, to the Lord he doth not regard it. He that eateth, eateth to the Lord, for he giveth God thanks; and he that eateth not, to the Lord he eateth not, and giveth God thanks."

Conceding the right of private judgment—frankly confessing imperfect knowledge—let both judge charitably. The kingdom of God is not meat and drink, but righteousness, peace, and joy in the Holy Ghost. There may be, there is unity in the great principles of Christian morality, and yet a difference of judgment and practice in little things. We are not to despise one another because of this diversity, nor, though fully persuaded in our own minds, harass a brother by the vexatious obtrusion of our peculiar notions. His liberty is not to be bounded by our prejudice, nor his conscience regulated by our superstition. The law of love not only requires good-will, benevolent affection toward all men, but stretches its authority over our opinions, our moral judgment, our estimate of character. We are not to perplex the weak with doubtful disputations, nor incur the risk of imbittering our own feelings by urging our ultraisms as essential to salvation. Life is too short to be wasted in frivolous disputes, even about matters of conscience. Christianity is too precious and noble and vast to be scandalized by contentions in the Church about meats and drinks, the tithing of mint and anise and cummin. As Christians, we are public men. We live for our race. The Lord is our Judge. Great principles are to be avowed, maintained, diffused, established. God and our generation are to be served—the one to be glorified and the other to be saved.

"For none of us liveth to himself, and no man dieth to himself. For whether we live, we live unto the Lord; and whether we die, we die unto the Lord; whether we live therefore, or die, we are the Lord's." The text is a comprehensive description of a Christian's life, a decisive test of character. It is the language of one who well knew what Christianity is, and who himself exemplified its principles and spirit.

Avoiding minute details, we proceed to fix the meaning of the terms "living unto the Lord" and "dying unto the Lord."

"Living unto the Lord" may be considered as implying that we distinctly recognize the will of God as the rule of life. If I may so express it, as the natural subjects of the Almighty we are bound to serve him to the full extent of the powers he hath given us. He has an unquestionable right to our obedience. This results from our relation as creatures. He made us and he preserves us. This original obligation, instead of being relaxed and impaired, is confirmed and intensified by purchase and redemption.

The will of God is to be sought in the statute law of the gospel—the plain and express decrees which define and regulate our duty. It is important to notice and remember that the service we are to perform is not left to our choice. We have no rights of legislation in the premises. Our task is assigned us, divinely appointed. "Lord, what wilt *thou* have me to do?" ought to be the inquiry of every human spirit. The word of God gives the answer: "Thou shalt love the Lord thy God with all thy heart, with all thy mind, with all thy soul, and with all thy strength, and thy neighbor as thyself." This is the law and the prophets, the true philosophy of life, the first and second commandments. On these hang all the subordinate requirements of "judgment, mercy, and faith." The precepts of Christianity are so wisely and graciously adapted to promote the private interests of individuals and the general welfare of human society that many who are disaffected toward the divine government will, for their own sakes, choose to do many things which are just and kind and beneficent. These things are comely, reputable, of good report among all men; and a man cannot, therefore, serve himself more effectually than by practicing the great virtues of humanity. Man's chief controversy is with God—against him he wars. He is not naturally the enemy of his kind. While some fierce and unsocial passions occasionally break out and startle us by the atrocity of some monstrous individual crime, and while nations wrought into fury sometimes quench their hate in blood, yet commonly the social instinct, and the love of ease, and the fear of retribution, prevail over what is hostile and malignant in our nature. In the absence of injury or provocation, men generally wish others well, and are even disposed to do them good. To some of the duties of Christianity there is therefore no natural aversion, no active repugnance. And it is greatly to be feared that many are basing their hopes of heaven upon their exemption from the vices that corrupt and embroil society, upon their amiable feelings and kind relations, upon neighborly offices and charitable expenditures. But those virtues which are merely human, educational, conventional, cannot save. In this world they have their origin, their use, and their reward. The great element of piety is wanting. There is no reference to God. And here is a marked difference between the man who lives for himself and the man who lives unto the Lord. The one obeys a constitutional impulse perhaps—consults his reputation, his business, his influence; or, it may be, rising a little higher, he may rightly estimate his responsibilities as a father or as a citizen, and so is honorable, moral, refined. But he is without God in the world. O the loneliness and destitution of such a spirit! Atheism is his religion, if not his creed; or at best he is an idolater, himself the idol. The other realizes the divine authority, and obeys *because* God commands. The relative duties of life are performed not to gratify a native generosity, or eke out a dubious popularity, but as part of the service and homage due his Maker. Over the whole circumference of his engagements, in the bosom of his family, the busy marts of trade, the retirement of the closet, the worship of the sanctuary, the citizenship of the world, there presides a solemn recognition of the Divine Presence, his being and his empire, and every step is taken in reference to him as a witness and a judge.

I know that many profess and seem to be religious on lower principles. Public opinion, consistency, ease of conscience, to shun hell, to gain heaven, all operate, and they supersede and dethrone the higher law in the text—not that these motives are illegitimate, but partial and inferior. They ought not to become principal and paramount; and they cannot without a deleterious unhingement of character, and a transfer of our duty from the ground of what is divine and authoritative to that which is human and self-pleasing. The motive in the text is comprehensive, embracing all lower ends; harmonizes all, yet subordinates them all to its own sovereign sway. Like a conqueror at the head of his battalions, it marches forth to subdue the insurgent elements that would dispute its dominion. It is the "stronger man" keeping his goods in peace. Without it, there can be no consecration; and with it, no compromise of duty. The failure to recognize and adopt this great principle of morality has fearfully diluted the experience of the Church, and embarrassed every department of Christian service. "I will run in the way of thy commandments, when thou shalt enlarge my heart," said the psalmist. No man can rise above the constraining considerations which spring from interest, feeling, safety, pleasure, in reference to all minor questions of duty, save as he resolves religion into some great general principles and purposes, from the decision of which there is no appeal.

These principles, wisely adopted and well understood, will marshal all the chances and changes of life, all its untoward events, all its interfering agencies, so that they shall fall into ranks like well-trained soldiers under the command of a superior officer. They simplify religion, disentangle it from all purely selfish influences, from the bias of worldly interest, from the guile of passion, and leave a man free to glorify God according to the Scriptures. How simple and sublime the character, deriving its greatness and worth from God and duty! How grandly independent is he who knows no fear but the fear of God, who seeks no favor but the smile of Jesus, and whose single eye scans all things, great and small, in the light which no shadow can eclipse! His life regulated by one great pervading law and purpose, he escapes all the trials by which feebler and less decided Christians are tormented and impeded. His heart, consecrated in all its plans and purposes, falters not at sacrifice or peril or suffering. Difficulties and doubts he has none. His religion is to him a law that never changes. His heart is fixed, trusting in the Lord. His plan of life settled scripturally, advisedly, and in the fear of God, he is not to be bought or bribed, frightened or defeated. Turning neither to the right nor left, he moves right on. If along his pathway the den of lions opens, he lies down and lodges for the night, and in the morning tells how the angel kept him. If the furnace be kindled to test or to destroy him, he walks unburned in the flame, and comes forth without the smell of fire upon his garments. Escaped from the shallows and the breakers where so many toil with unavailing oar, he has launched on the deep, and, favored by wind and tide, looks with lively hope for an abundant entrance into the everlasting kingdom of our Lord and Saviour Jesus Christ.

But the principle I am discussing, considered as a test of character and a rule by which to adjudicate our Christian claims, is worthy of enlargement. Living unto the Lord implies that we make the approbation of God our governing aim, that we study to please him, and that, whatever we do, we do all to his glory.

Religion to be saving must be supreme. "My son, give me thine heart." "He that loveth father or mother more than me, is not worthy of me." God claims the body and the spirit. He will not divide the empire which is his by right with invaders and usurpers. Unless, therefore, his approval is the predominant motive, we not only base our Christianity upon mistaken apprehensions of the Divine claims, but we repudiate the only principle which can subjugate the rebellious elements and passions of our fallen nature. Before conversion we form attachments and allow indulgences wholly inconsistent with a life of devotion. To do well we must first cease to do evil. The flesh, with its affections and lusts, must be crucified. Self-denial is the first law of discipleship. Who would submit to have the right hand cut off, the right eye plucked out—much less perform the operation upon himself—unless, by the expulsive power of a new and holy affection, these enemies which encamped within his heart shall be routed and taken captive? There must be the ascendency of another and a higher principle than any which is merely human to break down the dominion of appetite and passion and habit. Flesh and blood are sad counselors in the work of God. To consult them is to betray our spiritual interests. The multitude do evil; we must dare to be singular. But who will come out from the world, brave its scorn, defy its persecution, disdain its blandishments, and rebuke its ungodliness by declining its fellowship? None but those who feel that God's smile amply remunerates for the world's contempt, and that the testimony that we please him outweighs all earthly treasure, and outshines all earthly glory.

To live for Christ and to live for ourselves is utterly impracticable. The union is a moral impossibility. We love a good name; but they that will live godly in Christ Jesus shall suffer persecution. We are rich, but the command is, "Sell all that thou hast, and give to the poor, and come follow me." We love home and friends; but Christ calls to absence and labor and sacrifice. Religion is popular—you embrace it; the Church is fashionable—you join it. The people shout, "Hosanna!" and Jesus is escorted by a worshiping multitude—you say, "Lord, I will follow thee whithersoever thou goest." The Master replies: "The foxes have holes, and the birds of the air have nests, but the Son of man hath not where to lay his head." What will you do now? Go away sorrowful? or, having counted the cost, go on to build? "Choose ye this day whom ye will serve;" or have you settled this question long ago in favor of duty and Heaven? Are you living unto the Lord? You are making a fortune—is it that you may do more good? You are rising in the world, seeking title and honor and influence—is it that you may enlarge your sphere of usefulness? O brother, if the carnal affection grows along with the carnal interest, thy prosperity may destroy thee! Or, if thou art seeking thy own pleasure, gratification, and advancement, thou hast fallen from grace. Even Christ pleased not himself. Paul obeyed the heavenly vision immediately, conferring not with flesh and blood. And every man who would fulfill the great purposes of his creation and redemption must make God's approving judgment the motive of all his actions and the goal of all his efforts. O how the saints of the Bible luxuriated in this element of devotion!

"One thing have I desired of the Lord, that will I seek after: that I may dwell in the house of the Lord all the days of my life, to behold the beauty of the Lord, and to inquire in his temple." "I count all things but loss, for the excellency of the knowledge of Christ Jesus my Lord." These exemplars illustrate our subject. They lived unto the Lord. In his favor was life. "A day in his courts was better than a thousand." The world's parade and pomp paled before the glory of the sanctuary. The festal charms, the music, and the mirth of the tents of wickedness were despised, and the lowest place in the house of God preferred. They felt that they did not live at all except as they lived unto the Lord.

This is the spirit of the text. Life is not to be measured by days and months and years, but by a succession of services to Him that loved us and gave himself for us. I have no doubt that when the last hour comes—that hour for which earth has no comfort and philosophy no hope—when the spirit, disenthralled from the seductions of time, the witchery of sense, shall stand face to face with the realities of an eternal state, then even life's most serious engagements will all seem as vacancies, like the hours passed in sleep, and the pleasures of the world like the vagaries of sleep itself. Go buy, sell, get gain, build a name, rear houses, add field to field, project public improvements, locate railroads, plan empires—this is all labor and travail, vanity and vexation of spirit.

This is to breathe, not to live; to work, not to enjoy. "All flesh is as grass, and all the glory of man as the flower of grass;" "but he that doeth the will of God, liveth and abideth forever." To love God, this is joy; to know Christ, this is gain; to do good, this is life. Mortal man! child of the dust! this vain life which we spend as a shadow is but the vestibule of being. Here we die while we live; the cradle rocks us to the tomb. We spend our strength for naught. Riches fledge and fly away. Honor is but a dew-drop, glittering in the morning ray, exhaled by the very beam that makes it shine. Love and friendship—the heart's best affections—wounded, pine; or, bereaved, they dwell among the dead, like Mary, weeping there. O where is the bloom without the blight? the sun without the cloud? Lord Jesus, thou wilt show me the path of life; in thy presence, though dimly seen, is unutterable joy; and where thou art in glory visible, is heaven.

"Whether we die, we die unto the Lord." This is an important declaration, "wholesome and full of comfort." "Precious in the sight of the Lord is the death of his saints." The death of a good man is of too much import to happen by chance. It is an important instrument in God's plans of mercy and judgment. The event is big with instruction. Not to lay it to heart when the righteous perish is criminal insensibility—a wicked indifference to the dispensations of Heaven. Such a death is a public calamity. It is not a sparrow falling to the ground, a flower fading in the field, "the sear and yellow leaf" afloat upon the autumnal gale, and then descending to the earth, where its mates of the forest lie hueless and dead. A light is quenched, and the darkness grows deeper. The world is bereaved of a conservative influence. The prayers he would have offered are lost; and if "the fervent effectual prayer of a righteous man availeth much," how great the loss! The family loses a guide and guardian, the Church an example, the country a benefactor. He serves the country best who loves God most. He is not the patriot who fights the nation's battles, right or wrong, but he who leads a life of quietness and peace, in all godliness and honesty. He is not the most important man who projects your laws, marshals your parties, and leads in politics, but he who, by faith and prayer and power with God, averts the wrath our sins provoke. David did more for Judah when he bought Araunah's threshing-floor, built an altar, offered sacrifice, and stayed the pestilence, than when, with kingly authority, he dispatched Joab to quell the rebellion of Absalom. The intercession of Moses when, with holy boldness, with daring confidence, he rushed between the offending Israelites and the Almighty, girded for battle and extermination, and prevailed for their salvation, wrought a greater wonder than when, obedient to his magic rod, the parted waters returned in vengeance upon Pharaoh's pursuing host. Elijah was the chariot of Israel and the horsemen thereof—the bulwark of the nation. The clouds of heaven hung their keys at his girdle, and the widow's meal and oil multiplied beneath his blessing. A good man! O ye men of royal birth, ye sages, statesmen, heroes, ye glimmer faintly beside the saint shining in the image of God! His wisdom is divine, his lineage heavenly, and greater than he who taketh a city, for he hath conquered himself. I admire architecture, painting, sculpture, the wonders of the chisel and the pencil. I love nature in her mountain majesty, the rolling ocean, and the woodland vales—all that is lovely and sublime—but God is witness I would go farther to see a good man, to hear him talk of Jesus, enter into his communion, feel the moral grandeur of his destiny, than to behold any achievement of art or scene of nature. These change and perish; he is immortal. He thinks, he feels, he loves. His body is the temple of the Holy Ghost, and his spirit is bathed in the glory of the shekinah — the symbol of the presence and worship of God. The departure of such a man is a token of displeasure. It is the voice of Heaven in judgment. But, though the family is afflicted, the Church in mourning, and the nation smitten, *he* " dies unto the Lord" and "in the Lord." With him "it is well."

Or the text may find its fulfillment in that God hides him from the evil to come. I knew a good man who, in dying, said, "My God is housing me from a storm;" and the declaration was prophetic. Soon evils that would have broken his heart and brought him in sorrow to the grave came upon his family in overwhelming disaster. Dangers—spiritual dangers—are coming; domestic calamities draw nigh; national troubles are fermenting; God sees the clouds gathering, the elements brewing; and, while yet the cloud is as a man's hand, and the winds are murmuring afar off, he transfers his faithful servant to the repose of the blest. "In his hand are all my ways." Delightful thought! He directs my steps, hears my sighs, chooses my allotments, numbers the hairs of my head, is about my bed and my path, and knoweth how and when to deliver. "Whether we die, we die unto the Lord."

But it may be asked: "Why, if the righteous are so dear to Christ and so valuable to the world, are they doomed to death at all? Why does not religion, which saves us from a thousand other evils, release us from this law of mortality?" In answer, I remark: The reasons are obvious on reflection. Exemption from death as a reward of piety would appeal so strongly to the love of life—the quickest, most enduring instinct of our being—as to override the freedom of choice, and thus make rational, voluntary piety impossible. We should adopt it as a starving man would clutch offered bread, or the man dying of thirst would seize the cup of cold water. And besides, the violence done to our nature in making the propensities decide a question belonging, under the present economy and in the proper fitness and adaptation of things, to the intellect, the heart, the will, the incongruity would follow of proposing a carnal, earthly motive for a spiritual life. On such a plan, Christianity must approve what she now repudiates; and the holy considerations by which she now seeks to win us from error to wisdom, from earth to heaven, would all be neutralized and lost, and the world to come be doomed to borrow the forces of time to achieve its noblest victories.

The evil of sin cannot be shown but by its punishment. This conclusion is legitimate from what is revealed of the divine administration, and from what we know of the processes of conviction in the mind of man. God hates sin. It is a blot upon his dominions. But he has not left the world to learn the fact even from the awful denunciations of his word, but he has written it in the catastrophe of nations. The deluge, famine, pestilence, fire and brimstone from heaven, have been the messengers of his wrath and the instruments of retribution. And where, save in the crucifixion of Christ Jesus and the damnation of the guilty, will you look for a more impressive demonstration of God's justice and his indignation against sin than in the dying agonies of infant innocence, or the mortal convulsions of him who dies unto the Lord? It is written, "The body is dead because of sin," even when "the spirit is life because of righteousness." But death, with all its antecedents and consequents, the mournful harbingers of its approach and its power, the loathsome desolations of its victory and its reign, to the saint of God is no longer death. It is but dissolution—a departure. Sad in its aspects and accompaniments, it is nevertheless a release. A pillar of cloud and fire, its shadows all fall on this side the grave; beyond, all is light and life and glory. We die unto the Lord, and—may I not add—for the Lord. The death of the good preaches terror to the wicked. "If the righteous scarcely be saved, where shall the sinner and the ungodly appear?" O we ask not "Enoch's rapturous flight nor Elijah's fiery steeds" to bear us away, if by dying we may help to convince the world of sin and judgment! We would do good even in death. As we wish to live to serve Him " who loved us," so would we die to make his glory known—" the justice and the grace."

"Mark the perfect man and behold the upright, for the end of that man is peace." "The chamber where the good man meets his fate" is a scene of glory. See his patience under suffering—the calm submission, and often the joy unutterable. Is this human fortitude, the stoicism of a blind philosophy, the outflashing of sentiment and fancy? No, no. It is the fulfillment of promise; grace abounds. It is the conviction that the Judge of all the earth will do right. "Though he slay me, yet will I trust in him." It is the knowledge of the Redeemer in his pardoning mercy, his purifying spirit, and in the glory soon to be revealed in its fullness and eternity. It is an argument for religion that it ends well. "Let me die the death of the righteous, and let my last end be like his." The prophet's prayer finds an echo in every heart not lost to hope and heaven. Who that looks upon a dying-scene where Christianity wreathes the pale face with smiles of rapture, and inspires the failing tongue to utter its last articulations in the dialect of heaven, does not breathe from his inmost soul the wish, Even so may I meet the last enemy? In life, being strong in faith, we give glory to God; so in the final struggle he is glorified in us and by us. "These all died in faith;" immortal record, epitaph of the good, and interpreter of their doom. Living and dying, "we are the Lord's"—his property—absolutely, in every change, walking upon the earth and sleeping in its bosom. He made us and he loves us. He is "not ashamed to be called" our God. Life, probation, and death are all ministers employed by him to do us good. If he prolong our days, it is that we may serve him and our generation by the will of God. If he afflict us, it is "for our profit, that we may be partakers of his holiness."

If he call us hence, it is that we may "see him as he is, and be like him forever." Our bodies may inhabit the house appointed for all the living, and our very name perish from the records of time, but he looks down and "watches all our dust till he shall bid it rise." We are the Lord's—the jewels of his kingdom and the travail of his soul. He hath said it, and it shall stand fast—"they shall be mine;" "because I live, they shall live also." "We are the Lord's." Let us rejoice in our relationship, and walk worthy of our high descent and our immortal destiny.

The principle and spirit of the text were beautifully exemplified in the life and death of our beloved brother, Bishop Capers. I have never known a man of more simple, single-hearted, uncalculating devotion. Born of God while yet a youth, his life was consecrated unreservedly to the service of Christ and his Church. Through all the changes of his career—youth, maturity, and age; single, married, and surrounded by sons and daughters; on circuits, stations, and districts; a deacon, an elder, and a Bishop—he exhibited the same steady, onward devotion, a man of God, of faith, of zeal. His steadfast purpose never faltered, no change of fortune modified the entireness of his dedication, no accumulation of cares relaxed his efforts to do good. He lived unto the Lord. Absence from home might entail loss, afflict feeling, tax affection; no matter, he had set his heart within him to finish his course with joy, and the ministry which he had received of the Lord Jesus to testify the gospel of the grace of God. On more than one occasion he might have secured to his family a home rich in comforts, and to himself honors and emoluments, by separating himself from the itinerancy he loved and consenting to serve a people who proved their esteem by the largeness of their offered liberality. But attached to our Church and its economy by conviction and choice, salary was no temptation to leave it, or even to modify his relation to it; and, in the face of all the sacrifices and privations and labors of a traveling Methodist preacher, he declined a city home and a well-filled purse.

My acquaintance with our dear departed brother—I ought to call him father—began while I was but a boy and he was in the meridian of his strength and the blaze of a renown such as few attain. The impressions made upon me then, by his humble manner, his sanctified conversation, and his unwearied labors, were fully justified by the familiarity of intercourse in after years. He seemed to me to be dead to the world, its gains and honors, and alive only to the glory of God and the salvation of souls. While his name was upon every tongue, and crowds were rushing from appointment to appointment, and the whole country was in a fever of curiosity and admiration, he seemed to shrink from fame and the exultation by which a common mind and a common heart would have been lifted up in his case was lost in an overwhelming sense of the responsibility his position entailed. He was one of the very few men I have known who was not injured in his piety and preaching by great popularity. To seek popularity as an object, in a minister is a crime; to bear it meekly when it comes unsought, is a virtue of rarest value.

This virtue characterized, distinguished William Capers in the freshness of his youth, the glory of his noon, and in the mellow ripeness of his sanctified old age. He was clothed with humility. It was his beauty and his strength. The praise even of the lowly oppressed him. Courted and caressed by the rich, the great, the mighty in the land, he shrunk from their embrace, lest he might seem to others to be seeking great things for himself. His faith was never hindered by seeking the honor of men, his fidelity never compromised by the adulation of the Church or the world.

Who ever heard him tell of the mighty works he had done, the great sermons he had preached, the wondrous revivals he had carried on? Who ever saw in his air the conceit of success, or detected in his language the self-gratulation of a praiseworthy deed? He was not the hero of his narratives, nor did he talk to make the simple wonder or the great admire. Like Paul, whose visit to the third heaven was kept a secret for fourteen years, and revealed at last only to vindicate his apostleship, he said but little of his own experience, save in the retirement of private life to the ear of intimate companionship. Astonishingly fluent, he talked much, but always well. He never forfeited in private the reputation he had made in public. Cheerful without levity, and easy without familiarity, he never degraded the ministry into the trifler, nor reproached the sanctity of his profession by foolish talking or jesting, which are not convenient. As a man, his nature was alive and gushing with all noble, generous impulses. Kind, affectionate, full of sympathy, he rejoiced with them that rejoiced, and wept with them that wept. In his family, gentle without weakness, and fond without improper indulgence. His wife—herself a model woman—revered while she loved, and honored while she served. His children, feeling themselves favored of Heaven in the virtues of such a father, obeyed his commands, consulted his wishes, and felt his smile to be a meed and a recompense. No man loved his children more. He regretted in the last hour that so few of them were present, and yet rejoiced that he had seen them so recently. Lovely family!—children honored in their parents, and parents honored in their children. God's best blessing continue with them to the latest generation.

It is not amiss to say that Bishop Capers was in manners a gentleman—bland, courtly, refined. In him the polish of the courtier and the simplicity of the saint beautifully blended. His politeness did not consist in the formalities and ceremonies which, in certain circles, are dignified as the insignia of the well-bred and the fashionable, but it was the outgushing of a heart which knew no rule but the promptings of its own benevolence. It was the outward expression of an inward disposition, a mode of action which a loving spirit instinctively prescribed, the free, untaught, unconstrained operation of Christian courtesy. In the parlor and the pulpit, the street and the sanctuary, he was minutely regardful of the proprieties of life; and while the simplest rustic found no affectation, the fastidious critic discovered no fault.

I must not omit to mention his excellence in prayer. Whether we consider his power as a gift or a grace, he surpassed most men. In his devotions there was so much of the evangelical element that a heathen man might have learned the plan of salvation from any one of his public exercises. On his knees he knew nothing but Christ. The cross was his all-prevailing plea. He urged it with fervor, affection, and faith. He was himself an intercessor, filled with yearning sympathies for his fellow-men. And sometimes his power with God would remind us of Jacob and the angel, of Israel and his blessing.

To describe him as a preacher belongs rather to his biographer than to the sketch of a funeral discourse. He was a scribe well instructed in the kingdom of God, an able minister of the New Testament. He brought forth out of his treasure things new and old. Rich in thought, fertile in matter, there was no sameness in his discourses, even when he preached from the same text—which he often did. I never heard him use the same illustration twice, or falter for a word. Copious in language, apt in selection, and inexhaustible in variety, he was always ready and always new. It is difficult to classify his style as a preacher. His sermons were not essays nor expositions, nor were they narratives with reflections interspersed, nor yet topical exactly; still, all these sometimes—except the first—were mingled by him. Perhaps the word textual will fit his manner best. His sermons grew out of his texts—not by formal divisions, but by an artistic development, a verbal evolution of their meaning. Under his peculiar management many a verse or passage to the untrained eye dark—or at least obscure—became instructive, beautiful, most interesting. Gifted with wonderful versatility and readiness, he excelled all I ever knew in adapting his text and discourse on a sudden call to all that was peculiar on the occasion. He often awakened attention by the announcement of a verse which none but he would ever have chosen. In this, however, he was not fanciful or eccentric, but simply obeyed the impulse of a mind unique in its conceptions and modes of thought. In thought, language, style, he was original, yet without eccentricity; called no man master, and yet violated no rule of the books; always accurate, always simple, but elegant in his simplicity. His sermons were often ornate, but there was no florid coloring, no exuberance, no glare. There was a delightful propriety, a minute beauty, a neat, chaste, graceful arrangement of every part. His flowers were not artificial; they all had roots, and they were redolent with the morning dew, fresh and fragrant as a vernal garden in the early day.

It is but just to say that his pulpit efforts were very unequal; yet, in his driest, darkest moods, he was William Capers; all the mental characteristics of the man stood forth; a familiar acquaintance could not fail to recognize them. He possessed the singular faculty of speaking with fluency, grace, and propriety when his mind was barren and empty, and his hearers listened well pleased, even when they got nothing to carry away. But at other times he was transfigured, his very form dilated, his eye beamed with celestial beauty, soft with the light of love, yet radiant with the joy of his rapt and ravished spirit, and his voice, mellowed by emotion, spell-bound while it inspired the hearing multitude. When the Spirit of the Lord God was upon him, when the angel touched his lips with a coal from the altar, O he was a charming preacher! I have heard him when the consolations of the gospel distilled from his tongue as honey from the rock, and the message of salvation came down like the angelic song upon the shepherds of Bethlehem. Anon I have seen him clothe himself with terrible majesty, as when a prophet proclaimed the vengeance of the Almighty, and then the thunder of the violated law pealed from his lips like the trump of doom, and the pallid, awestruck assembly told that the preacher had power with God and prevailed with men.

For the mourner in Zion, the grief-stricken, the bowed, the desolate, he had the tongue of the learned and the heart of a seraph. O the pathos of his sympathy, how touching and tender! It was a healing oil, a soothing balsam. Beneath its magic charm desolation bloomed and tears were turned to rapture. Many a way-worn pilgrim, weary with life's heavy burdens, faint yet pursuing with faltering steps, felt his hopes revive and his courage grow strong while this "old man eloquent" discoursed of providence and grace and heaven, of the cross, the mercy-seat, and the crown of life. These were the themes on which he loved to dwell; they were the rejoicing of his heart and the staple of his ministry. But the harp is broken, and all its music gone. The pleasant voice is hushed, and he who played so well upon that wondrous instrument, the human tongue, lies low in cold obstruction and dumb forgetfulness. Bishop Capers is no more! His place at the council-board of the Church he loved is empty. The pulpit shall know him no more forever. The grave's dark eclipse rests upon that beaming face, and that venerable form that moved among us but a little while ago, shrouded, coffined, buried, sleeps in death—thank God, in Jesus too!—awaiting the descent of the judgment angel and the revelation of the Son of man.

The circumstances of his decease have been so widely published, are so generally known, that I need not detail them now. Suffice it to say that having finished his last episcopal tour, visited his children, he returned to his quiet home to rest for a season in the bosom of his family. O the sober bliss, the grateful joy of such a meeting! It was a mercy that allowed him this last interview. Death found the soldier in his tent, recruiting for another campaign. At midnight the spoiler came. The sleeping household were roused by the trembling cry of the wife, the mother, in the agony of her alarm. They rushed to the good man's chamber, and found him sitting up, but writhing in pain. "Make my blood circulate," he said. They essayed the task, but failed. Seeing their alarm, and feeling that his end was nigh, he said: "I am already cold; and now, my precious children, give me up to God. O that more of you were here! but I bless God that I have so lately seen you all." But see how principle and duty and devotion to the Church worked at the last and to the last. Bathed in the dew of mortality, enduring untold agony, longing for the faces of those he loved, gasping in death, he said: "Mary, I want you to finish my minutes to-morrow, and send them off." Duty was his law in life, his watch-word at the gate of death. Partially relieved by the physician's skill and the power of medicine, he asked the hour. When told, he exclaimed, "What! only three hours since I have been suffering such torture? Only three hours! What must be the voice of the bird that cries, 'Eternity, eternity!' Three hours have taken away all but my religion." Health gone, strength gone, hope gone, life almost gone, but religion abides steadfast and stronger. Retreating from the shore where stand wife, children, and friends waving their last adieu, but my religion goes with me. All the foundations of earth are failing me, but my religion still towers amid the general wreck, securely firm, indissolubly sure. Glory to God for such a testimony from such a man!

For a little while nature seemed to rally, the king of terrors to relent. His children retired to rest at his urgent entreaty. On the morning of the 29th of January he proposed to rise and dress himself, and insisted that his devoted wife should seek repose. She reminded him of the doctor's prescription, and besought him to keep his bed. He took the medicine, drank freely of water, pillowed his head upon his arm, and breathed his last.

> So fades a summer cloud away;
>   So sinks the gale when storms are o'er;
> So gently shuts the eye of day;
>   So dies a wave along the shore.
>
> Life's duty done, as sinks the clay,
>   Light from its load, the spirit flies;
> While heaven and earth combine to say,
>   "How blest the righteous when he dies!"

In the history of our honored, beloved brother there is no vice to deplore and no error to lament. I say not that he was perfect; but I do say a world of such men would liken earth to heaven. I say not that he had no infirmities, no human frailties; but I do say that his self-sacrificing spirit, his humble, holy, useful labors, his unwearied zeal, and his spotless example are to his descendants a noble patrimony, and to the Church a priceless heritage. Alive, he was a demonstration of the power and truth of Christianity; being dead, he yet speaketh, proclaiming to all that God is faithful. He left all and followed Christ, but never lacked any good thing. Counting all things but loss that he might win Christ, God gave him friends and fame, and honor and usefulness. A messenger of God, his visits were blessings. The country admired him and the Church loved him. His death fell like a shadow upon many a hearth-stone, and his native State became a valley of weeping. Cities struggled for the honor of his burial, and Methodism, in mourning, repeats his funeral to prolong her grief and consecrate his memory. O brethren! we have lost a friend, a brother, an advocate, an example, a benefactor. Earth is growing poorer. There is now less faith, less zeal, less love in the world. The righteous are perishing, the good are taken away. O ye venerable fathers of the Church, contemporaries and fellow-laborers of the ascended Capers, your ranks are broken! The friends of your youth are gone, and relics of a generation well-nigh past, ye still linger among us. God bless you, we love you very much, but we cannot keep you much longer! Your sands are running low, your change is at hand. You, venerable sir,* are almost the only bond that binds the preacher and the congregation to the pioneers of Methodism in this broad country. That bond, fretted and worn by more than three-score years and ten, is well-nigh threadless, attenuated, and ready to break. But God is with you. The raven hair, the ruddy cheek, the vigorous arm, the enduring strength, are gone—all gone—but *your religion too*, thank God, is left you! Leaning upon that staff, you are waiting your summons. Heaven bless you with a smiling sunset, a pleasing night, and a glorious morn! And you, hoary veterans of the cross—one and all—heroes of a glorious strife, remnants of an army slain and yet victorious, if we survive when ye are gone, how bereaved and solitary our lot! But ye are going; the wrinkled brow, the furrowed cheek, the halting step re-

---

* Bishop Soule.

spond, Yes, we are going. Pray for us while you live, and bless us when you die.

And you, brethren—middle-aged and young—let us imitate the example, catch the spirit, of our glorified brother and fellow-laborer. He felt himself a debtor to the wise and the unwise. The white man, the Indian, and the negro all shared his counsel, his labors, his sympathy, and his prayers. The white fields are yet ungathered, and the strongest reapers are falling. The mournful event ye commemorate cries, Go work to-day in the Lord's vineyard! This is our duty, and ought to be our only business. We are here, as officers and ministers of our branch of the Church, to inaugurate our great missionary and publishing interests under new auspices. But the cold shadow of death falls darkly upon our council-chamber. Its presence is a warning. We have home interests we may not live to supervise; there are plans of usefulness we may not help to execute; for we too are passing away. What we do must be done quickly. Let us live unto the Lord. Let us live unto the Lord more than ever. Let us be more prompt, self-denying, and laborious. Let us be steadfast, unmovable, always abounding in the work of the Lord, forasmuch as we know that our labor is not in vain in the Lord. What we lay out he will repay. Amid our toil, inconveniences, and trials, be this our consolation: "We are the Lord's." If we live till our physical powers decay, the dim eye may still read our title clear. On Jesus' bosom we may lean the hoary head, and in death's sad struggle feel our kind Preserver near. God will not love us less because "the strong men bow themselves," and "the keepers of the house tremble." His love endureth forever. His claim is undeniable; his title indisputable. The grave's effacing fingers cannot mutilate the handwriting. Time's ponderous wheel, as it grinds the world to dust on its march to judgment, cannot destroy the record. "A book of remembrance is written before him"—safe beyond the desolations of earth and the triumphs of the sepulcher. Heeding, then, the solemn providence which bids us weep a brother deceased, let us go forth bearing precious seed, sowing beside all waters—we shall rest, and stand in our lot at the end of the days. "Whether we live therefore, or die, we are the Lord's." Living and dying, dead and buried, we are his—his when we rise, his when heaven and earth are fled and gone, his in the New Jerusalem forever and ever!

"Servant of God, well done!
  Rest from thy loved employ;
The battle fought, the vict'ry won,
  Enter thy Master's joy."
The voice at midnight came;
  He started up to hear;
A mortal arrow pierced his frame:
  He fell, but felt no fear.

Tranquil amid alarms,
  It found him on the field,
A vet'ran slumb'ring on his arms
  Beneath his red-cross shield.
His sword was in his hand,
  Still warm with recent fight,
Ready that moment, at command,
  Through rock and steel to smite.

The pains of death are past,
  Labor and sorrow cease;
And life's long warfare closed at
  His soul is found in peace.
Soldier of Christ, well done!
  Praise be thy new employ;
And while eternal ages run,
  Rest in thy Saviour's joy.

Why Women Should be Well Educated.*

THE rage for female education in Georgia is a phenomenon, an anomaly, almost a mania. It is strange, wonderful, well-nigh unaccountable. Regarded as a great social fact in the progress of the times and the people, it has no parallel in the past. History records no such movement. The oldest civilization of the Old World furnished no such development. Poetry, romance, chivalry, never dreamed of such devotion to woman. It is a monumental fact, the acknowledged memorial of tardy justice, and the significant index of popular conviction and purpose.

The history and philosophy of this movement, with some suggestive reflections, will constitute the topic of this address.

The college at Macon, first known as the Georgia Female College, since the Wesleyan Female College, stands first upon the list in the order of existence. Projected in 1837, organized in January, 1839, it still lives unencumbered and prosperous. It had its embarrassments and its foes, its debts and its disappointments, even while its classes were full and its annual contributions to society were brilliant and useful. Itself an experiment, it has vindicated the wisdom of its projectors, confounded the predictions of its enemies, and I might say has revolutionized public opinion, corrected its errors, enlightened its estimate of woman's influence, and brought into play new elements of power, conservative and efficient. A peculiar public spirit has been awakened;

---

* Delivered July 10, 1856, in Madison, Ga., during the commencement exercises of the Madison Female College.—EDITOR.

parental ambition has been roused. Village vies with village, city with city; the State is adorned with buildings, all beautiful, some magnificent. Decayed towns are revived, and this empire commonwealth is made the glory of her citizens and the wonder of her neighbors. Eastern, Middle, Western, Northern, and Southern Georgia are well supplied with these instrumentalities of education. A "female college" has come to be the index of progress in the line of social advancement; the exponent of civilization, the front banner in the march of mind; the central diamond in the diadem of that wondrous age we glorify as the nineteenth century. As a stone cast into the bosom of the sleeping waters agitates them to their utmost boundaries, so the refluent waves of the movement in Macon seventeen years ago are sweeping out in circles wider and wider still. Already the undulations are beating at the base of your farthest mountains, rolling unchecked over your southern plains—on, still on, knowing neither weariness nor rest. Who shall, who would stay the tide? Albeit, we know not whereunto this thing may grow, who fears the consequences? Let it alone; there is healing in its wave. It is waking the pulse of vitality in the stagnation of ages. It is pouring its crystal waters into the old Dead Sea of ignorance and prejudice, on whose blasted shores no flower could bloom, and whose only fruit was but bitterness and ashes. Let it alone; it is bearing upon its bosom the intellectual fortunes of unnumbered families, and is freighted with blessings for thousands more.

This extraordinary development, however peculiar in some of its phases, is yet explicable on the most obvious principles of the human mind. Through long centuries and in every land woman has been strangely underrated as to her intellect, her influence on mind, character, society, and government. Even in Christian countries, where juster views of her individual claims prevail, she has been appropriated and confined to a sphere of action which, although legitimate to her sex and her relations, nevertheless circumscribes and forestalls the powers capable of nobler deeds and more useful expansion. The opinion which restricts woman to the kitchen and the nursery, or which brings her forth on gala days—days of ceremony and festal gladness, just as we gather flowers to wreathe an arch or garland a bridal-hall—results from a radical misconception of woman's nature, of God's design, and of the world's social interest. Indeed, all the exclusive and restrictive theories of society and education which do not recognize woman as an intellectual helpmeet for man affiliate with that Asiatic barbarism which cloisters her when at home and veils her when she walks abroad. But "time, which overthrows the illusions of opinion and establishes the decisions of nature," has been working out a revolution of sentiment which, in the progress of knowledge and Christianity, will achieve and vindicate a new order of things. Like all other revolutions, it has its foes and its defeats, its rapid triumphs and its sudden arrests. But, from the day in which it was graciously conceded that women had souls at all, the world's opinion has been approximating the truth; and, as the light brightens around it, it is correcting its former estimates, and providing for them more liberal arrangements. Now, when a great truth long hidden bursts upon the human mind it startles, electrifies, impels. Forcing itself upon our convictions, in the light of its own demonstration, we wonder that what is so plain was not seen before, and, mortified by the disclosure of our stupidity, we make haste to repair the damages of our delinquency. The sense of injustice made palpable to our understanding, and intensified by the noblest feelings of our nature, suggests the idea of atonement; and we labor to obliterate the memory of our neglect by heaping kindness on the victims of our error. Such a mood, it is true, is not favorable to a just discrimination, to wise plans; and sometimes it exhausts itself in well-meant but very injudicious enterprises. Nevertheless, an ill-managed movement, if underlaid by fundamental truth, will rectify its own defects as experience reveals them, and will evolve at last, from its formative processes, a well-organized system, symmetrical, efficient, and abiding.

The public mind of this country is now in this excited transition state. That woman, as one of the important agents in the constitution of society, needs and deserves culture and development is the common sentiment of Christian lands; but the mode and the measure of her education are points concerning which there is great conflict of opinion. Although immense practical issues are involved, the question is speculative—a controversy in which there is no umpire but experiment. But that the experiment may be fair and conclusive, it is essential that those views which insist upon a thorough and extensive education of our daughters should prevail till results shall prove them unsafe and unwise. If lower and more rudimental standards should be adopted, the possible capabilities of woman's mind may never be developed; and the evidence which such a partial system affords against deep and thorough training and in favor of superficial education, on the assumption of the constitutional incapacity of women for any thing better, is all negative. It proves nothing. The practice, though conformed to the theory, does not confirm it, because the opinion, which it ignores and denounces, is still left untested; whereas on trial its wisdom and its truth might be demonstrated. The loss to the world by this one-sided, tentative process has been immeasurable—loss of character, influence, and power. When, therefore, the advocates of a low, contracted, partial system appeal to society, its history, progress, and results, although they find many things apparently well adapted to their purpose, a closer examination will reveal the fallacy of their arguments, and turn even their proofs against them. That women, under a meager, restricted system, should have exhibited so much judgment and taste, good sense and refinement, is evidence strong as demonstration of what they might be and would be under a liberal and enlightened economy of instruction. What they have achieved is not the limit of their power; what they are is not the perfection of their nature. That they have not been degraded in intellect and grown imbecile under all the disadvantages of their lot only shows that they are the inheritors of a moral and mental economy so celestial as to be exceedingly hard to spoil. That they have made good housewives, prudent mothers, and interesting companions, under a programme of duties and relations which taught them that it was their business to feel and not to think, to sew and not to write, to look pretty and talk nonsense, rather than to aspire to knowledge and the legitimate influence of a social being, ought to close the argument and regenerate the policy of the world.

Much has been said of the intellectual equality of the sexes, and this mooted question still arrays its combatants on either side. In this tournament I break no lance. The party which wins the victory grasps a barren scepter. If there be inequality, the difference is not greater than among individuals of the same sex; and in my judgment the whole theory of accommodating education to what is peculiar and distinctive in either boys or girls, to the exclusion of every thing for which there is a supposed inaptitude, is impolitic if it were practicable, and impracticable if it were politic. Minds, all minds, differ in many respects. Some are tardy, some are precocious in their development; some reach their maximum of attainments and strength almost at a bound;

others toil on, step by step, and are accumulating for a lifetime. These peculiarities manifest themselves only in the progress of life and education. They cannot be determined by the sagacity of the teacher, nor foretold by the science of the phrenologist. Besides, it is the business of education to aid nature, to remedy her defects—directing what is strong, and strengthening what is weak. The truth is that voluntary, earnest, persevering, protracted mental action is the chief secret of becoming wise and great. By it, a feeble mind may be trained to energy and distinction; without it, a mighty intellect will degenerate into imbecility. The differences of aptitudes and exhibition among men and women are not strictly constitutional, but referable mainly to their mental habits. Allowing—as I think is just and proper—a diversity of mental organization, yet I insist that all the elements of mind are common to both.

The original combinations of these elements are endlessly diversified; but the characteristic results are not more marked as between men and women than between men and men. The dissimilarity, which I concede, if not created by education—the education of the fireside, the school-house, and the world of social life—is essentially modified by woman's social relations, and the passions and affections incident to those relations. The human mind is expanded or contracted, corrupted or refined, waxes into vigor or wanes into feebleness, according to the subjects of thought with which it is most familiar; and if women are not capable of strong thought, of deep analysis, of prolonged research, it is rather from mental desuetude than original incapacity. Compelled by the necessities of her allotment to think much of little things—meeting all the expectations of society, as now constituted, without effort, and perhaps disqualified by a defective education for high and sustained mental action—it is not marvelous that so few women are distinguished for great acumen and vigor of intellect. Even among men those are most distinguished for power of thought and felicity of expression whose professions and pursuits most constantly tax the thinking faculty on the high themes of statesmanship, philosophy, and religion. The deep thoughts, the mature judgment, the continuous reasonings, for which the great among men are celebrated, are not natural or spontaneous—the facile, untrained working of original powers. They are acquisitions, habits, the results of hard study and long practice; and, after all our boasted preëminence, very few reach high distinction in the departments where we claim to excel. Profound thinkers are rare—the prodigies of their generation. The present age is wofully degenerate; the race of great men is nearly extinct. England has now no Pitts or Peels or Wellingtons; France no Mirabeaus, Talleyrands, or Napoleons—or at most but one, and he is only "the nephew of his uncle." America has no more Calhouns, Clays, and Websters.

Even in the world of literature the chief actors have acquired notoriety rather than fame—like Dickens, by the quaint, outlandish titles of his books; like Thackeray, the strolling retailer of old court scandal; or like Carlyle and Emerson, by the most affected, arbitrary, and unnatural use of their mother-tongue—beguiling the world into the belief that they are deep, when they are only dark; profound, because they are unintelligible. In my humble opinion there is more mind, more sound wisdom, more wise, practical ideas in Hannah More's works than in all the ponderous tomes of the boasted German philosophy. The truth is, very great minds are rare in either sex; but the inference that all the rest of mankind are constitutionally incapable of great improvement would not be deemed a fair conclusion. Various solutions—natural, obvious, easy—can be found to explain the fact without charging all the rest of us with mental impotency. So I say in relation to women. Though not generally distinguished for intellect beyond the circle of their families and friends, yet the sex is not without representatives in all the varied walks of literature. The reasons for this are to be found first in the nature of their duties and the subjects with which they are most familiar—subjects which tend to fetter and dwarf the mind, and duties which leave no time for attention to any thing beyond the graceful, the light, the imaginative. No wonder, therefore, that females figure most in those departments most accordant with the delicacies of their physical and mental constitution, and to which they are restricted partly by the appointment of nature, but mainly by the decree of popular opinion.

Society has not only denied to women the motives for strong mental effort, by which the ambition of men is roused to action, but it positively offers the temptation to rest in inglorious mediocrity as the more respectable and attractive. The love of admiration is natural to the human heart, nor is the passion stronger with women than with men, save that the former are more dependent for their personal influence on their personal attractions. This common instinct of our nature seeks its gratification in those modes which observation and experience teach to be the most direct, the best adapted to popular taste. While, therefore, girls are made to believe that there is more power in a curl than in a thought, more witchery in complexion than in language, more attraction in graceful motion than in general knowledge, just so long the conventional notions of the world repress intellectual development and foster frivolities of character. The grave, the good, the great, are all parties to the policy which assures the female world that dress, figure, grace as to their persons, light conversation, frothy commonplaces, vapid inanities about beaux, courtship, and marriage, are about all that is expected of them, and that she who excels in these things is the belle of the hour. Even wise men, in their gallantry, talk nonsense to women, as though politeness required them to condescend to those of low intellectual estate.

Under the fallacious views which prevail, the young people, in all their social intercourse and at every festal gathering, seem to have conspired to ignore knowledge, taste, ideas, worthy of our rational nature, and to have resolved the charms of society into idle prattle, as unmeaning as the chattering of swallows. This abominable fashion does gross injustice to both parties. Men degrade their intellect in compliment to the fair, and the fair are betrayed by the compliment into unworthy estimates of themselves. This style of address, though intended to please, is actually an insult, as it implies an incapacity to appreciate any thing more sensible and exalted. Instead of listening well pleased with the twaddle of their obsequious admirers, I wish that women would resent this imputation upon their good sense, and compel the lords of creation into more rational conversation. I would as soon look to find the garden of Eden with its fruits and flowers on the icy shores of the circumpolar sea as to expect the emancipation of the female mind from the disabilities of the ruling fashion, unless women themselves pioneer the reform. But, ladies, in resenting the indignities which are perpetually offered you in life's daily walk, you must learn to discriminate. Amid the crowd of attendants who wait upon your smiles there are some with whom there has been a long, long famine of ideas. There is but a handful of meal in the barrel and a little oil in the cruse, and no prophet in the land to bless the scanty store. "They give you all; they can no more, though poor the offering be." *Spare these*, and keep your wrath for him who voluntarily makes a fool of himself because he is talking to a woman.

But that I may not be over-tedious, I will proceed to give positive reasons for the sound, thorough, extended education of woman. My first argument is scriptural and, I think, conclusive. The divine plan, as manifested in creation and in the significant title by which Eve was designated, indicates the true theory of the sexes as to their moral, intellectual, and social relations and duties. God made man and put him in the garden of Eden—a sacred inclosure, a paradise of delights. Eden and paradise are the synonyms of bliss—the types of heaven. Adam, the royal tenant, "made a little lower than the angels," was "monarch of all he surveyed." Earth fed him with her fruits; the crystal river that flowed through the midst of the garden furnished him with drink; the birds of the air regaled him with their songs; the beasts of the field acknowledged his supremacy. Innocent and pure, he walked and talked with God. But this unfallen intellect, this son of the morning, this occupant of a sinless world, sighed in solitude. What was wanting amid the munificence of his Creator's gifts? What did he need? A helpmeet. *A helpmeet?* Why; he had no house to be set to rights, no bread to bake, no garments to mend, no stockings to darn. None of the grave duties to which some theorizers would restrict the female world, for which we are told they were made, and for which alone they are fit, had any place in Adam's primal home. A helpmeet! Yes; the first man was alone, and it was not good for him. The glorious sun, the green earth, the sportive birds, the submissive beasts, were not companions. They could neither think nor talk nor feel. He sighed for sympathy, communion, bright eyes that would glow with admiration as they gazed with him on Eden's bloom; a soft, sweet voice to mingle its minstrelsy with the harmonies around him; a heart attuned with his to love and praise; a mind to think and soar and wonder amid creation's marvels; and with him to bow in adoration to the One who made them all. He wanted his other self—his better half. So God made another, not like him but of him—a process, an emanation, an improvement of himself, a completion of the circle of being, himself duplicated and refined: Adam and Eve, man and woman, identical in their nature, their minds and hearts, their interests and desires. Such was the Divine idea of a helpmeet for man, and such was Adam's understanding of it. Any other mode of relief would have been alien to him, the sources of sympathy would have been unlike, the bond of union wanting, the *help* would not have been *meet*—suitable—the twain could never ha e become one.

Exalt the mind of man as you may, a helpmeet for him must partake of the dignity. Glorify his affections, ally him with angels in his religious nature, she whom God has given him as a partner and companion must share in his inheritance. Whatever high and holy trusts have been committed to man—trusts dependent for their fulfillment not only upon sympathies and affections, but on mental oversight and guidance—it will follow that no order of help unaccompanied with high intellectual endowments would have been suitable. Now, the argument is that if our Maker, in the original constitution of the sexes, adapted them to each other as companions and counselors, each with mind to think, heart to love, soul to aspire, then any system of education which exalts the one and circumscribes or degrades the other is wrong in principle and policy.

That men ought to be educated is an accredited doctrine. The more they know the better. On this subject public opinion is a unit. Let me ask, then, Is an uneducated woman a helpmeet for an educated man? Is it right in society to foster a mode of instruction which dooms the noblest intellects to dwell alone or live ill-matched and unhappy? The evils of such a state of things are not incidental or partial only; they are inevitable and wide-spread. They disjoint the economy of nature, pervert the design of Heaven, in the only institution which has survived the doom and desolation of Eden. Marriage is honorable in all. It is of divine ordination, the origin of families, the nucleus of nations. No union is so intimate, no obligation so binding. Its consequences are momentous. The opinion which would degrade or abolish it is "a doctrine of devils." The sentiment, however modified, which enfeebles its bonds or contracts its enjoyments is inimical to morals and social happiness. Constituting as it does an absolute communion of wishes, joys, and sorrows, it must be founded in those views and affections, cherished by those affinities of sentiment and taste, which make the parties capable of mutual association. He is an unhappy husband who would rather his wife should be seen than heard, knowing that she will make a better impression by the grace of her robes than by the poverty of her discourse. She is a poor wife who cannot get a good dinner, who does not keep her children clean and well-dressed, her person and her house neat and tidy; but then a man wants intellectual communion—thought responsive to thought, soul kindling with soul, the joyous swell of kindred emotions and all the heaven of friendship, radiant with intellect and love. Leave woman untaught, her mind undeveloped, unenriched, and you bereave marriage of its significancy, and make her whom Heaven intended as a helper, companion, and friend a mere convenience and a toy. And the wretched man who, fascinated by her maiden charms, is betrayed by his fancy and his passion into indissoluble wedlock finds that he pleased his eyes, but broke his heart. Honor, self-respect, awe of public opinion, and, it may be, the fear of God, will hold him on to his fidelity; but the charm of wedded life is gone, the spell of love is broken, and, amid the blank desolation of the future, never returns to cheer him even with the memory of its smile. A marriage for money is a crime. A marriage for convenience is a life-long blunder. As long as human beings are sordid or sensual these ill-assorted unions will occur under the wisest and best social economy; but it is unquestionably the interest of individuals and society to harmonize as far as possible the intellectual condition of the sexes.

In my opinion no little moral obligation is here involved, whether we seek to prevent evil or promote happiness. Such harmony is important as an agency in diminishing the probabilities of unwise, unequal matches, and especially as it gives to woman the power to perpetuate her influence when the illusions of fancy have fled and stern reality comes to test her worth. Mind commands homage, and human nature pays its tribute of respect often even where virtue is wanting. How much more readily and profoundly when its honors crown the loved one to whose graces and virtues the heart has already yielded its devotions. When the rosy light of young beauty has faded from the cheek, the lustrous eye paled with the sorrow and cares of maternal life, the rounded figure grown lank and languid, and shrunk from its voluptuous fullness, then that woman who presides at the domestic board is a crownless queen, unless intelligence be there to renew the dominion which beauty has lost. When wrinkles have furrowed the once fair and beaming brow, the raven hair grown thin and gray, and life's green leaves are all sear and yellow, then mind beaming forth, like sunlight upon a ruin, gilds age with splendor, and gives to love's fervid day a bright, tranquil, balmy eve, leaving the contented husband in doubt whether life was happiest in its morning raptures or now amid its sunset joys

So profound are my convictions on this subject that, in the further prosecution of the point under discussion, I venture the declaration that the general education of women is more important to society than the general education of men. Or, if you like the negative form of the proposition better, the world would suffer less in its most vital interests from the common ignorance of men than from the common ignorance of women. In all that concerns morals and duties, the Bible is the only authority I acknowledge. To it I make my appeal; from it I derive my argument. From the general account of creation, and especially from the specific directions which that Holy Book contains, it is plain that God regards the rearing and training of children as a paramount duty, a duty requiring mind, enlightened mind, mind educated and sanctified. The religious nurture of the young, wise family discipline, next to our personal salvation, and intimately connected with that, is life's chief duty, whether you regard its influence on mind, heart, character, society, government, or the triumphs of the gospel of the Lord Jesus. The neglect of this is to-day the curse of the Church, the bane of society, a calamity to the world. Almost all the evils in the country that either sadden or alarm us—irreverence, profanity, insubordination, restlessness under legitimate authority—all originate here. Other evils are incidental, this is radical; they are effects, this a cause—the cause which is fast multiplying sinners and crimes, undermining the law of the land, and defeating the Christianity of the Bible. I cannot believe that parents, Christian parents particularly—and these are as criminal as the rest—are positively indifferent and reckless as to the behavior and moral fortunes of their children. Much of the evil of which I complain doubtless arises from ignorance, defective views of parental obligation, the inability to discern principles and to forecast consequences, and much perhaps from the intrinsic embarrassments of the task itself.

To raise a child aright requires more sense than to manage the affairs of an empire. It is easier to solve questions of finance, commerce, agriculture, political economy, than to weigh the effect of a look, a tone, a word, upon the susceptibilities of a young, fresh, impressible, immortal spirit; far easier to negotiate treaties, to unravel the complicated relations of one country with another, than to graft a right principle upon a wicked nature and make it live and grow; than always to tell when and how to punish an offending child; than to measure with scrupulous exactness the language of reproof and praise. Now, that very much of this subtle, intricate, embarrassing task devolves upon woman all agree; and that too at the very period of life when the difficulties are enhanced and complicated by the child's infancy of person and thought, and its ignorance of language—the very time anterior to those developments which indicate at once the defects of constitutional character and the disciplinary remedies which the case demands. The God of wisdom never committed the high destinies of man and government and eternity to woman without the endowment of those natural intellectual gifts which, duly cultivated, would enable her to accomplish her lofty mission.

Allow me to say that if I were forced from a want of time and means to select from the curriculum of a polite and finished education, I should prefer languages to mathematics, a complete belles-lettres education to a partial one in any of the sciences, either for a boy or girl. Of course, if I could have it so, it should be thorough—universal for both. But I want to insist that the education of girls should be minute, careful, profound if possible, in one department which has been long neglected, or very partially attended to. I do not mean housewifery, important as it is; nor mantua-making, for Solomon in all his glory was never arrayed like one of our American lilies; nor millinery, for the ladies have carried that to such perfection that putting on a bonnet and taking it off amount to very much the same thing. No; I mean mental philosophy in all its departments—psychology, logic, or mind, its laws and powers, the passions and affections of our spiritual nature, the intellect, the will, the sensibilities.

If the proper training of children demands, on the part of those who direct and govern them, deep knowledge of human nature and its secret springs of action, ability to trace actions to their principles and principles to their results, and wise discrimination of the effect of the same truth and of the same discipline on different minds and temperaments—and this no intelligent person will doubt or deny —then the argument is at an end, the proposition is established: women need all the light that learning can give. That authority may be intelligent, discriminating, efficacious, the duties to be performed must be apprehended in all their magnitude and minuteness, and instruction and government adapted to what is peculiar in the moral and mental structure of the subjects of this embryo empire. That education ought to be suited to the nature of woman, her relations and duties, I concede; but, in the name of the rising generation, I protest against the popular practical inferences that are drawn from the doctrine. A woman ought to be skilled in every department of domestic economy. Let her rival Dorcas in garment-making, equal Martha in getting up a dinner, excel Queen Esther in an evening party, but let her learn all this at home from maternal instruction and example. Never incorporate them with the school or the college. Let the manual labor humbug be counted with the things that were. We have tried study and farm operations and failed; we should fare no better with books and trays, music and dress-patterns, recitations and millinery.

Far be it from me to undervalue good bread, clean houses, neat, graceful housewifery. These things are essential to female dignity and respectability, important to domestic happiness. I admire them all, and pity the man, whether single or married, who has to live without them. But then, comparatively speaking, these are but low attainments, and to excel in them—however creditable—but a meager ambition. Woman has a higher, holier, nobler mission. Manners, taste, literature, laws, constitutions, all depend upon her sanative influence. She is "the power behind the throne" which mends or mars society. Her home is the fountain-head of influence—molding fashion, regulating morals, inspiring public sentiment. Without her alliance law is weak, the pulpit powerless, opinion a reed shaken with the wind, and all the boasted conservatism of society no more to the rush of passion than a spider's web to a lion's leap. Woman is Heaven's fiduciary trustee of the world's best interests. To her guardianship God commits the newborn spirit in its cradled infancy. The heart expands in the light of her love as a flower in the sunshine. Mind buds and blooms beneath her smile. Under her plastic hand the moral and intellectual elements form themselves into character, and society itself reeks with corruption or beams in virtue as she may be good or bad. To fell the forest, to guide the ship, to marshal the embattled hosts, to control the machinery of government, to wear the crown of eloquence, belong to man; but to woman God has intrusted *man himself*. She molds the warrior and the hero, she inspires the patriot and the orator, she gives to genius its noblest impulses and to virtue its loftiest aims. To the hallowed ministry of her love the world is indebted for its happy homes; home, for its sweet attractions; childhood, for its guardianship; man, for his happiness and repose; sickness, for its solace; the dying-chamber, for the last earthly light that beams amid its grief and gloom; the grave, for the sweetest memorials that bloom upon its pulseless bosom; and heaven itself, for thousands of the countless multitudes who shall swell the anthems of its eternity.

Now, must all these high, holy tasks be abandoned to the intuitions, the untutored sensibilities of untaught women? Never; unless we mean to arrest the improvement of the world, extinguish the hopes of humanity, blight household joy, and restore the reign of night. The notion that the affections are contracted, the sensibilities indurated by knowledge, and that high mental training would unsex woman, giving her a heart of stone for a heart of flesh, deserves to be placed along-side of that modern discovery of some French philosopher that the earth is receding from the sun, growing colder, and will become a ball of ice, uninhabited and uninhabitable. What! high cultivation unveil modesty, dethrone love, ossify tenderness, wear off the downy bloom of female character, convert the American fair, the loveliest of Eve's descendants, into Amazons? Why, knowledge constitutes the chief difference between savage and civilized life! Where do we find the noblest sentiments, the refinements of taste, the most unselfish impulses; benevolence, with its wine and oil; love, bearing the burdens of age, cheering the sorrows of childhood, making home glad with its music and all life radiant with its charm? Not among the ignorant, the vulgar, but amid the arts, habits, comforts, and laws of well-educated human beings. The power to think and the power to feel go together. A superficial head and a frivolous heart lie side by side. The shallow soil makes a barren field that never teems with the generous harvest, the very grass withereth "before it groweth up—wherewith the mower filleth not has hands, nor he that bindeth sheaves his bosom." A vain, silly, giddy woman has no head, and cannot think; no heart, and cannot feel. In the garden of her soul there is neither bud nor blossom, flower nor fruit. But the modest, intelligent, refined woman "opens her mouth with wisdom, and in her tongue is the law of kindness; she looketh well to the ways of her household, and eateth not the bread of idleness. Her children rise up and call her blessed; her husband also, and he praiseth her." Sensibility and wisdom, delicacy and strength, are not incompatible.

Woman's heart is her glory and her crown; but her emotional nature will not lose its tenderness in the light of knowledge. The sunflower, and not the night-blooming cereus, is the type of her soul and its sensibility. Does the brook cease to run because the day-beam comes down to lave in its bright waters, making the pebbled bottom reflect the glory of the sky? No, no. Nor will the radiance of learning repress the genial current of woman's gushing emotions; but rather, in the gladness of their flow, they will flash with superadded charms. Educate her worthily and wisely, and the very instincts of her being will rise to the dignity of sentiment. The vine, which is wont to creep, and soil itself with the dust of the earth, will be lifted up; twining its tendrils around the elevated mind, will unfold its blossoms in beauty, and emit a fragrance sweeter than "the balm of a thousand flowers." Educate her worthily and wisely, and the affections, which else had grown rank in wild luxuriance, all pruned and trained, will hang their rich clusters in the sunshine, and—if you will allow me the language of heathen mythology—the juice will be nectar for the gods. Educate her worthily and wisely, and every American home shall have its priestess and its altar, where patriotism shall learn its earliest lessons and religion burn its purest incense. The generations to come, blazoned with the heraldry of virtue, shall proclaim the sanctity and the success of her mission, and, by the blessing of God, a world reformed shall be the appendix to her life's precious poem of love, tenderness, and truth.

Paul's Commission to Preach.*

BY DR. LOVICK PIERCE.

"For Christ sent me not to baptize, but to preach the gospel; not with wisdom of words, lest the cross of Christ should be made of none effect." (1 Cor. i. 17.)

AS all Scripture is given by inspiration of God, and is profitable for doctrine, we may place our text at once upon its proper basis, and proceed to adjust its terms and explain its rather singular aspect according to our view of its import.

And first, were it meet to call any one of the apostles of our Lord Jesus Christ an appointee of his by eminence, we think all would unite on Paul. His epistles are nearly all prefaced with the same great governing fact—"Paul, an apostle of Jesus Christ;" once adding, "Not of men, neither by man, but by Jesus Christ, and God the Father." And he once says he was "set for the defense of the gospel." Putting all these evidences of his divine credentials together, and then seeing how slightly attached to the commission of preaching was the work of baptizing, there is much room left for wise suggestions, none for silly speculation.

The commission of St. Paul to preach the gospel was either a perfect commission, without an absolute order to baptize, or else he preached under an imperfect commission, and pleads its origin and authority to be divine. Every

---

*This sermon appeared in the Smithson Collection of Sermons. It fairly represents Dr. Pierce's method and style when in his prime. —EDITOR.

one not mentally disabled to judge by an incautious surrender of principle to creed will admit the first member of the proposition—to wit, that St. Paul had a perfect commission to preach the gospel, exclusive of an absolute order to baptize. And if this be ceded as a fact, it calls us all, with due distrust of many long-settled notions about baptism, to review old theories and conclusions, and see whether we may not in some way be "teaching for doctrines the commandments of men."

One thing we assume as certain—viz., that if there may be issued a perfect commission to preach the gospel without an absolute order to baptize, then baptism as a thing or act is not an integrant portion of what the Scriptures mean by the charming epithet "gospel." For if it were, then would a commission to preach shut up every preacher of the gospel to the necessity of baptizing as a part of his office, and of preaching baptism as a part of the gospel. This will furnish the reason why so many self-deluded preachers preach baptism so much. It is because they look upon baptism—by which they mean immersion—as a portion of the gospel; not as an incidental appendage of a Christian Church, but as a part of the very gospel. If they did not so understand it, they could not preach immersion as one of Christ's commands under the general commission, "Go, preach my gospel." And yet there are thousands of worthy preachers who preach this dogma as a portion of Christ's gospel. As a proof point-blank that they do so understand it, they deny the existence of a gospel Church in the absence of immersion, and hold that a pure and legitimate administrator must derive his right from his place in a regular descending line of the duly immersed. They also make obedience to this feature in the gospel they preach indispensable to Christian communion. In a word, immersionists demand more and yield less at this point than anywhere else. A candidate may be a liberal on almost any point of general faith, but on the question of immersion, as demanded by eminence, no modification can be allowed. All must yield to one mode, and then hold every one not immersed as a stranger and a foreigner in the family of Christ.

That any thing as subordinate to the gospel as baptizing is made in Paul's commission to preach, as set forth in the text, should have been exalted by men to such importance, is a point entitled to manly and fearless consideration. For let it be understood that the obligation of a minister to perform baptism cannot fall below the value of baptism itself; and if the necessity to be baptized is to be enforced on the same ground that we enforce the obligation to believe, then there could not be any such subordination of baptism as that which is provided for in St. Paul's commission. But if baptism, like circumcision, is a mere certificate of interests secured to the holder anterior to its institution—obtained without and entirely independent of it, it being only a sign, or seal, of an interest arising from a simple reliance on the covenant of grace through Christ Jesus—then Paul's failure to baptize was no infraction of any primary law or ground of saving faith. Thus to ignore baptizing was not to discard baptism as wrong or idle, but to declare its great inferiority when compared with preaching the gospel, it being at best only an outward rite, valuable as a testimonial of an inward grace, but perfectly worthless in itself. And if such a deduction is at all legitimate, it follows as a matter of course that the individual right of Christians to communion in the household of faith does not proceed in anywise from baptism in view of original dependence of the one upon the other, but from the possession and exercise of that faith which justifies the ungodly into the groundwork and reason of which baptism did not and cannot enter. The whole value of Christian baptism is found in its representative and social signification. In the first, it is the visible sign of imparted purity; in the second, it is the fraternal sign of the household of faith, and of the consociation of converted souls in the Church of the living God, and derives its importance and authority from the divine law and rule of order. It is to be regarded as the initiatory step into Church relationship; in taking which the initiated is understood to admit all the rights of the Church, and to pledge himself to a Christian observance of all the rules and regulations thereof. Hence it is conceded as a self-evident fact that any denominational law or usage in the establishment of an exclusive mode of baptism cannot have any force beyond their own limits as a reasonable ground of brotherly fellowship until they prove that a legitimate membership in the Church of Christ cannot be secured without a special mode of baptism, and that all variations or modifications of that mode render nugatory and an usurpation the claim of any person for brotherly communion and Christian fellowship—the claimant not being in the Church. Our conclusion is that every such assumption of right and power in a Church is but a beguiling of Christ's children in a voluntary humility, a subjection of them to an usurped authority, and a policy of bigotry at war with Paul's directions, "Let no man therefore judge you in meat and drink," or in any thing immaterial to the faith that justifies and saves. Every such surrender of a great principle is the inauguration of an element of arrant bigotry.

But the commission of St. Paul suggests another important idea—viz., that the office of baptizing may, by an overestimate of its necessity, minister to divisions in the Church, and that as an inferior office it may and should be laid over until this evil is cured. We assume this apostolic example as convincing proof that baptism can never have importance enough to justify divisions in the Church; and therefore all such divisions founded on mere differences about baptism are evidences of bigotry on a larger scale than they are of orthodoxy. It is true that Paul ignored baptism for reasons stronger than could easily be shown in our day; but it is sufficient for our purpose in all cases where the evil is presumptively evident. Paul's movement in this instance is not alleged on higher ground. He only feared, as a possible case, that some one of the self-styled Paulites might, in partisan heat and folly, claim to be baptized in the name of Paul. But let not any imagine that Paul feared the formula of baptism would be altered so that the officiating minister would say, "I baptize thee in the name of Paul, the apostle of Jesus Christ." No; this was not what he feared, and what he so nobly deprecated. He feared that he would seem to be making disciples unto himself; this was what he meant by baptizing in his own name. There was the carnal leaven of envy and strife working lustily in Corinth. It was a choice time and place for a factionist. The revival—or, to speak more properly perhaps, the great religious awakening in Corinth came up under Paul's preaching; so much so that he afterward, in vindication of his ministerial success there against his calumniators, asserts his preemption right to the whole of them as his converts. But, waiving all advantages from position and priority, he nobly lived and labored only for Christ. He was one of a very few preachers, as I fear, who know that there cannot be an over-appreciation of themselves but at the deadly cost of an equal depreciation of Christ. He knew that the leaven of Paulism in the Church would be no less harmful than would the leaven of Herod. He counted a refusal to baptize his converts a saving policy demanded by Christ himself when set up against the error and idolatry of man-worship which enters into all these excessive admirations of men. In how many ways and in how many instances, think you, are baptisms virtually administered in the name of a Paul? I tell you I am not utterly mistaken, nor do I speak uncharitably, when I say that there are now in our midst preachers who would rejoice more at the conversion of any old or prominent member in another Church to the belief that immersion is the only mode of baptism—indeed, that it is the thing itself—than they would at the conversion of a sinner who had this sectarian faith before. Now, candor and conscience compel me to say that I want no other proof of the carnal origin of any ecclesiasticism of this kind than these two—the bigotry that disowns and the zeal that proselytes with a gusto. And these little carnal outgushings can be found in no Church unless some strict orthodoxy of creed or punctilious observance of order not recognized by other Churches as of such intrinsic value is raised to preëminent importance, and becomes a matter of glorying. There are thousands of these misguided immersionists who have imbued their spirits with admiration of this bantling idea until they really believe themselves the chosen sentinels of the ark of the covenant. Thus, every one who defends an idea under the belief that he is defending a divinity naturally becomes a sort of spiritual idolater.

It is evident that Paul was too cautious in his course, or else many of his successors are far too incautious; either he was over-scrupulous in guarding the great doctrine of grace, of exclusive grace in human salvation, or else we are generally too indifferent about the dangers of its corruption. I fear there is too much glorying in men and modes for the purity of the Church. It is no better to make a sectarian now than it would have been in Paul to make a partisan. He determined to do neither by any official act of his; and therefore, after baptizing Crispus and Gaius, and subsequently Stephanas and his household, he practically ignored baptism, lest any should say he baptized in his own name—that is, baptized his converts as his own disciples and the friends of his party. Against such a chance, he said that Christ sent him not to baptize, but to preach the gospel—not to raise up a Paul party by going on to baptize, while some said, "I am of Paul," and of course would wish to be baptized by Paul as their champion leader. No; he ceases to baptize any of them, knowing that if they thought baptism was any better at his hands, because he was their man, than it would be at the hands of any other minister, they were not religiously worth baptizing. And if they were baptized as much to honor Paul as to be honored by him, they were to all practical ends baptized in the name of Paul. Here was a preacher for you—a model preacher. Where shall we find his successors? Can no such man be found in our times? Can we find anywhere now a warm-hearted immersionist who, when about to immerse an uninformed subject, would say: "Christ did not send me to baptize, but to preach the gospel—that is, baptism is so little a thing that I do not look upon it as contained in the spirit of my commission; it is only added as a thing of practical utility to the outward Church; and if I thought you would look upon yourself as any more acceptable to Christ, any more worthy or welcome a member in his Church on account of this immersion, I would now desist." Baptism, like circumcision, is nothing—nothing in the same sense. Who ever heard any immersionist labor to convince his subjects that immersion, as a spiritual agency, was empty, dead, worthless in itself; that it was a mere religious form, and could not, by its mode, make religion more valid? Now, brother, it were as well for you to make water itself your savior as the mode of applying it in baptism. We modestly say that if our immersionists would talk thus to their numerous disciples—and it is their absolute duty to talk so to them—there would be a decline in the estimated value of immersion. But right here arises the difficulty which presses so fearfully upon all sides of this question. The practical working in these days of all sectarian and partisan movements is exactly the opposite of Paul's course. We risk wrong notions about certain things—for instance, immersion itself—rather than depress them to their proper measure for fear of unsettling some views already extravagant in devotion to this mode. Paul's idea was that non-baptism was a less evil to the Corinthian Church than baptism, with idolatrous elements wrapped up in it. Our modern immersionists recommend and defend their idolized mode of baptism as if satisfied that an error in mode is more to be dreaded than an excess of confidence in its God-pleasing letter. Hence, an ultra immersionist never thinks too much passed to the credit of immersion until you say it is meritorious enough to supersede Christ's merit; then, alarmed and horrified, he raises his wail. So you do not reach the point where you may say: "There is no gospel obedience without it, no Church without it, no ground of Christian communion without it. It is Christ's chosen and only mode of baptism Christ has the same views of immersion and preference for it that we have. And I believe that God is just as much pleased with me on account of my having followed him through his 'liquid grave' as I am with myself." Every immersionist that does not feel and think thus enough to justify him in saying so ought to be ashamed of his adhesion to his party; for if all this is not true, the whole ground of modal baptism is only a delusive mirage. But the delight with which every water-worshiping spirit hears the immersionist extol and magnify the mode of his baptism is proof conclusive of his devotion to mode. The credentials under which he acts must, therefore, differ from those which Christ gave to Paul in so far as to make baptism a part of the gospel and its administration a paramount duty. Hence, a stress and meaning are placed on every phase of this wonderful symbol so as to magnify a mode.

But once more we will return to our stand-point—the division of the Church in connection with baptizing. Have not these latter days furnished men of popular ministerial prominence who have rent in twain a Church of years and of well-earned fame on the ground of baptism? Not indeed about its mode, but about sequences involved in the extravagant notions entertained concerning the mere mode. The Church as it was made immersion indispensable to gospel obedience. The great reformer desired the Church to go farther and increase the necessity for this obedience by making immersion, when believingly received, the guarantee of regeneration; thus seemingly denying the doctrine of baptismal regeneration, and yet teaching that the Spirit is so resident in the word, or letter, as to render obedience to the letter indispensable to the offices of the Spirit, and those offices a never-failing certainty upon such obedience. It was a magnificent idea for such as labored under the modal lunacy. It is a matter of wonder to me how Mr. Campbell came to make immersion such a central point in this brief programme of spiritual development. It is, however, retrospectively a very suggestive incident. The germ of Campbellism is found in the overestimated value of immersion. Whenever an enhanced value is attributed to outward forms of religion, it always leads to theoretical dogmas or to sacramental sanctification. The Campbellite heresy is the fullest development of what we understand to have been the evil deprecated by St. Paul—"the baptizing in his own name"—which the world ever saw. But who supposes that Mr. Campbell ever felt this horror of having disciples baptized in his name as a champion and a leader? And yet to prevent a similar evil Paul was commissioned to preach the gospel without baptizing, because to baptize and make a hobby of it would have ministered to party feuds; and baptism was considered of too little value to the Church to be practiced at such cost of vital principle.

The argument up to this point has been to show that baptizing in Paul's commission to preach was only incidental and not imperative as though it were essential in carrying out the high behests of Heaven, as some seem to regard it. And being so clearly a contingent duty, it cannot be exalted into a consideration of such intrinsic value as to constitute a *sine qua non* in settling the ground of Christian fellowship, thereby rendering null and void all higher and more spiritual qualifications, such as spiritual regeneration. And if the whole question of baptism is too insignificant to justify divisions in a Church, the mode of baptism must furnish still less justifiable ground for discord and division in the whole Church of the Lord Jesus Christ. This much for the conditional part of Paul's divine commission. Next comes the positive and imperative. He was sent to preach the gospel. How did he do it?

Paul's preaching of the gospel was marked by three distinguishing features: in its matter, in its manner, and in its extent. To each of these let us pay a passing notice.

"Christ and him crucified" was his constant theme. His first public discourse was in the synagogues at Damascus to prove that Christ was the Son of God. As he increased in strength, he mightily confounded the Jews, proving that Jesus was the very Christ. Here was to them the rock of offense, and here he applied his arguments. At Thessalonica he entered into their synagogue, "and three Sabbath-days reasoned with them out of the Scriptures, opening and alleging that Christ must needs have suffered, and risen again from the dead; and that this Jesus, whom I preach unto you, is Christ." Most of his epistles open with the recognition of Jesus as the Messiah of God. To the Romans his salutation is: "Paul, a servant of Jesus Christ, called to be an apostle, separated unto the gospel of God (which he had promised afore by his prophets in the Holy Scriptures), concerning his Son Jesus Christ our Lord, which was made of the seed of David according to the flesh; and declared to be the Son of God, with power, according to the Spirit of holiness, by the resurrection from the dead." Here is a brief view of the gospel as Paul preached it. He began with Christ and ended with Christ.

To the Church at Corinth he said: "For I determined not to know any thing among you, save Jesus Christ, and him crucified." To the Galatians: "God forbid that I should glory, save in the cross of our Lord Jesus Christ, by whom the world is crucified unto me, and I unto the world. For in Christ Jesus neither circumcision availeth any thing, nor uncircumcision, but a new creature," or a new creation. Thus he teaches us that in the mighty work of the soul's regeneration there is nothing that counts save Christ himself. For this most sufficient reason he says to the Philippians: "And be found in him, not having mine own righteousness, which is of the law, but that which is through the faith of Christ, the righteousness which is of God by faith." He preached Christ as the end of the law for righteousness to every one that believed. The law of the Spirit of life which makes believers free from the law of sin and death he placed in Christ. Deliverance from the noisome body of death he ascribed to Christ. Such, indeed, was his estimate of Christ that he proudly declares his loss of all things—a loss too which was the result of deliberate choice—for the excellency of the knowledge of Christ Jesus his Lord. Nay, more; he gloried also in the marks of the Lord Jesus which he bore in his body—the marks of whips and the enduring scars of stonings, all suffered for preaching Christ. He preached this gospel from prison and prison-bounds; he preached it in chains. He was transported in this condition from Jerusalem to Cesarea, and from Cesarea to Rome. To the Romans he declared in his epistle: "For I am not ashamed of the gospel of Christ; for it is the power of God unto salvation to every one that believeth; to the Jew first, and also to the Greek." He preached Christ, the wisdom of God, and the power of God. He declared that in Christ dwelt all the power of the Godhead bodily, and that believers are complete in him— need no other ingredients in their religion, Christ being all and in all. To his merit nothing could be added, especially nothing by ceremonial washings. Jewish ablutions were all annulled, and Jewish sacrifices abolished, and the kingdom of heaven was set up. But outward things could not become of any more worth after the setting up of the Messiah's kingdom than they were before. How could they? Could Christ make water baptism of more value in the Christian religion than circumcision was in the Jewish? Surely not. For this would have been to put away one ceremonial on account of its unprofitableness and substitute it by another equally worthless as a saving element. If no saving virtue could be imparted to circumcision, none can be to water baptism. The two impossibilities are just equal. Here we see further evidence that Christ did not send Paul to baptize. Paul wrote and spoke on every essential principle of salvation, and yet there is not a word from him on this now mooted question, except an incidental disclaimer to the Christian validity of John's baptism as related in Acts, nineteenth chapter. And this may safely be regarded as one of many instances in which Paul, being set for the defense of the gospel, interposed his apostolic authority against the incorporation of any one element of Jewish religion into the gospel of Christ. Paul knew that to admit these twelve disciples into the fellowship of the Ephesian Church upon the authority of John's baptism would be construed as accepting a rite which did not demand the acknowledgment of the trinity in unity of the everlasting Godhead, a circumstance which demolishes forever the baptism of John as an example for Christians. It is perfectly immaterial by what mode John baptized; all must confess that his baptism passed away with his peculiar office and dispensation; and with his baptism, its mode. Its effete and imperfect character was declared by the order of Paul that those disciples should be baptized in the name of the Lord Jesus, which was done by some other minister besides Paul. But Paul ceremonially laid his hands on them, and they then received the Holy Ghost, of whom they had significantly learned in their Christian baptism. In view of these and other considerations not less grave, it is to us a most surprising fact that, ever since our earliest recollection, there have been persons claiming the right of teaching as if by eminence, who hold the preposterous notion that Christ's baptism by John before the public was an example to be followed by his disciples, and who have taught in all cases of immersion under their auspices that the gist of the thing consists in its being obedience to Christ's example. And yet a mind not crippled by prejudice will see at once that it was impossible for Christ to be baptized, at any time or in any mode, simply as an example for his followers. Neither his character nor his order left to him the possibility of receiving John's baptism or his own as an example for believers. Example proper cannot be set in cases where the conditions and moral obligations are essentially dissimilar. Where, we ask, in the name of unprejudiced candor, is it found that Christ's ceremonial consecration to the office of God's High-priest on earth, in the river Jordan, by John the baptizer, the only official of God who could befittingly perform this consecration of Jesus to his public office as a divine teacher—where, we ask, is it found that this *sui generis* baptism, or Jewish priestly washing, was done or designed as an example for Christians to follow in their baptism? I confess that to meet with men of good capacity in other respects, who can doggedly defend the idea that Christ took up John's baptism, grafted on to it a different ceremonial, and then made his own baptism by John an example for believers' baptism, leaves me less ground of confidence in the reliability of human opinion, where prejudice exists, than I am willing to admit.

In all Paul's preaching there is little, very little, heard of baptism. Not a word did he say about baptism as if it were a doctrine proper, or any thing like a doctrine, of the gospel. Not a sermon did he ever preach in vindication of baptism in any way or as to any mode. What he did say referred to the spiritual truths acknowledged and vows assumed by baptism in the name of Christ. It only went to prove this one thing: that the baptized renounced sin, and professed full and implicit faith in Christ Jesus, and in all the grand and gracious benefits of his death; so much so that they were said to be baptized into Christ's death. Now, I would like to know why any mode of baptism may not lead the mind, by ceremonial allusion, to the death of Christ. May not the man who is baptized in the name and as the disciple of Jesus Christ thus manifest his sole reliance on the cross, and his obligation to die unto sin, without any literal resemblance between the mode of his baptism and the mode of Christ's death?

We come next to speak of the manner of Paul's preaching. This was of no less decided a character than was the matter. The general manner of Paul's preaching, as to style, was argumentative. We judge that his epistles afford unquestionable specimens both of the matter and manner of his synagogue discourses. Luke, in the Acts, tells us plainly that he did preach after this form. His reasoning seems to have been after the fashion of Christ's instruction to his disciples after his resurrection—namely, that if they had understood the prophecies concerning him, and had believed them, they would never have felt a jostle in the groundwork or in the frame-work of their faith. Hence, beginning at Moses and all the prophets, he expounded to them in all the Scriptures the things concerning himself. O what a discourse that must have been! How often have I felt inclined to wish that I could have heard it! But we have the rich skeleton of it still unimpaired. It was somewhat after this divine model that Paul preached the gospel. At Thessalonica, for instance, he entered the synagogue, and three Sabbath-days reasoned with the Jews out of the Holy Scriptures, opening and alleging that Christ must needs have suffered, and entered into his glory. "And this crucified Jesus, about whom Jerusalem and all Judea have been so excited and confounded, is the veritable Christ—the Christ described by your prophets. Look and see. No one but Jesus, whom you have crucified, could ever answer the description given of Messiah by Isaiah."* Go, guilty unbeliever, compare notes with these delineated characteristics of Christ, and see if you can conceive of a mere Jewish prince entering upon his glory without suffering, and make such a prince the promised Prince of peace. God's Messiah is foretold by all your prophets so minutely that his entrance into Jerusalem upon an ass, and the foal of an ass—as the prophet had phrased it; probably a young, unbroken ass—was as necessary to meet that vastly significant monosyllable "needs"—Christ must "needs" suffer, and enter his glory—as was his crucifixion upon the hill of Cal-

---

* Isaiah liii. 3.

vary. It was necessary that all prophecies concerning Christ should be literally fulfilled; and all were so fulfilled; and then he cried, "It is finished!"

But Paul's manner of preaching the gospel, as it regards style, is more fully set forth in his first letter to the Corinthians. Corinth was one of the proud and populous cities where this missionary apostle broke ground himself—a city where false apostles tried to oust him, and made it necessary that he should boast himself a little. They sought to depreciate Paul by ridicule and by insinuations derogatory to his integrity. But all these attempts were weakened into mere pestiferous breath by his apostolic signs and seals, to which he could so undeniably appeal. He claimed to have begotten the whole of them in Christ Jesus; so that, however many instructors they might have, they had only one ministerial, spiritual Father. On this ground he claimed their Christian affiliation. But as Corinth was a hot-bed of factionists, it afforded a fine opportunity for proselyters. But how did Paul break ground in Corinth? He says: "I came not with excellency of speech or of wisdom, declaring unto you the testimony of God. And I was with you in weakness, and in fear, and in much trembling. And my speech and my preaching was not with enticing words of man's wisdom, but in demonstration of the Spirit and of power; that your faith should not stand in the wisdom of men, but in the power of God." Whether Paul intended any difference between his speech and his preaching, and if so, what, we are not advised; but we suppose the terms to have been used then, as they are now, to distinguish between a sermon proper and a hortatory address on the general subject of religion. But be the difference what it may, his style was the same in each. It consisted in the recital of God's testimonies, or truths, as found in the Scriptures of the Old Testament. These were brought forward, and their application to Christ and their fulfillment in him and by him were simply declared. None of the apostles seem to have felt it a duty or a necessity to prove God's word true. They simply assumed and affirmed its truth, and called upon sinners to believe it, and to deport themselves accordingly. They did not stand at the door of a sinner's heart and plead with him to yield to the chances of a verdict against himself; but that they took a verdict already found, and walked into the heart's guilty chamber and, exhibiting Jehovah's bill of complaints, called upon him to plead "guilty" as to his conscience, was clearly the fact, and judgment was at once entered up.

This manner of preaching, it is to be feared, has been too long neglected, and a reliance on logical reasoning, such as might appear well in a lawyer before a court and jury, or in a statesman before his peers and his country, has been substituted for that faith which declares God's testimonies, and leaves him to work out their verity by the demonstration of his Spirit and power. Or if there should be any approach to it, it is done rather in the way of a professional performance than as a mere agency to be made powerful and efficient by the Holy Ghost. We do not feel that we are, in a peculiar sense, laborers together with God—embassadors for Christ, sent not so much to negotiate about terms as to demand submission. It will require the disclosures of the last day to tell what has been lost to the Church by the error of her ministers in placing too much reliance on the wisdom of words. The hope of demolishing the fortresses of unbelief and sin by mental troops or logical detachments is a vain hope, at least in our general warfare. Sinners must be arraigned before the law and the testimony of God, charged with a consciousness of their guilt, and left to the demonstration of the Spirit and of power. This is the way in which ministers ought to preach; and at this point arises the need of prayer by the Church, for the want of which much preaching is lost. The Holy Spirit is given in answer to prayer.

But it is time for us to subject our text in another of its peculiar aspects to a more critical examination. Paul's commission to preach the gospel, as it seems in the language of the text, made his obligation to baptize so contingent that he did not consider it a part of his call at all. Strange procedure this, if baptism is what our Baptist friends claim it to be—the door into the Church and the ordeal of obedience. But his call to preach the gospel was a positive call in two aspects: first, he was to preach it; and secondly, he was to preach it without wisdom of words—that is, without any connection with the philosophy of Greece or Rome, or any dependence upon mere excellency of speech. This is no denunciation of a pure and good style in preaching, but a simple declaration that the style of preaching, so far as it concerns grammar and rhetoric, or even logic, philosophy, and oratory itself, is not the medium of spiritual power and success. This medium is found in the divine testimonies themselves. Wisdom of words cannot energize the truth with such power as dead souls demand. Indeed, if wisdom of words could add any thing in the way of saving energy to the word of God's grace, then would it be settled that the divine word, like a musical instrument, gives forth better or worse sounds according to the artistic skill of the performer. Not so, however, with the minister of the gospel. He strikes the keys of gospel truth and grace; and, disdaining all the artistic rules which the fastidious taste of the auditors of the age may seek to impose upon him, he thunders from Sinai or weeps and wooes from Calvary as he judges best, and quietly leaves all issues to God's Holy Spirit.

But there was a positive prohibition in Paul's commission

to preach. This negative part of his obligation is couched in terms of such import as to demand investigation with godly jealousy. The temptation to preach the gospel with wisdom of words was never greater than at this time; and the reason of its forbiddance is not entirely transparent to all minds. It is lest by wisdom of words we make the cross —or what we may consider the preaching of the cross itself—of none effect. This danger of burying the cross out of sight by wisdom of words, so as to destroy its meaning and power, is utterly unintelligible to carnal minds. They have not learned to distinguish between the proud delight they take in the poetic drapery cast about the cross by the delicate imaginings of their preacher and the cross as it exhibits the love of the Father in the gift of the Son, and the love of the Son in dying for sinners. And yet in seeing and feeling this very distinction lies the very life of the cross. It is possible for a master of oratory so to drape the cross as to lead listeners to honor and glorify themselves, either in their heroic censure of the scribes and Pharisees for the cruel treatment of Christ, or else in their enthusiastic admiration of his life and death as the Prince of philanthropists. But with him as the Lamb of God, taking away the sins of the world, they feel no adoring sympathy. The cross, in this high sense, is made of none effect.

This prohibition, so justly imposed by Christ upon his preachers, while it deprecated as weak and unavailing the wisdom of the world which had labored—but with constant failure—to make God known in former ages, looked no less to the more modern inventions of a proud philosophy seeking to rid itself of the necessity of dependence on the doctrine of a positive inspiration of the Scriptures for faith and salvation, with the special view of avoiding that mystery of godliness, *the incarnation*, and of bringing Christianity sufficiently under the auspices of some school of German neology to make the story of the cross more of a carnival for the revelry of reason than a kneeling-place for penitents. This tendency to bring the great central doctrine of the gospel—Christ crucified, crucified vicariously—into pleasant odor with a rationalistic philosophy is diffusing itself more and more into every new modification of theology. It is to be detected wherever it gains a foothold by frequent gentle insinuations that there is a great deal of the human as well as of the divine mind to be looked for in the Bible. And they soon learn to make this want of inspiration as broad as the flattered cravings of a worldly spirit may demand. Many of these American neologists are strangely wrapped up in a modernized Swedenborgianism. They are wonderfully familiar with ideal spirits; can almost see and feel them; have no dread of them. But watch these religious lunatics, and if they belong at all, in their own classification, to the rationalistic philosophers, they are apt to wind up their rhapsody with a most respectful and religious announcement of their Bible creed: "I believe in one true and living God." This is Deism as it is cultivated in the Church by the Unitarians of our day. Deism used to manifest itself by epithets of abuse lavished against Christ; since its baptism and reception into the Church, it only believes in one true and living God. But its wisdom of words has made the cross of none effect.

There remains one other view of this subject to which we desire to call particular attention: it is the sense in which we should understand "excellency of speech" to be forbidden in Paul's commission to preach the gospel. There does not seem to us any sense in which it can be taken as contradistinguished from "wisdom of words," except that of composition; or, if there be any other or further sense, it must be that of fine elocution. Now, how is it that either or both of these pleasant accomplishments can make the gospel of none effect? There are several ways in which they might lead to such a result. There might be in the preacher himself such a looking to mannerism as to vitiate simple faith in the word; or there might be in the Church such a readiness to account for success by the charming style and captivating eloquence of the preacher as to render it necessary that God should withhold his Spirit in order to save the Church from this man-worship, and to preserve unmixed to the end of time the pristine view of efficiency—"It is God that giveth the increase."

But our thoughts lead us to the conclusion that this excellency of speech may be applied directly and without any forcing to the practice—in these days too common among us—of writing and reading sermons. Why, we ask, do so many ministers of a certain order of taste go to the trouble of writing their sermons—for it is troublesome when viewed in connection with life's many calls—if it is not for "excellency of speech or of wisdom." I do not think, after all the ingenious excuses given by the advocates of this pernicious practice, that but one ruling reason can be found for its adoption and use, and that is desire to attain excellency of speech and of wisdom. If these polished preachers believed that they could, by carefully conning over their rising thoughts and entering the pulpit from knees of wrestling prayer, produce an extemporaneous discourse which would elicit as much praise from the élite as one they can bring forth in manuscript from their studies after days of thinking, does any one suppose that they would write and read their sermons? Certainly not. There is not one of them who imagines that truth is any more truth because it is first written; and certainly it does not add any thing to the sublime grandeur of the pulpit to see a preacher thumbing down his sermon for fear that a puff of wind will blow out his light, or fixing his eyes on every change in his position as if he revolved on an axis. And if no vital advantage is to be gained by writing a sermon, why do it? We answer again, It is for the sake of excellency of speech and of wisdom. It is not that the sermon may be more impregnated with truth, but merely that it may accord with grammar and rhetoric, and be pronounced a chaste and beautiful piece of English composition. And here, my dear brother, let me tell you for your mortification that I often hear men who are men pronounce your discourses very beautiful compositions but very poor sermons.

But we do not play off, because we are either afraid or ashamed of our position—which is that, as a general result, the writing and reading of sermons for the common uses of preaching make the cross of none effect. Does not the history of the pulpit everywhere prove beyond the possibility of denial that discourses first written and then read, or written and pronounced, are somehow shorn of their wonted power? Who ever saw under this form of preaching any of that heart-stirring influence which precedes and accompanies revivals of religion? And does not every one know that a simple sermon of that sort—to say nothing of a series of them—is deprecated as an evil in times of revival? There is, as a matter of necessity—doubtless of necessity—an absence of that peculiar unction which seems to give a sort of almightiness to a gospel sermon when it gushes like a crystal stream fresh from the baptized heart of the preacher. Here every emotion expressed is a truthful thermometer of love divine within. But tell me nothing about it; my mind is clear that it must often happen in the delivery of written sermons that the emotions are merely artificial. They may appear in the right place in the programme, but they are unnatural and unable to call up their kindred tribe in others.

The ground I take involves so much that is exceedingly delicate that modesty itself restrains me. This much, however, I must say for myself: that whether mine is an abnormal mind or not, one thing is certain, I cannot feel under a written sermon as I can under an extemporaneous one; and I believe that the common sense of mankind has, by a general disapproval of the practice, given a verdict against it. It is an innate desire, partaking of the nature of a simple appetite, to crave feeling in all public addresses which would lead us to action in matters of interest. The extent to which a speaker can carry our active sympathies with him is the measure of his probable success. And if nearly all the results of speaking are in favor of extemporaneous discourses as most efficient, why will ministers who could if they would extemporize well persist in this dull round of reading, disliked by nine-tenths of mankind, if it is not for the eclat of excellency of speech? I do fear for all my friends who are about to inure their minds to this incubus on fine natural powers of speech. It is true—certainly true—that if a sermon-reader could have in his manuscript every word just as it would have risen in an impromptu discourse—fresh gushings of a present, internal fountain of feeling—yet when read those words would fall on the ears and hearts of his audience like weary, worn-out winds. The curse of inefficiency has been universally stamped upon written sermons when read to an audience and called preaching. If badly read, it is murder; and if well, it is agreed that the man in the desk is a good writer and a fine reader; but no one ever regards any thing as preaching proper unless it is generated and delivered as an impromptu production; all else is called preaching merely by grace. Every congregation that requires the pastor to serve it with prepared sermons—that is, sermons prepared to be read—is found to be as unmoved in all the emotional springs of piety as a skeleton. Indeed, the underlying and prompting motive in those cases is generally quietism. But in these time-serving movements, as they creep in among us, there is an unsuspected element of vainglory. I have never conversed with a volunteer in this line of Methodist preaching who did not leave me decidedly under the conviction that ambition after excellency of speech and of wisdom was the real motive prompting him in the premises; and the avowed motive is to insure the esteem and gain the ear of the well-informed. This all looks well—looks right; but somehow it does not work well. It is condemned by the comparative practical results. There is some way in which this reliance on excellency of speech vitiates the gospel, some way in which the cross is made of none effect. Hence, St. Paul would not preach the gospel with excellency of speech or of wisdom. If he had pertinaciously adhered to all the school rules of composition and oratory as practiced by lawyers and senators, his power would have been located in his oratory, using the word "oratory" in its generic sense. But, waiving all these facilities of speech, he simply declared God's testimonies. He planted himself on the truth of God's revelation, and demanded belief in it and conformity of life to it. He never gave himself any trouble about the strict conformity of his speech and preaching to every law of grammar and every rule of rhetoric, but declared the testimonies of his God in demonstration of the Spirit and of power. In his preaching the cross was undraped; it stood out naked, the center and soul of the gospel, and the only hope of sinners.

Having considered what seems to have been optional and what imperative in Paul's call to preach the gospel, to wit, the work of baptizing, and also both the positive and the negative parts of what was imperative in his commission, and having shown moreover how he did preach, both as to matter and manner, we come finally to say a few things on the extent of his labors.

There were but few features in Paul's personal ministry more striking than the extent and abundance of his preaching. Referring to abundance, he says: "In labors more abundant." In reference to his field he says: "So that from Jerusalem, and round about unto Illyricum, I have fully preached the gospel of Christ. Yea, so have I strived to preach the gospel, not where Christ was named, lest I should build on another man's foundation; but as it is written, To whom he was not spoken of, they shall see; and they that have not heard shall understand." "Circuit-rider" was once the sobriquet of a Methodist preacher. It was then used as a depreciative term. Circuit-riding was regarded as a low employment. But here was a precedent in circuit-riding—or perhaps in Paul's case it was circuit-walking—which fully justifies the Methodist in riding circuits. It is the best plan in the world for the wide and easy spread of gospel truth. It seeks to break new ground all the time. It is in exact accordance with the aggressive genius of the people. Paul's circuit—from Jerusalem round about to Illyricum—was perhaps more than one thousand miles in length; but whether they were in direct line or not, he fully preached Christ in cities and in country. His theme was "Christ crucified." Before the preaching of the cross, superstition, idolatry, and systems of false religion, venerable in years and powerful in patronage, fled like morning mists before the orb of day. He says that this style of preaching brought forth fruit in every place; that God always caused him to triumph through Christ. This was the effect of preaching Christ then, and has been ever since. Preaching must be done upon the simple basis of faith—faith in the word, faith because it is the word of the Lord that endureth forever. Our faith must not be in the logical arguments used, not in the captivating style, not in excellency of speech or of wisdom, but in the great doctrines of the cross. And if we catch the proper inspiration of this doctrine, like Paul, we will restlessly strive to make Christ known to such as had not heard of his name in this relation before. Whatever we may or may not do in this aggressive line, if the spirit of preaching the gospel to every creature is properly upon us, we will show our divine calling by our labor in the lanes of poverty and in the destitute districts of the country. A preacher who can content himself through life to sit down in some good pasture and write off and gracefully read off a sermon or two every Sunday, and feel no call to preach to the destitute that lie all around him, is surely not a minister of Jesus Christ. No such pastors and preachers are reported to us in the New Testament. Look and see. The extent to which a minister preaches the gospel, he being able to choose his course, has much to do with the evidence of a divine call to the ministry. A man may have a local charge, but no man can do his duty by giving himself to one congregation while there are large numbers of neglected souls in easy reach of him. But we will here close this humble sermon. We have glanced at one or two things which lie without the beaten pathway of our predecessors in exposition. Our great desire is to wake up in all our preachers a jealous, just concern to guard against all the chances of making the cross of none effect by wisdom of words.

Let Paul's account of a gospel ministry be our motto: "But if all prophesy, and there come in one that believeth not, or one unlearned, he is convinced of all, he is judged of all; and thus are the secrets of his heart made manifest; and so falling down on his face, he will worship

God, and report that God is in you of a truth." If any one ever saw the like of this under a sermon read, no matter what its excellency of speech, he has seen what I have not. Let us prophesy—that is, declare the testimonies of God.

The Word of God a Nation's Life.*

"That he might make thee know that man doth not live by bread only, but by every word that proceedeth out of the mouth of the Lord doth man live." (Deut. viii. 3.)

"THE things which were written aforetime were written for our learning, that we through patience and comfort of the Scriptures might have hope." The narratives of the Old Testament are not to be regarded as simple paragraphs in general history, mere links connecting in consecutive order the events of the olden time, but as embodying great principles in human society and in divine administration, vital alike to the well-being of the one and the uniformity of the other. God is always the same; and the Bible, while it records the actions of men, is really the history of God, and as "with him there is neither variableness nor shadow of turning," we learn from his past procedure what we may expect as to his present and future government. This fact being fully apprehended, we have a key to the dispensations of Providence, and need not greatly err in interpreting current events or in speculations as to the future. While in the Mosaic economy there were many statutes, local and temporary, having their origin and use in what was peculiar to an introductory dispensation, yet among them are laws of universal and permanent obligation, principles ordained of God for all time, and perpetuated for the instruction of mankind in the lasting records of the Church.

---

* Preached before the Bible Convention of the Confederate States, Augusta, Ga., March 19, 1862.—EDITOR.

Government is an institution of heaven; the powers that be are ordained of God. It is true the Scriptures do not designate any particular form of government as best, nor are they eclectic as between the various theories which have challenged the suffrage of mankind; but as the condition precedent to the Divine blessing, the duties of rulers and subjects are distinctly defined, and conformity to them urged by all that is precious in a nation's hopes, and by all that is fearful in the just judgment of Almighty God. It is true that many features of the Jewish polity were rudimental, introductory, and intended to teach the great lessons of dependence and obedience, as well as to meet for the time being the local necessities of tribes and families. Patriarchal supremacy, the subordinate authority of the chiefs of clans, and, under them, the heads of houses, were all necessary to local government, but were wholly inadequate for general purposes. Similarity of institutions was too feeble a bond of unity, and the elements of discord and disintegration were too strong to be neutralized by the perpetually diluting memories of a common descent and the traditional marvels of Egypt, the wilderness, and the land of Canaan. Before their settlement in the land of promise, the children of Israel, however distinct as a people, were not a nation in the organic sense of that word; and their governmental condition was elementary, and the forms of authority were simple, yet sufficient for order and prompt action. While the law did not abrogate these institutions, and the theocracy to be inaugurated did not supersede them, God was all the time educating them to broader views of their destiny, and to more exalted conceptions of their spiritual relations, and of the high functions they were to perform as a chosen people among the nations of the earth.

The disciplinary process by which the Jews were conducted through their singular history from bondage to national independence, power, and prosperity looked to two grand objects, one of which has been largely overlooked in our perusal of the historic records of the Old Testament. One purpose, and the primary one, was to train up a people to a nationality, favorable in the plans of Providence for the introduction of Messiah's kingdom; the other and the collateral one—secondary in order, yet vastly important to mankind—was that, taking the Jew as the type of his race, God might develop the sources of weakness and danger, the probable points of departure from the true and the right way, the temptations most likely to corrupt and deteriorate, the elements of decay, overthrow, and extinction. The Jews, with all their folly, ingratitude, and perverseness, were fair specimens of human nature; and an impartial record of individual experience or national history would show pride, unbelief, and forgetfulness of God in forms as revolting and under circumstances as provoking as any furnished by Ephraim or Judah.

Moses, in the address of which the text is a part, exhorts the children of Israel to obey all the commandments of the Lord their God; reminds them of the way along which they had been led, of the afflictions which they had endured, and the deliverances wrought for them; interprets for them the programme of Divine Providence, and declares the ulterior object to have been that they might know that "man doth not live by bread only, but by every word that proceedeth out of the mouth of the Lord doth man live."

The lowest construction which these words will bear—and doubtless the doctrine is true—is that man's animal-physical life is not sustained by bread alone, but by any thing that God may appoint and sanctify for nutriment; that his blessing first gave the earth its fertility and continues it, and if he were to command the air to sustain us, it would be equally obedient.

But the text has a higher meaning. It teaches that not only our being, but our well-being depends upon conformity to the divine word; that life, in its lowest gradation as predicable of man, is not sustained by the natural law of adaptation of means to ends, and can neither be developed, prolonged, nor made happy outside of the will and word of the Lord; that bread, though ordained as the staff of life, does not nourish by virtue of its chemical properties, but by the blessing of the Lord; that the transgression of the divine law by intemperance, excess in the use of what God supplies or allows, poisons, destroys, entails disease and death; that life is to be regarded not as a physiological fact, but a moral endowment, deriving its dignity and value from its religious use, the moral appropriation of its powers, its spiritual relations, and its possible eternal sequences. The words "man liveth," though a simple form of speech, are nevertheless compound in their signification. "Man" is a generic term, and stands for the race; "liveth" is concrete, and includes man as an individual being, as a member of the community, as a citizen of the country; and the whole comprehension of the phrase is that man considered as an independent personality, that human society in its aggregate, the Church as an ecclesiastical organization, the State as a body politic, are all under the same general law of dependence, subjection, and obedience, as the condition of life, honor, prosperity, and perpetuity.

We have assembled under very peculiar circumstances. As a people we are in the midst of revolution. Our secession from the old Federal Union and the inauguration of a new Confederacy have not only dissolved the political ties which connected us with the Northern States, but have broken up our religious societies, our benevolent institutions, and thrown us upon new organizations to meet our responsibilities as a Christian people to the world around us. It has seemed to me appropriate, therefore, to waive in the discussion of the subject chosen the special views and individual applications which the words would justify and even demand under ordinary circumstances, and to content myself in a brief discourse upon a few leading ideas as they apply to society and the State.

The chapter opens with the implied doctrine that the test of true allegiance to God and the security of a quiet and peaceable life in all godliness and honesty is in universal obedience to the Divine commandments.

This is a broad, perhaps a startling, proposition; but it is the starting-point of all sound and safe reasoning on the question of duty, either personal, social, or political. Obedience, to be sincere, must be entire. Neither God's authority nor man's real interests will allow of any limitation. All religion consists in recognizing the law and glory of our Maker, submitting to duty because it is his will, and not because it is a decision of our reason. The authority of the divine statute must be most solemnly regarded; otherwise, outward conformity is no proof of inward loyalty. To prevent delusion, this thought must be borne in mind, or the sacrifices we make to our own pride and selfishness may assume the name and claim the reward of religious service. While the will of God is absolute and binding, even when the reasons of its enactments do not appear, still, to manifest the nature and perfection of his government, he has been pleased to declare the benefit of his laws, and these appeal so strongly to our instincts and our solicitations of interests as to constrain our admiration and homage, and, under powerful impressions of reverence and fear, we sometimes resolve upon and pledge fidelity and service. But God, who knows the latent propensity of evil in our nature, may often address us as he did the children of Israel when they vowed to do all that he had commanded: "The people have well said all they have spoken; O that there were such a heart in them, that they would fear me and keep all my commandments always, that it might be well with them and their children forever!" To prove them, to know what was in their hearts, whether they would keep his commandments or no, he humbled them, suffered them to hunger and thirst, led them through a variety of difficult circumstances, favored them with many miraculous deliverances. They were thwarted and they were indulged, disappointed in their expectations and surprised by their mercies, punished for their sins that they might be admonished, and pardoned that they might be encouraged. But they were slow to learn the lessons of Providence. Distrust, murmuring, ingratitude, disobedience, marked all their history. Failing in the fundamental principle of submission and reference to God, they sought out many inventions. To say nothing now of the evil leaven of pride, self-will, the imitation of the multitude to do evil, which permeated their domestic life and social manners, very soon forgetting all the precautionary counsels by Moses, all the wonders of their own marvelous annals and their peculiar covenant relations, the practical recognition of their invisible king became an abstraction, a tradition without authority and a fable without a moral. They sought to live by bread alone, to prosper without virtue, to fight without divine warrant, and to conquer without celestial aid. The word of the Lord was buried amid the rubbish of their desecrated temple. The altars, the high places, every green tree, the enthroned abominations of the heathen, revealed a nation of backsliders and adolaters, and finally of captives and exiles.

To conserve a nation, that word of the Lord so often announced in the Bible, "*The Lord reigneth*," must be recognized, acknowledged, practically believed. Incorporated in the constitution, confessed by their chief magistrate, re-echoed by subordinate rulers, pervading the legislation of the country, presiding over public opinion, it will be a safe-guard in revolution, a guide in peace, a Pharos beaming light and hope upon the future. Political morality would never have been deemed a thing of no concern, an article of barter, bandied about the market-places of the land, if men had not first imagined that the Most High did not regard the actions of men and administer justice among the nations. A perverted public sentiment, largely tinctured with atheism, which excludes God from the affairs of earth, and confines him—if it admit his existence at all—to heaven and heavenly things, is a fruitful source of venality and corruption in high places and low places, of insubordination, of commercial fraud and infidelity to contracts, of impious legislation and wide-spread contamination. Our republican fathers wisely separated the Church from the State; their degenerate successors madly separated the State from heaven. It has been the fashion to theorize and decide on politics as if Christianity were not a superior, supreme law, and as though God had abandoned his book and his rights to the chances of a doubtful contest. Statesmanship has become an earthly science, a philosophy without religion, and a system of expediency without a conscience. In discussing systems of finance, commerce, tariffs, international relations, who insists on moral causes, on the dependence of the nations on Him who turns the seasons round, dispenses the changes and destinies of governments, and cannot and will not be forgotten, without rebuke and judgment?

Loose and licentious notions of liberty are the legitimate outgrowth of ignoring the supremacy of God. Vicious maxims in trade become current; capital is invested in enterprises which war against morality; vice puts on the livery of fashion, and becomes bold by patronage; the administration of justice grows lax, in morbid sympathy with a false philanthropy; unpunished crime gangrenes society; and deified wealth rides over principle and merit and talent; and a hollow, heartless selfishness holds carnival over the wreck of every virtue.

The voice of the multitude, the example of the great, the power of money, constitute an inquisition so virulent and overbearing that reproof is dumb, the testimony of the Church is paralyzed, and if from the wilderness which popular sin has made there comes out some fearless prophet of heaven, threatening the wrath to come, society, demoralized by indulgence and blinded by long impunity, rains upon his honest head the epithets, "bigot," "enthusiast," "fanatic," "hypocrite," and rushes on unchecked to its doom. Men may philosophize, speculate, declaim, but God will reign. He never abdicates or dies. His glory he will not give to another. We are not our own, but men under authority. In morals we have no rights of legislation. We have a Master in heaven. His title to reverence is indisputable; his claim to homage and obedience is inalienable. We must render to God the things which are God's. If we would be a Christian nation, what the law commands or allows must never contravene the behests of Heaven. Nations have a sort of collective unity, and between rulers and people there is a reciprocal responsibility; and if there be connivance in evil, each is amenable for the guilt of the other. If the executive or legislative or judicial department bring the law or policy of the country into conflict with the revealed economy of God, the people should remonstrate, vindicate the divine right, exhaust the remedies in their power, and, if they cannot reform, at least fix the burden where it belongs. If the people grow corrupt, impious, and claim the natural right to do moral wrong, then the government must set itself to honor God, by becoming a terror to them that do evil. Rulers must not bear the sword in vain if they would fear God and live by his word.

The Church too must cease to shrink before the cant of those godless demagogues who, when the good seek to array public opinion against vice, and to bring law into harmony with the Bible, preach liberty of conscience, all the more vociferously because they have long since ceased to have any conscience or rule of life save selfish indulgence. Her testimony against evil must be clear, intrepid, meek but firm, patient but unwearied. The insane cry of popery and priestcraft must no longer smother the thunders of the pulpit; and the theory of a Christianity which converts people without a change of heart or life, liberal enough to let men do as they please for the sake of their name and their money, which grants indulgences for sin rather than be thought uncharitable, relaxes by an apocryphal canon the stringent, inexorable rules of purity and self-denial, must be met, routed, exiled; and the sacramental host must know that if they would drink of the river whose streams make glad the city of God, then must they fulfill the commission of his lips. The impregnation of government, law, art, commerce, civilization, with her own pure, gentle, peaceable, loving sentiments, is the predicted triumph of Christianity; and we approximate the glory of that millennial age when we honor the divine word by believing its promises, fearing its threatenings, adopting its counsels, practicing its morals; when we magnify the Lord and exalt his name; when we recognize his providence, beseech his aid, deprecate his wrath, by confession, petition, and reformation. I am glad that our young republic acknowledges God in her constitution, and calls on him to witness the rectitude of her aims and objects. I am glad that our President in several official acts, "seeing that we have no might against the great multitude coming upon us," has sought to turn the eyes of the people to the Lord their God; and that in his late inaugural he concludes with an earnest appeal to God and a thrilling declaration of his own abiding trust in the justice and mercy of the Lord Almighty. I am glad that the people have responded again and again to the call to fast and pray with unwonted earnestness and universality. Amid much that is discouraging to the pious, in view of abounding iniquity, these national acts, interpreted by scriptural examples, inspire hope that God will vouchsafe to the intercessions of the faithful few our deliverance and liberty. O my countrymen! let us reverence the Lord of Sabaoth; and let us remember that our country is to be preserved and perpetuated, not by science, wealth, patriotism, population, armies or navies, but by every word that proceedeth out of the mouth of the Lord. "Hear me, Asa and all Judah and Benjamin: the Lord is with you while ye be with him; and if ye seek him, he will be found of you; but if ye forsake him, he will forsake you."

Another word of the Lord by which society is to be improved and the nation exalted to healthy, happy life is his statute on the religious training of the young. On this subject for a series of years the policy of the country has been wrong and growing worse, the testimony of the Church has been timid, wavering, and inconsistent. In relation to it the commandment of the Lord is explicit. The admonitions and counsels of the Bible are frequent, earnest, and pointed; but a proud and petulant philosophy, full of conceit and flippant maxims, has corrupted both opinion and practice, and circulated ideas full of deadly poison, blighting to character and fatal to all government. The primal cause of well-nigh all the evils which afflict society is to be found in defective family discipline, example, and instruction, and in a nearly total disregard of the injunctions of the Bible, the word of the Lord upon this subject. To train up a child in the nurture and admonition of the Lord is a lofty commission, a moral duty of the highest grade, next in responsibility to our personal salvation. To fulfill it in perfection requires the highest order of intellect and the deepest work of grace. According to the capacity given, or that might be acquired, every parent is bound by the most solemn considerations, both personal and relative, temporal and eternal, to do what he can in developing the immortal mind committed to his charge into the highest style of character. Admitting the intrinsic difficulties of the task, I cannot forbear remarking that the embarrassments most complained of chiefly arise from substituting the divine by human plans; the sternness of authority, arbitrary, imperious, and passionate; turbulent temper, venting themselves in petulance and scolding; an indiscriminate use of the rod, or the bribery of weak compliances or irredeemable and unredeemed promises, or the postponement of all effort till the day of salvation is gone; and all these in the face of God's word, which says: "Fathers, provoke not your children to wrath," "forbear threatening," "put away lying," "be not hasty in thy spirit to be angry," "he that loveth his son chasteneth him betimes." The Bible not only gives specific instruction in all these things, but is itself the best instrument of discipline. Its doctrines are to be taught, its principles explained, its motives urged, its promises applied, its threatenings announced. "And thou shalt teach them diligently unto thy children, and shalt talk of them when thou sittest in thy house, and when thou walkest by the way, and when thou liest down, and when thou risest up." For, says the psalmist, God "established a testimony in Jacob, and appointed a law in Israel, which he commanded our fathers that they should make them known to their children; that the generation to come might know them, even the children which should be born; who should arise and declare them to their children; that they might set their hope in God, and not forget the works of God, but keep his commandments." How wise, how benignant, how conservative this statute! A father dies without a will, the division of his estate is settled by the arbitrament of law; but if he failed to communicate the knowledge of God, who shall supply his omission or make up to the wronged or defrauded child his lost heritage? How natural and beautiful the divine plan for transmitting truth! Every parent a historian and preacher, every habitation a temple, every path a school-house, every bed a pious retreat, where age sinks to rest with the language of piety on its lips, and youth is hushed to repose by the music of love in the words of heaven. O if the people would live by every word that proceedeth from the mouth of God, what families, how happy! what children, how lovely! what Churches, how pure! what a nation, how great and wise and strong, having God so nigh in all that we call upon him for!

What a departure from the word of the Lord must that be which has accredited people with religion—Bible religion—and yet allowed them to live in the neglect of a primary duty integral to personal piety, essential to Church progress, fundamental to public order and national greatness! Verily, the bread which we have been using may continue breath and being, but it is scanty, husky fare, and will fill the land with moral skeletons, tattered, hungry prodigals, too feeble to stand in virtue's ways, and too far off to return to our Father's house. If we would have our sons as plants grown up in their youth, our daughters as corner-stones polished after the similitude of a palace; if we would enjoy the fatness, the sweetness, the wine of life, we must live by every word of God. We must come back to the law and to the testimony, and renouncing and denouncing all the pert infidel sayings of the times, all the cant of irresolution, the pleas of sloth, the pretenses of mock humility, set ourselves to realize that prophetic scene, bright with celestial promise—"And all thy children shall be taught of the Lord, and great shall be the peace of thy children."

It is due to the subject and appropriate to the occasion to say that the whole education of the country should be Christian. During the formative period of life it is obviously the will of God and to the interest of society that the rising generation should be taught the knowledge of God, the mind developed in the light of the Bible, and the heart guarded from the contagion of bad example, and trained under a system decidedly evangelical. Science and religion should be united in indissoluble wedlock. The sanctities of the parental roof and the memories of pious instruction should be perpetuated in the school-house, the academy, the college. The interests at stake are too precious to be jeoparded by any omissions or lapses or intervals of neglect. The infidel policy of leaving the youthful mind unbiased and free is unsound in principle and impracticable in fact. It is a stratagem of the enemy of souls, too shallow to deceive a thinking man, and ought to inspire the good to an instant occupancy of the ground, and a tenacious holding of it, by all the arts of love and mercy, the most assiduous, painstaking care, and the most devout supplications to God for needed help. The Christian denominations of the land have been seeking to do somewhat in this direction; but they have largely modified their plans to forestall the charge of sectarianism and escape the apprehended edge of reproach from their enemies. What! is it sectarian to teach a youth to fear God, to do right, to love the country? sectarian to urge patriotism, benevolence, personal purity, by the sanctions of revealed religion? My brethren, if we would live by the word of the Lord, we must no longer compromise our duty to God and the country by diluting our systems of education to suit carnal taste and worldly wisdom. We must prepare for the future. The conflict for dominion between light and darkness is progressing; the crisis is at hand. We must come up to the help of the Lord against the mighty. The young should be enlisted as conscripts of the kingdom. Catechisms, Sunday-schools, family religion, pastoral care, religious education, should all be levied upon, pressed into service, if we would save the landmarks of morality from the inundations of vice and draw over the nation the shield of Omnipotence. Put the Bible in every house, an evangelical teacher in every school, a man of God in every pulpit; stir up, vitalize, intensify every agency for good in the Church; multiply by faith and prayer revivals of religion; seek, O seek the instruction and conversion of the young; and then, when this terrible war is ended, and peace reigns in all our borders, we shall have a state of society so bright, beautiful, and blessed that time shall have no emblem of it in the past but Eden, and eternity no type in the future but heaven.

This history of the past, as well as the suggestions of the text, constrain me to add one more illustration of the general truth I have been expounding. The life of a nation, in the sense of stability, honor, credit, prosperity, depends largely upon the moral character of its rulers. Nor are these results regulated by merely natural causes. History, sacred and profane, attests that God's blessing is upon the good, and his curse sooner or later upon the bad. In the political creed of this country a man's morals, his relations to God, have scarcely been thought of in his elevation to office. Party, party service, order in rotation, have often determined the candidate, and, albeit he was the victim of notorious vices, the wire-worker reckoned advisedly upon rallying the strength of the party to his support through his affinity with the vile on the one hand and the unscrupulous devotion of all the rest to the platform on the other. We are the victims to-day of this ungodly traffic in vice, of unscriptural theories of government, of selfish schemes of power, of the fanatical ambition to enthrone an idea born in the seething brain of a pseudo-philanthropy, which boldly avows that the Bible is a lie if it does not teach its creed, and God to be rejected if he does not indorse it.

The word of the Lord is: "Provide out of all the people able men that fear God;" "The wicked walk on every side, when the vilest men are exalted;" "When the wicked beareth rule, the people mourn." On the other side, a ruler "is a minister of God for good," "a terror to evil-doers, and a praise to them that do well." "Righteousness exalteth a nation, but sin is a reproach to any people"—especially when sin is exalted, honored, enthroned in the high places of the land. In the divine administration rulers are contemplated as the head and representatives of the people, even in hereditary governments; and it must be eminently so in an elective one. It is to be remembered, therefore, that the people must share in the judgments which the sins of rulers provoke. When these proud transgressors challenge the Divine Being by their reckless impiety, the retribution is often sudden and overwhelming, as when he smote Herod with worms; or a gradual blight, a living death, as in the days of Jeroboam, the son of Nebat, who made Israel to sin. One mode of divine punishment—and perhaps the most to be dreaded—is to abandon a people to corruption, leave the disease to work its course without check, permit them to fill up the cup of their iniquity, and, when sin puts on the glare of renown and the robes of office, and dances in festal gayety under the patronage of the great; when the flood-gates are open, the impediments are gone, and pollution rolls like a flood, then the clouds of wrath brew in the heavens above, and the Dead Sea makes ready her grave beneath. Another mode is to make the people mourn their folly through the passions of their rulers, and then come wars, taxes, oppressions, waste of blood and treasure; or the clouds of heaven are sealed and the parched earth responds not to the tiller's toil; mildew blights the ungathered harvest, pestilence wastes population, or the red rain of battle drenches the land with sorrow, and captivity is the doom of the nation. We are beginning a new career. God help us to avoid the errors of the past, and, throwing off the shackles of parties, conventions, and platforms, to abide by the word of the Lord. Let us have a Christian nation in fact as well as in name, that God may be as a wall of fire round about this young Confederacy, and a glory in the midst of her.

There is one other departure from the word of the Lord common to the policy of the country, adopted and pursued by well-nigh all, which demands and deserves rebuke. I mean the greed of gain, the deification of money. The subject is too large for discussion now, but a word to the wise will not be amiss.

In this very chapter Moses admonished the people against the self-same evil into which we have sadly run, and notifies them that the only security against the temptations of an all-surrounding abundance was to remember, fear, and obey God. "Beware, lest when thou hast eaten and art full, and hast built goodly houses and dwelt therein; and when thy herds and thy flocks multiply, and thy silver and gold is multiplied, and all that thou hast is multiplied; then thine heart be lifted up, and thou forget the Lord thy God." Alas! this is the crime and the curse of America. We have prospered, grown rich, luxurious, proud, and have said in our hearts, "My power and the might of my hand hath gotten me this wealth."

The history of the world confirms the testimony of the Bible as to the moral dangers of accumulated treasure. Wealth is favorable to every species of wickedness. Luxury, licentiousness of manners, selfishness, indifference to the distresses of others, presumptuous confidence in our own resources—these are the accompaniments of affluence whenever the safeguards of the divine word, both as to the mode of increase and the proper use, are disregarded. As to the higher forms of character and civilization, unless regulated and sanctified by Scripture truth and principle, opulence has always been one of the most active causes of individual degeneracy and of national corruption. Under the influence of its subtle poison, moral principle decays; patriotism puts off its nobility and works for hire; bribery corrupts the judgment-seat, and justice is blinded by gifts; benevolence suppresses its generous impulses, and counts its contributions by fractions; religion, forgetting the example of its Author and the charity of its mission, pleads penury, and chafes at every opportunity for work or distribution; covetousness devours widows' houses and grows sleek on the bread of orphans; usury speculates on providence and claims its premium alike from suffering poverty and selfish extravagance; extortion riots upon the surplus of the rich and the scrapings of the poor, enlarges its demand as necessity increases, and, amid impoverishment, want, and public distress, whets its appetite for keener rapine, and with unsated desire laps the last drop from its victim, and remorselessly sighs for more. The world counts gain as godliness, prosperity as virtue, fraud as talent, and money, *money*, MONEY is the god of the land, with every house for a temple, every field for an altar, and every man for a worshiper. The Church, infected by popular example, adopts the maxims of men, grades the wages of her servants by the minimum standard, pays slowly and gives grudgingly, and stands guard over her treasures as if Providence were a robber and they who press the claims of Heaven came to cheat and to steal.

Whenever the conservative laws of accumulation and distribution as presented in the Bible are ignored, then not only does the love of money stimulate our native depravity, but the hoarded gain furnishes facilities for uncommon wickedness. The attendant evils are uniform. They have never failed in the history of the past. When commerce, manufactures, and agriculture pour in their treasures, then, without the counteracting power of Scripture truth and gospel grace, they infallibly breed the sins which have been, under God, the executioners of nations. Such is the suicidal tendency of unsanctified wealth that the greater the prosperity of the people the shorter the duration. The virulence of the maladies superinduced destroy suddenly, and that without remedy. Now, mark how apposite, how prophetic, how descriptive the word of the Lord: "They that will be rich fall into temptation and a snare, and into many foolish and hurtful lusts;" "He that maketh haste to be rich shall not be innocent;" "He that hasteth to be rich hath an evil eye." How these passages rebuke the spirit of speculation, the greedy desires, the equivocal expedients, the high-pressure schemes of the people! "Lay not up for yourselves treasures upon earth." "Charge them that are rich in this world, that they be not high-minded nor trust in uncertain riches." O ye who make and save, and hide and hoard, hear ye the word of the Lord: "Your riches are corrupted, and your garments are motheaten. Your gold and silver is cankered, and the rust of them shall be a witness against you, and shall eat your flesh as it were fire." O ye who strut and shine in plumage plucked from the poor and needy, "ye have received your consolation;" "weep and howl for the miseries that shall come upon you."

One of the moral secrets of this wretched war, as we call it—perhaps it may turn out to be merciful—in my judgment, is to arrest the corruption of prosperity; to unsettle, agitate, break loose the people from their plans and hopes; dethrone their cotton idol, and, by upheaving the incrustations imposed by long years of peace and security, to let into our darkened minds the light of truth and ventilate the dormant conscience. Infatuated by the love of the world, sensualized, fast-rooted in our pride and forgetfulness of God, the Spirit of grace has been shut out, the hearts of men were impervious through the power of dominant, overmastering habit, and the preaching of the gospel as fruitless as would have been the tinkling of a cymbal. The Church has been sliding into the world; the broad scriptural lines of demarkation were well-nigh passed. Piety had grown thin, meager, unreal. Christian manhood was merged in a mawkish spirit of compliance—a supple, sickly liberality ready to break down the last barrier to the encroachments of fashion and the demands of an ungodly age. We needed reform. The shocks and vibrations of war's terrible batteries were necessary to shake the drowsy, stagnant atmosphere, to change the currents of thought, to break down the dominion of old ideas, and set us free from the selfish policy of the past. To this end God has "stirred up our nest," pushed us out from our resting-places, unhinged the whole machinery of life, and called us to privation, sacrifice, and peril. O that this bitter discipline, this fiery ordeal, may prepare us for a liberty better regulated and a religion more spiritual, active, and useful!

Hear now "the conclusion of the whole matter." The sum of this teaching is that man liveth not by bread only, not by natural means, not by human philosophy, not by expediency, by time-serving—the shifting policy of earth—but that if we would be good, prosperous, useful, happy, safe, we must live by every word of God. My brethren, we are not mere life-time creatures, born to graze over the world like beasts of the field, or to flit about in gayety and song like the birds of the air, but subjects of discipline, spirits on probation, where great deeds are to be done, heroic sacrifices to be made, the distresses of others to be relieved, and our generation to be served by the will of God. The earth we inhabit is not a mere physical frame-work, but a theater of religion, of devotion to Christ and service to man. Breath, digestion, growth, sumptuous fare, titles, names, rank, power—these are not life, but semblances, mockeries, all. No, no; life is a boon of grace, the gift of God, capable of high achievement and noble destiny. To save our souls and to serve our race—this is our task; and to fulfill it is "life and health and peace." Love to God and man is our highest dignity, the divinest charity, the surest preparation for duty and death. While the wise and rich and mighty glory in their possessions, let us give all for "the pearl of great price." While the wavering minds of an unbelieving world toss restlessly upon a sea of doubt, let us hold fast by the oracles of God, the sure word of prophecy and promise. Precious Bible! Here is treasure which never waxes old. Here is knowledge without decay, truth which endureth forever. From it comes all pure morality; out of it proceeds all the sweet charities of life; in it is the motive-power that is now reforming, and by and by will achieve the reformation of our race. The old man leaning upon his staff and tottering to the tomb reads it, and thanks God he was born to die. The gray-haired matron soothes her sorrows by its record of love, and the light of her hope, kindled by its inspiration, projects beyond the desolations of death. Childhood and youth pillow their heads upon its truth in nature's last struggle, and die with their fingers between its promise-freighted leaves. In the house of mourning its footstep is noiseless as an angel's wing, and its power to cheer more potent than an angel's tongue. At the grave of the buried it chants the hymn of hope, preaches the patience of faith to mourning friendship and stricken love, exhales and crystallizes the tears of sorrow, and gems the crown of life with these transfigured mementos of earthly suffering.

To devise a plan for giving this Book of books to the world is the object of our meeting. Under present circumstances we can do but little. Our country is in trouble. War is upon us. We can, however, consult and pray, renew our expression of faith and love, strengthen the bonds of unity, and make ready for the future. It is a time for preparation. Let us provide a treasury for the gifts of the Lord's people, organize for effective action when peace shall come, give the New Testament at least to our soldiers, and show to the Churches and the world that we covet the eulogy pronounced by our Lord upon Mary when he said, "She hath done what she could." Let us declare our will and purpose to coöperate with the other associations of Christendom in the work of printing, publishing, and circulating the sacred Scriptures without note or comment; and may God speed the holy work and hasten the day when the Bible shall be the creed of every people, the text-book of every statesman, the constitution of every nation, the joy and excellence of all the earth!

Make Full Proof of Thy Ministry.*

"I charge thee therefore before God, and the Lord Jesus Christ, who shall judge the quick and the dead at his appearing and his kingdom; preach the word; be instant in season, out of season; reprove, rebuke, exhort with all long-suffering and doctrine. For the time will come when they will not endure sound doctrine; but after their own lusts shall they heap to themselves teachers, having itching ears; and they shall turn away their ears from the truth, and shall be turned unto fables. But watch thou in all things, endure afflictions, do the work of an evangelist, make full proof of thy ministry." (2 Tim. iv. 1–5.)

IT is needful sometimes to stir up even a pure mind by way of remembrance. The solemn charge of the apostle to a minister so zealous and faithful as Timothy indicates his estimate of the importance of the ministerial office, of the temptations which assail it, and the fearful consequences either of infidelity or negligence. His language implies that the responsibilities of this divine vocation are always grave, delicate, and difficult, but that they are seriously augmented and complicated often by the events of history, the state of the Church, the modes of thought, the prevailing tastes, the evil tendencies which constitute and characterize what we call the "times."

---

*Preached before the Georgia Conference, in Mulberry Street Church, Macon, Georgia, November 19, 1865. Few Conference sermons ever made such an impression as this sermon delivered at the first meeting of the preachers after the war. All were acquainted with poverty and hardship, and the outlook for all was dark. By God's blessing, this sermon did unspeakable good in confirming the purposes and rekindling the zeal of the preachers.—EDITOR.

In the text there are two leading ideas. The *first* is *preceptive*, and sets forth the duty of the ministry, both official and personal. The enumeration of particulars is at once minute and comprehensive. "Preach the word; be instant in season, out of season; reprove, rebuke, exhort with all long-suffering and doctrine." "Watch thou in all things, endure afflictions, do the work of an evangelist, make full proof of thy ministry."

The *second* is *prophetic*, and proclaims the on-coming of a degenerate age—great corruption in the Church, alienation from the truth, love of novelty, disgust with faithful preaching, and a hunting after teachers more liberal and accommodating. "For the time will come when they will not endure sound doctrine; but after their own lusts shall they heap to themselves teachers, having itching ears; and they shall turn away their ears from the truth, and shall be turned unto fables."

The legitimate inference is that stern, honest, heroic preaching is both preventive and conservative. Preventive in that, while native depravity, long-cherished idolatries, prescriptive superstitions, an engrossing worldliness, multiplied and multiform errors and delusions, the energies of passion, lust, and crime, all embodied against God and truth, may limit the usefulness and largely defeat the benign purpose of the ministry, fidelity to duty may nevertheless postpone the evil day, and neutralize the evil agencies of it when it comes. Conservative because it strengthens the hands and nerves the hearts of the faithful few who remain unseduced, uncorrupted amid the general contagion, and thus maintains and perpetuates a living piety in the midst of defection, backsliding, and moral death.

Whether the perilous epoch the apostle describes has passed, or is coming, or is now upon us, I shall not undertake to determine. Ecclesiastical history records many declensions from doctrinal truth and practical righteousness. These dark seasons sometimes lengthened into ages, and again these long winters of ice and death were relieved by tongues of fire and Pentecostal showers which ushered in the vernal seed-time of the summer harvest. I propose to deal not with the past, but with the present—our own times, ourselves. It is not to be denied that as a denomination we have lost ground—I do not mean comparatively, but absolutely—in experience and practice; the aggressive policy has been arrested, stagnated; revivals have been few, short-lived, superficial; our increase has not kept pace with population; the tendency to change, disintegration, laxity in morals and discipline, has grown into a potent evil, and signs of evil omen are shedding a baleful light upon the present and the future. The moral causes out of which this state of things has grown have been augmented by the convulsions of the country and the demoralization of war. To retrieve what we have lost and prevent further damage, to restore the Church to its pristine efficiency and prepare her for future triumphs, there has been much talk of change, the readjustment of our machinery, the obliteration of the obsolete and the effete, the economic revolution of our system and the better adaptation of its agencies to the existing phases of society. All this sounds well—smacks of philosophy, and carries the charm of plausibility with it. I am no enemy to those modifications which experience has shown to be necessary, but I desire to utter the sentiment here to-day, with all the emphasis which reading, thought, and observation can give it, that no legislation will either touch the seat or abate the symptoms of the disease that is praying upon Methodism. Neither improved architecture, nor pews, nor organs, nor lay delegation, nor extension of the pastoral term, nor the abolition of class-meetings and probationary membership, nor the multiplication of bishops, will achieve the consummation we all devoutly wish. Some of these changes would be harmless—nay, positively useful; others very unfortunate; yet others, as I believe, disastrous in the extreme. The facts which alarm and depress the pious and intelligent observer show the kind and the malignity of the disorder, but are themselves the effects of causes which are not to be arrested and extirpated by mollifying ointments or by a dietetic régime adapted to the caprice of an abnormal palate. In truth, the remedy must be applied not to the symptoms, but to the disease. Cure the latter, and the former will cease of course. The causes which are working evil among us are numerous. Some seemingly too insignificant for mischief upon a large scale, nevertheless illustrate the maxim that a little leaven leavens the whole lump. Others are more potent and imposing, but equally subtle and efficacious in their corrupting power. This is not the time and place to specify; it is not needful by way of information, nor yet expedient in view of the interest of this occasion or the future prospects of our beloved Zion. Our business now is with the duties which promise to be remedial and reformatory. Profoundly convinced and deeply distressed as I confess myself to be with the long stagnation which has been upon us, with the irregular, fitful, feeble, and unsatisfactory operations of Methodism in many respects, I am not a convert to that despairing view which declares that Methodism has had its day, lost its adaptation to society, grown superannuate, must subside into the organization of which it was originally an offshoot, or change its platform and remodel its economy, not by the ingenious and vigorous invention, the creative faculty of a living mind wide awake and equal to the emergency, but by readopting the cast-off, the effete, the fossil ideas of the formal past, the very slough of a defunct age. Spirit of progress, forbid, in the name of God, this backward revolution! Our business, my brethren, is not to paint and garnish the sepulcher of the dead, but in the name and by the faith of Jesus to say to the buried Lazarus: "Come forth; take off the grave-clothes; loose him, and let him go."

According to my capacity, I am accustomed to take as strong views of what is wrong and of what is wanting among us as perhaps any of my brethren, but I do not believe that the preachers are all degenerate or the people all backslidden. Like Martha, we have been cumbered with much serving; and like Peter, when he paltered with the Jews in the house of a Gentile, we have compromised with the world, and are to be blamed, but "there is life in the old land yet." Our work is not yet done; the tokens of the Divine presence and favor are not all withdrawn; the shout of a king is still heard occasionally in the camp; the pillar of fire still burns in the heavens, and the pilgrim cloud which pioneered our fathers on their way to Canaan, though long stationary, I believe is about to move. Put on your sandals, gird your loins; let every man take his staff in hand and wait the signal. And now, brethren, I charge you before God and the Lord Jesus Christ, who will judge the quick and the dead at his appearing and his kingdom, prepare, get ready, for the work assigned you. Our salvation as a people, our usefulness in the world, our future glory and power, depend, under God, mainly upon two things—FAITHFUL GOSPEL PREACHING and a SCRIPTURAL ADMINISTRATION OF DISCIPLINE. These two topics branch into many particulars. I shall confine myself mainly to the first, and shall include the latter only incidentally, if at all. The order of the text will be the order of the sermon.

"Preach the word." By the word we understand the revelation which God has made of himself and of his mind and will to mankind respecting their salvation. This revelation contains doctrines, precepts, promises, threatenings. These are all related; there is an interdependence among them, and taken together they make up the "word of faith" which we are to preach. We cannot ignore, omit any without infidelity to our high commission. In the Acts of the Apostles we learn that the burden of apostolic ministry was Jesus and the resurrection. St. Paul tells the Corinthians that he had determined to know nothing among them but Christ and him crucified. But, interpreting these peculiar expressions in the light of the New Testament, we are not to understand that these early preachers confined themselves, either in their epistles or sermons, to a single topic, an isolated fact. They preached Jesus, warning every man, teaching every man in all wisdom, that they might present every man perfect in Christ Jesus. The cross of Christ was the grand central idea. Around this revolved every thing distinctive and peculiar in the Christian scheme. The question comes up, Who was Christ? The word answers: God over all, blessed forever; God incarnate—the Word made flesh; the Star which Jacob saw beaming in hallowed prophecy over the fortunes of Israel; the Shiloh unto whom the gathering of the people should be; the Desire of all nations; the Prince of peace; the only-begotten Son of the Father—full of gracious truth; the Root and Offspring of David; the Morning-star; the Sun of righteousness; the Saviour born; the sinner's Friend; the Advocate; the Redeemer of the world; the Resurrection and the Life; the glory of heaven and earth. Why did he suffer and die? To make atonement for sin; to solve the problem which had confounded all created intellect—how sin could be remitted without infringing the rights and tarnishing the honor of the divine government; how the guilty could be rescued from wrath without a forfeiture of the divine veracity. The humiliation of the Son of God makes manifest the malignity, the atrocity of sin, the Divine abhorrence of all iniquity, and at the same time the exhaustless treasures of redeeming mercy. Calvary! mysterious mount, altar on which the Eternal Lawgiver offered himself as a ransom, compendium of law and gospel, at once the Genesis and the Apocalypse of human salvation.

To preach the word we must make a full disclosure of the entire depravity and helplessness of human nature. This doctrine lies at the very foundation of Christianity. The great salvation was made necessary by the corruption of our race, the dominion of death, and the sentence of condemnation. This doctrine, I fear, though affirmed, is not taught. It is assumed, but not explained, emphasized, urged. Round, dogmatic assertion upon this subject will rarely convince; more likely to revolt, offend, provoke denial. Self-deception is one of the attributes of human depravity, and the softening, modifying influences of civilization concur with our conceit and complacency to cover up the fact of the desperate wickedness of the heart. The preacher must tear away the specious veil, dissipate the delusive dream. He must bring the probe and the scalpel to the work of dissection, and hold on till he has made the startling revelation of that hideous sight, a naked human heart. Men must see their corruption before they will admit the necessity of atonement. They must feel the sentence of condemnation in themselves before they will fall as suppliants at Jesus' feet. This doctrine is fundamental to gospel repentance. The people must believe it. The preachers must declare it, prove it, pile scripture on scripture, concentrate the rays of light till they burn with focal power upon the sinner's heart. Meager, shallow, rationalistic notions will ruin all our revivals, dilute the piety of the Church; reduce repentance to a transient emotion of regret, conversion to a name; brand spiritual religion as weakness and superstition, and leave the strong man armed to keep his goods in peace.

The dependence of all saints and sinners upon the enlightening, renewing influences of the Holy Ghost must be distinctly taught, ardently believed, earnestly enforced. This doctrine is radical to Christianity. Christianity is the dispensation of the Spirit. Its presence and power are the promise of the Father. The Spirit alone can unseal the book, quicken the letter, give demonstration to truth, persuade the rebellious will, and triumph over Satan and sin. The minister of the Lord Jesus should not forget that the Spirit never sets his seal to any thing but *Bible truth*. All excitement produced by mere human appeals, by meretricious pathos, by professional tricks and expletive maneuvers, is spurious, transient, deceptive; betrays both preacher and hearer into a false position, and numbers the Church with the unconverted, the unbelieving, and the unstable. You may *get up a revival* by management, by sounds, by anecdotes, by appeals to social instincts and family affections, by fanciful pictures of reunion of the departed in heaven, but you cannot bring it down from heaven but by the power of faith and prayer and the blessing of God upon his own truth faithfully, affectionately preached. Revivals to promote the Church must not only partake of the Pentecostal type, but they must be identical in origin, power, and fruit. The true glory of the Church is not, as we vainly imagine, in numbers, wealth, and extension, but in holiness, consecration, love of the truth, spiritual experience, the faith which overcomes the world, abiding communion with God. A statistical table is not an infallible index. Our glorying is not always good, even when the figures show an increase, nor grief wise when they report diminution. I have sometimes thought if we were to report conversions instead of numbers—prayer-meetings, with the proportion who attend regularly, instead of revivals in which so many joined, and alas! are never counted but once—we should get much nearer to a right understanding of the true status of the Church.

"Preach the word"—the word, not philosophy, nor politics, nor science, nor human speculations. Do not read essays, nor deliver orations, nor substitute critical lectures for evangelical sermons. Thank God, I need not expand on this point before the Georgia Conference! You, brethren, have neither perverted nor prostituted the pulpit to any selfish, foreign, unholy purpose. You have been content to let the potsherds strive with the potsherds of the earth; you have not supplemented the gospel with party cant and earthen ideas till no gospel was left. Like Nehemiah, you have refused to come down from the walls of Jerusalem and leave the work God gave you to do, to stand still while you wrangled at the base with the enemies of Israel in unprofitable debate. But, brethren, might not our ministry be rendered more effective? It is a singular fact—and I think very suggestive—that the earlier years of a man's ministry are generally most fruitful of visible results. It would seem fair to conclude that as a preacher increased in knowledge, piety, reputation—all elements of power—his usefulness would be enlarged. The popular belief is that it is so; and in the absence of visible fruit, and under the pressure of mortified feelings, casting about for comfort, the preacher argues or concludes it must be so. Where is the evidence? Conjectural estimates will not answer. Logical sequence of natural causes may vindicate theoretic hopes, but where are the signs following? Tell me not of crowded houses, admiring audiences, newspaper eulogies, petitions from the churches for your services. I ask for revivals, for converts, for disciples confirmed, for churches consecrated, alive, burning with zeal and abounding in liberality. Can a minister of the Lord Jesus be satisfied with less? In hope against hope, shall he believe not only without evidence, but against evidence, that he is useful? Ah, brethren! I know you have many a heart-ache at this point. You mourn in solitude with tears over your unprofitableness; but still the harvest responds not to the tiller's toil. Your gifts are prized, admired; you read, study, pray; you have left all to preach, and yet the seed you sow seem to fall upon the barren rocks. Why is this? Among many minor reasons, I think there are two leading causes. First, the Church unduly magnifies your gifts, overrates your influence, expects more from you than you are able to perform; transfers her faith from God to you; trusts in manner, eloquence, talent, popularity; and God cannot bless your labors without *indorsing a vital error in the Church*, and giving his glory to another. The Church all over the land is cursed with this Corinthian spirit. One is for Paul, another for Apollos, another for Cephas; some want preachers, some want pastors; some want style, some want songs; some want tears, some want revivalists. Who, what are all these? Reeds shaken with the winds; poor, powerless instruments. People of Christ, never mind the star preachers; send off for God Almighty. If he bring the golden-mouthed Chrysostom, well; or, if he speak through a ram's horn, the walls of Jericho shall fall, and victory crown the hosts of Israel.

Second, the reason perhaps is to be found in our own ministry; in the change of topics and of style; in substituting argument for exhortation, the edification of the Church for the awakening of sinners; giving undue prominence to the conservative over the aggressive, watching the fold when we ought to have been hunting the lost. On this subject I affirm nothing—certainly do not mean to dogmatize—but I suggest in order to awaken inquiry. I am satisfied that the ministry is losing power and the Church being damaged in her piety by the prevailing ideas among preachers and people. The divine order is inverted, the great commission qualified by social claims and local ideas until the primary object of the Christian ministry has become subordinate to the secondary and collateral. Gospel preachers were intended, as a class, to be evangelists, not pastors; and while the progress of society may often make the combination of the two offices in the same person necessary, yet all parties must recognize the great leading function of the ministry to be aggression upon the world of sinners; while the sub-officers of the Church and the personal piety of the membership conserve the Church itself. The Methodist system was constructed upon this idea, and while we had class-leaders and exhorters and class-meetings, the Church flourished as the garden of the Lord and the ministry counted their converts as the dew of the morning. In my early boyhood I was struck with the fact that no Methodist preacher—old, young, educated, illiterate, on Sunday, every day, everywhere—ever preached, no matter what the text, without an appeal to sinners: Repent, or you will perish; believe, or you will be damned. When we were young, brethren, this was the burden of our preaching. We had good times—convictions, and converts, and revivals. But now for a long, long time, go where you will, hear whom you may, it is all calm instruction, edification of believers, experience, moral, some mysterious doctrine or great principle. And generally the grass is too short for the sheep to graze, and the water too stagnant to be refreshing. For all these things there is a time when the work is well done; but I tell you to keep a Church alive there is nothing like a revival. A bright, old-fashioned, sky-blue conversion will stir a heart under the ribs of death. An altar full of gracious mourners will cluster the angels of heaven in jubilant congregation, and pour the elixir of new life along the withered veins even of a lukewarm membership. And you, brother, when you had finished your grand argument, rounded your brilliant paragraph, swelled your last climax to its sounding close, and some admiring hearer told you it was "a splendid effort," did not feel half so well as when, mixing law and gospel in due proportion, you showed the sinner the plague of his heart, and pointed him to the blood which makes the wounded whole, some trembling penitent grasped you by the hand and said, with quivering lips, "Pray for me." The end of our ministry is the salvation of sinners. Woe to that man who contents himself with good places, fat salaries, pleasant society, and who, because he preaches the truth in beautiful language, congratulates himself on his well-doings! Once you looked for results, expected something; and if the dry bones did not stir, O how you prayed for the wind to blow! You did not ask, "Can these dry bones live?" and go to philosophy to justify your powerless prophesying; but you wept, you groaned, you cried, "Come from the four winds, O breath, and breathe upon these slain, that they may live."

The times demand a ministry thoroughly imbued with the light and the spirit of the Bible—men who have their intellectual and spiritual being in the Bible, who love to range in that element of vigor, that world of wonders. There lie the models to be studied and copied; there sleep the spirits to be recuscitated and brought back in fresh power upon the world. Out of it, in the sixteenth century, sprung the reformers—men who shook heaven, earth, and hell. Nothing but the Bible can make such men. Heart infidelity under cover of orthodox belief, the depressing influence of an almost illimitable worldliness, the cunning craftiness, the subtle beguilements of manifold errors, will defy every thing but the word of God, which is quick and powerful. Alas for the fancies, the theories, the inventions of men! Chaff before the wind. Take away your flowery garlands; tear off your swaddling-bandages; unwrap the two-edged sword—let its cherubic lightning gleam; come down with both hands on the monster sin; strike for God and truth and country. Our last hope is in the power of the Bible. The old foundations are broken up. Old institutions and customs and prejudices are dead. There is no reverence for authority or age or forms. The restless activities, the licentious spirit that burns unsmothered in the bosom of society, the fierce democracy of mind scorning alike the opinions of men and the authority of Jehovah, shut us up to this experiment with divine truth. The Bible has encountered kings, and overcome them; the institutions of ages have fallen before its prowess; it has fought with superstition and barbarism, and they have fled before its light; and now comes the last great conflict with unchained, unsanctified liberty. Soldiers of Christ, equip yourselves from this divine armory! "PREACH THE WORD."

"Be instant in season, out of season." One great drawback upon the efficiency of the modern pulpit is the stereotyped, monotonous order of every thing. Ofttimes the sermons are full of thought, replete with instruction, adjusted in logical order, adorned with rhetorical skill, but somehow they fail in doing Christ's work on the souls of men. There is about them the dullness of uniformity, the tedium of a set task, the drowsy tinkling which lulls and soothes. There is no freshness, vivacity, vim; no electric flash, no gathering of the clouds nor falling of the rain. All is bright, but cold—a moonlight sheen upon a field of ice. Effective preaching will cost the sacrifice of some scholarly notions, the leaving out of some stately words, the withering of some beautiful flowers. We must throw off the despotism of books and authorities, the shackles of a timorous and benumbing restraint. Adopt the language of nature, take counsel of the great heart of humanity. When will men be converted by philosophy or rhetoric or graceful speaking? The truth must be thrown into a living form of pungency and power. Preachers must take the naked gospel and preach repentance, the terrors of the law, the atonement, the new birth, eternity, to men with the same tact and earnestness that they preach the world in the heat of a bargain. We must speak to them, not of them—directly, closely to them. We must imitate not Eli in his faint, soft remonstrance to his vile, degenerate sons, but John the Baptist when he tore the imperial purple from the crime of Herod. Church and congregations will bear to be told that they are not quite perfect, that they might improve, that death will come one of these days; but gospel preaching is humbling, stripping, tearing work, dividing asunder the soul and the spirit, the joints and the marrow. We must probe the wound, lay it bare, give vent to its stench and rottenness, apply the knife and the caustic. Never mind the groans and the complaints—rub in the salt; the disease is mortal—the patient will die without a sudden, powerful remedy.

"Be instant in season, out of season." Ministers are too much accustomed to an undeviating method. Regular, as a clock, but dull as the pendulum—the same measured sweep, the same dull "tic-tack;" no variety, no music. O give us the blast of the bugle-horn as it rings of a dewy morning over hill and dale till the earth is alive with echoes!

You preach at stated times and accustomed places. But this is not enough; you must be prompt, earnest, unwearied; preaching when the chances are more favorable and when they are less so; to small assemblies and to large ones; to private circles; in obscure places, in highways and hedges; to one or to ten thousand; before friends and foes; when it pays and when it costs something. Embrace every opportunity that offers, and thank God for it; and when none offers, seek, make one. What would St. Paul have said to one of these dodging, skulking men, who never preaches if he can help it, who is always hoarse or sick—or thinks he will be if he is not—teasing, worrying everybody, anybody to preach for him; and when he is obliged to do it, does it reluctantly, like he was taking physic, and cuts short as if he was in a hurry to get to bed again? The lazy can always find excuses; the willing, earnest man knows no difficulties. It is the reproach of Christianity that some of her ministers dole out their services like a miser giving alms—pernicious, paltry, and seldom repeated. You ought to preach, preach often. You ought to love to preach. "If I could preach like some men, I would." Ah then, brother, you would preach yourself and not Jesus Christ! What has your reputation for talent to do with your duty? God knew your capacity when he called you to the work, and expects only according to what you have. Remember it was the man with one talent who buried his lord's money and slandered his master in making an apology for himself. Do the most and the best you can, and then if any thing be wanting, charge it to Christ's account.

The wants of the Church, the condition of the country, the state of religion and public morals, demand men of heart, faith, irrepressible energy, and indomitable heroism. Reprove, rebuke, with all long-suffering and doctrine. "*Reprove*," "*rebuke*," are not exactly interchangeable terms. The first means to convince by instruction, correct error, amend faults. The latter means to chide, bear strong testimony against; includes the sharp appeal, the unshrinking application, the close, cutting reproof demanded by the temptations of business and the flagrancy of crime. These duties belong to the pulpit, the private interview, and the official intercourse with the Church. By instruction and discipline the ministry must keep alive the impression that sin is not to be tolerated in the Church, that we have no fellowship with the unfruitful works of darkness, that no age or sex or title shall protect it from censure and denunciation, and without hearty abandonment, from excision. But, while rigid, unyielding, uncompromising, there must be long-suffering, patience, tenderness. If the sons of Levi make successful encroachment upon the empire of pollution, we must purge out the old leaven, get rid of Achan and his stolen gold and his outlandish garment; then we can make a bold assault upon the world, and may hope for glorious triumph. Long neglect of discipline, adulterous communion with the world, have grievously entangled the work before us. What sins we have to encounter!—venerable sins, legalized sins, fashionable sins, foolish sins, religious sins, sins which have become more extended and more firmly intrenched by the long and quiet sufferance of them. The pleasant notion of some that the world is growing better, that repugnance to holiness is subsiding, that false religions are trembling by the weight of their own absurdities, and that the subjection of mankind will soon be an easy task, is all an amiable delusion. The difficulties are undiminished—I fear augmented. Certain am I that the same vigorous element which conquered at first must come into play again before we hold our jubilee over a victorious Church and a world regenerated. O we want men of a meek, prudent spirit—wise men, who will preach the word, the whole gospel! In every unregenerate man there is some spot that pinches and galls, some habit when the truth checks and disturbs him; right there is his whole quarrel with revelation, and against that his passions and prejudices burn and boil together. We want men who will not shrink, but preach on till they have made a record for God in the heart, and left an arrow of anguish in the soul. We want men of unblenching intrepidity, who will charge idolatry in its securest fortress, assail sin in every refinement of its aspect, in all its respectableness of pretension and prescriptiveness of claim, in all its relations to wealth, culture, influence, and interest. We want men who believe that the world will never be made better but by insisting upon all that God requires, and that all compromise and accommodation of truth is a mortal sin. The conversion of the world is not a pecuniary transaction, a commercial enterprise, a diplomatic maneuver. The work is not to be achieved by books and money and machinery. We must all come down to simple praying and preaching. On these we must mainly rely. And when the Church apprehends her dependence, discards her arithmetic and philosophy, and takes hold upon the truth and strength of God, then may we look for the wonders of old, the years of the right-hand of the Most High.

"Watch thou in all things. This I understand to mean not merely the circumspection enjoined upon all Christians, but an intelligent observation of times and events, of opinions and principles. It is nipping error in the bud, scenting heresy in the wind, warning the citadel of the distant danger. It is to strengthen the weak places, admonish the endangered disciple, guard Zion from the insidious approaches of evil. Watch against the fond desire, the ambitious impulse, the selfish cravings, the plausible reasonings by which you may be corrupted, your ministry enervated, and the Church damaged. Take care that your good be not evil spoken of. Beware of filthy lucre, the love of gain, trade speculation. Shun a secular spirit as you would the plague. Strive against envy, jealousy, a hard, censorious, fault-finding temper. Do not think of yourself more highly than you ought to think. Be humble, modest, courteous. Let no man despise your youth or reproach your age. "Watch thou in *all* things."

"Endure afflictions." Make up your mind to bear with patience and equanimity whatever hardship, loss, or peril may come along in the regular, faithful discharge of your ministry. The time of persecution, in one sense, has passed. Our fathers bore the burden and heat of *that* evil day. Nevertheless, there are discomforts, inconveniences, and sufferings—mental and bodily, personal and relative—not a few in our itinerant life and labor. But what of them all? Christ endured far more for us—the cross and agony and shame. We bear our troubles for Jesus' sake.

> Jesus, I my cross have taken,
>   All to leave and follow thee;
> Naked, poor, despised, forsaken,
>   Thou, from hence, my all shalt be.

Homeless wanderers, with scanty fare and tattered raiment, but rich in faith and hope, how happy is the pilgrim's lot!

These times are hard. An inventory of the Conference now would astound the men of the world. So many men, such scanty means, how do they live? Ask the widow with her empty barrel and vacant cruse. By the blessing of God, we endure to this day! Some of you have eaten the bread of affliction and mingled your drink with weeping. And now, with the skies all dark, your pockets empty, an impoverished Church and country all around you, bound in spirit, you have come up to Jerusalem not knowing the things that shall befall you here. But none of these things move you, neither count you your life dear unto you so that you may finish your course with joy, and the ministry you received of the Lord Jesus to testify the gospel of the grace of God.

"Do the work of an evangelist." I have detained you so long, said so much about preachers and preaching, that I will not pause now to expound terms or draw nice distinctions. Suffice it to say that whatever the original difference between apostles and evangelists may have been, it is not important now to settle. Apostles now we have none; evangelists we have or ought to have in every man called of God to preach the gospel. We shall not wander far from the true idea if we interpret the expression, "Paul may plant, Apollos may water," in the light of the Acts of the Apostles, where the works of these holy men are recorded. It seems to have been the office of an evangelist to visit the churches; *churches* where there had been an outpouring of the Spirit and an ingathering of souls, that they might confirm them who had believed through the word; *lukewarm churches*, that they might fan into flame the dying embers, restore the vigor and beauty of earlier and better days, and wake the song of Simeon in the heart of some old disciple who had been waiting and longing for the salvation of God; *decayed churches* where discord, defection, and death had made a solitude to wake once more the hum of life, and to make of desolation a garden of the Lord; *waste places*, the "regions beyond" the fields already cultivated, the highways and hedges of the world, where wander in sin and peril the neglected, the outcast, the forgotten, that he may tell the prodigal of his Father's house, the weary of rest, the heavy-laden and sorrow-stricken of deliverance and salvation.

"*Make full proof of thy ministry.*" Improve every talent, cultivate every grace; rightly divide the word of truth, give every man his portion in due season; watch, pray, reprove, rebuke, exhort, with all long-suffering and doctrine. Go open the eyes of the blind, unstop the ears of the deaf, raise the dead if you can, but be sure you preach the gospel to the poor. Go convince the infidel, put to silence the ignorance of foolish men, soothe the anguish of affliction, bind up the broken heart, comfort the feeble-minded, but teach every man that he must be born again, that neither circumcision availeth any thing nor uncircumcision, but A NEW CREATURE. "Take heed therefore unto yourselves, and to all the flock, over the which the Holy Ghost hath made you overseers, to feed the Church of God." Feed the sheep, feed the lambs, guard the fold. Feed them with knowledge, pure doctrine, "sound speech that cannot be condemned." Neither adulterate nor dilute the truth. Do not neutralize your pulpit deliverances by colloquial levity or personal follies, nor neglect your pulpit preparations for social gossip or the etiquette of imperious fashion. "Stir up the gift that is in thee;" keep no dead capital; hide, bury no talent; work while it is called *to-day*. Never do the work of God deceitfully nor carelessly. Make your efforts exhaustive of the utmost capacity of your ministry for usefulness. Be not satisfied with routine performances. Look for results; pray for them; refuse to be comforted ti they appear. Better mourn for barrenness all your days than once to feel content with fruitless preaching. You are not lawyers, to put up with your fee though you lose your cause, but ministers of the Lord Jesus, who ought to feel that there can be, must be no offset or alleviation or apology for failure. The "burden of the Lord" must not be lifted by mechanical contrivances, nor eased by sympathetic padding, but with meekness, in tears, with irrepressible longings and agonizing intercessions, we must bear it till He who laid it upon us shall grant deliverance by making his pleasure prosper in our hands. God in mercy deliver the Church and the world from a barren ministry—preachers who neither sow in tears nor reap in joy!

And now, brethren, emerging as we are from a long, disastrous war—the Church disordered, the country impoverished, society revolutionized—your work demands great prudence, unflagging zeal, and the most unselfish devotion.

The Office and Work of a Bishop.*

BY DR. LOVICK PIERCE.

"Beside those things that are without, that which cometh upon me daily, the care of all the churches." (2 Cor. xi. 28.)

THE apostle might be regarded in these remarkable words as saying this much by way of defense against all that the false apostles laid to his charge: "If justice were done me in this controversy, it would be admitted at once that the burden which comes on me daily—'the care of all the churches'—is as much as any one man ought to bear. But in my case, besides these daily cares that originate in the care of all the churches over which I am appointed to exercise the pastoral office, there come in upon me all those 'things without'—things not pertinent to my universal pastorate, but made incident to it through persecutions allowed by the abuse of civil authorities and the inhumanities of 'false brethren.'" The "things without" alluded to by St. Paul, and that added so grievously to the burdens of his life, are very fully set forth in the details given us in the chapter in which our text is recorded. Paul, although he was both a modest and a sensible man,

---

*Delivered in Carondelet Street Church, New Orleans, April 29, 1866, by Rev. Lovick Pierce, D.D.; an ordination sermon upon the occasion of the setting to the "office and work" of Bishops in the Methodist Episcopal Church, South, of the following-named elders: Rev. William May Wightman, D.D., LL.D., Rev. Enoch Mather Marvin, D.D., Rev. David Seth Doggett, D.D., Rev. Holland Nimmons McTyeire, D.D. The preacher was then in his eighty-second year. —EDITOR.

could yet be driven into self-defense when the integrity of his character was assailed by pretender apostles or prejudiced countrymen. But this was always done more on the Church's account than his own.

It is a fact patent to all that most of the attacks made upon ministers of Christ for alleged personal faults are most generally the outcroppings of a genuine spirit of persecution, and are designed to bring the Church, through her ministry, into contempt. In such cases, therefore, self-defense ceases to be a mere privilege, and becomes a high moral duty. But as men of the world generally enter upon self-defense, it is justly denominated folly. Indeed, it seems to be conceded by sensible people that no one but a fool will force upon his friends a vindication of himself when no aim or end higher than self-laudation is involved. For these reasons St. Paul in such a case always classified himself as if he too were a fool. But in the present instance he took himself out of this category by declaring that they had compelled him to this course by their gross and base misrepresentation of him. As a rule, silence in such a case denotes a doubtful character or a coward.

Heroism is a trait in human character which, according to the credulous faith of the ancients, advanced its possessor farther into the sphere of godlike deeds than any other virtue common to great minds and hearts. When exercised in such cases as those in which St. Paul displayed it, it enters into the moral sublime. The waste of ages cannot dim its native luster; no incrustations of rust can ever mar the fine polish on its winning face. So long as the manifestation of heroism, divine in its origin and aim, shall continue to exalt humanity in its courageous endurance of suffering, and even of shame in defense of truth and justice, so long will it outrank any and every other virtue that can exist without the actual presence of religion. Indeed, genuine heroism approaches in its appearance so nearly to faith that if we were to see a man professing faith in God heroically bearing up as Paul did in his noble course against all odds, we would account for his heroism on the ground of his faith, even though it were purely a constitutional excellence. We conclude, therefore, that the highest style of heroism is Christian heroism.

Sustained by this exalted virtue, which, being sanctified by the faith of Christ, made it equal to any emergency, St. Paul says: "Of the Jews five times received I forty stripes save one; thrice was I beaten with rods [as we naturally suppose inflicted according to Roman law]; once was I stoned [of Jewish stonings we have an account in the Acts; this stoning was intended to dispatch the apostle as a public nuisance. They dragged him out of the city, supposing him to be dead; but while they stood round about him he rose up—rose up, no doubt, by divine providence in a way sufficiently supernatural to convince them of God's will in his life]; thrice I suffered shipwreck; a night and a day I have been in the deep." [This occurred, no doubt, in connection with one of these shipwrecks. He floated on a spar, or a plank, for twenty-four hours, and was saved, either by being picked up or else by being providentially drifted to land.]

But be these things as they may, we would never have heard of some of these catastrophes if Paul's enemies had not compelled him to become a fool—as he chooses to phrase it—and publish these evidences of his true apostolic character. He was no croaker. Indeed, our exalted conceptions of his Christian heroism would dwindle down into the contemptible drivelings of a mere politician if we could detect in all this wonderful experience of St. Paul's and its narrated ills any mere catering for popular sympathy. He made all these self-sustaining pleas only in defense of his apostolic character and mission. Hence, he might well say: "Neither count I my life dear unto myself, so that I might finish my course with joy, and the ministry, which I have received of the Lord Jesus, to testify the gospel of the grace of God." Here is a specimen of Christian heroism which stands out in bold relief in advance of all other of his fellow-laborers.

See again what he enumerates as common occurrences in his journeyings. These journeyings upon land and water were made in painfulness and want, in hunger and thirst, in cold and nakedness. In every way, as he tells us, he was constantly in peril—in peril by robbers, by his own countrymen, and among false brethren. Yet we see him pressing his itinerant ministry with a zeal that could not be cooled down to the level of a self-preserving caution. His circuit extended from "Jerusalem round about to Illyricum." Through this vast circuit this evangelical apostle swept in order, as he tells us, that he might break new ground all the time. His great heart could not stoop to the selfishness of a local pastorate and the comparative littleness of "rejoicing in another man's line of things, made ready to his hand." His soul went out into the regions beyond, where Christ had not been named.

This was once characteristic of every itinerant Methodist preacher I knew. Not one of us ever had appointments enough if an opportunity to establish another where Christ had not been preached occurred. I fear that this age of Methodism passed away—or began to pass away—with the end of the one-year law of pastoral service. Let no brother enter an objection here until he is satisfied that itinerancy in its original form was not as well calculated to carry the gospel into the regions beyond as it will be when it is separated—chiefly by a mere name—from a settled ministry. It admits of no controversy that if the apostolic mode of preaching was by divine appointment, and in many cases by specific divine assignment, strictly itinerant primitive Methodist itinerancy as a mode of preaching the gospel has for its authority apostolic example over all more restricted modes of applying the gospel to the wants of the world. Among the good effects of itinerancy are these: that it does away with the frequent evils of calling a preacher, saves the congregation from the burden of a pastorate too long continued, and avoids the disturbances that follow enforced separations. And it will always be a law of our itinerancy that, although a minister may remain four years on the same work, yet he may be changed every year, and must be reäppointed each year of the possible four. Hence, our people are quiet in the assurance that they may rely upon our Bishops to change pastors when it may be deemed best, or to continue them within the limitation of the law when there is good reason. A change once a year is the only ever-present, controlling law of our itinerancy. All extension of service is only a privilege; no Methodist preacher has any right to arrange for more than one year at a place. So long as our distinctive feature is itinerancy, if any extension of the pastorate ever becomes useful to the Church it must be on the ground of some sort of divine intimation that the ministry of the pastor is not fulfilled in his particular field. The extension, to be in harmony with the genius of Methodism, must be on the ground of ministerial fidelity and the needs of the Church, and not on any mere law basis, or clamor growing out of social popularity.

Tell me now who can of a single Methodist Church in any of our fashionable cities that is likely to ask the return of a pastor even for a second year on the ground of his fidelity in the administration of the moral discipline of the Church against all worldly and carnal amusements—evils which, by not a few among us, are now being defended as legitimate pleasures and pastimes. I hope there are a few such Churches, but I fear they are too few to save our holy form of Methodism from a worldly canker which, like the prophetic gangrene, only foretells the certainty of advancing death upon the vital organs of a once healthy constitution.

Our pastoral term cannot be extended by a mere law determination beyond one year at a time without damage to the spirit of our itinerant ministry. Such a ministry cannot be maintained intact after the spirit of compromise in the Church becomes so prevalent as to make compromises every few years with a body of preachers who, while proudly boasting of an itinerant ministry as the most effective instrumentality of "spreading scriptural holiness through these lands," are all the time approximating a settled ministry by the extension of the pastoral term within a theoretical itinerant ministry. Indeed, if the views lately defended in General Conference on this subject shall ever find their way into the Discipline, and the extension of the pastoral term becomes a matter of indefinite privilege, our itinerancy, as a great and happy conception of the best and surest method of speedily preaching the gospel to every creature, will be reduced to a mere thing of name, and men's devotion to the system itself will be graduated by the pliability of the Bishop and the chances of remaining indefinitely on some easy, remunerative work. I am sorry my judgment in this case is so constrained that I cannot substitute it by one that recognizes in preachers a loftier demeanor. I am not sure that I should ever have become an itinerant preacher at all under any such economy as this indefinite privilege proposes. Such ill-judged innovations upon the essential element in an itinerant ministry will lead in a quarter of a century to the elimination of every thing distinctive and effective in an itinerant ministry, and of course and by consequence virtually and, as I believe, really destroy our episcopacy, and make us sure enough—if we deserved a Church name at all—"*The Methodist Church.*"*

Now, I do not believe that any one among all the advocates of an indefinite pastoral term and of dropping from our denominational title its "episcopal" identity ever dreamed of these changes running by sequential law into such radical alterations in Methodist economy as to change in a few years the whole front of practical and aggressive Methodism. Yet I believed these ill results would follow, and therefore I voted against all measures which, in my opinion, if ever incorporated in our laws, would, by the natural issue of things, ultimately annul our itinerancy and our episcopal general superintendency. In both cases the issue might appear as accidental, while in reality it would be bound up in the law of cause and effect.

As it regards episcopacy I cannot conceive how any man with due self-respect could ever consent to be ordained a Bishop after his General Conference had made the pastoral term, to all intents and purposes, practically indefinite. In such a case every preacher would be at liberty—if from love of ease or in ignorance of his people's wishes he desired to return to his charge—to make his return or removal a personal matter between him and the Bishop. It is not worth while to tell me any thing about what Methodist preachers have been; it is what they are now, and what their legislative proclivities indicate, that forms the standpoint from which I take my observation. It is enough for me to know from personal observation that Methodist itinerancy has not achieved such ministerial wonders in the earth since the one-year pastoral term was extended to two years as it did before. Nor need any one wonder why this

---

*This name had been proposed during the General Conference instead of the old name, "Methodist Episcopal Church, South."—EDITOR.

is so. It is enough for us to know that whatever costs the most self-sacrifice—if the sacrifice be cheerfully made for the kingdom of heaven's sake—will receive the largest indorsement of divine approval, because it enters more fully into the divine rule of faith, and because it secures a more devoted ministry. All attempts on our part to soften this bed, or to lighten this burden which takes hold on self-sacrifice, is obliged to divest the ministry of some portion of its divine sanction; for God cannot sanction a system of service that allies itself with selfish motives.

The four years, where we now rest awhile, is only a compromise, an encampment between an itinerant ministry properly ordered and maintained and a nominal one, kept up by a lingering prejudice in favor of itinerancy because of its grand achievements when early Methodism was contending for its apostolic character. Strike itinerancy out avowedly and none, so long as the present generation remain, could ever again feel that they were in the original Methodist Church. These attachments will preserve a nominal itinerancy in our Church for years to come. But it will be mainly effected only in so far as a sacred judgment may be used in honor of a once renowned reality.

These successive movements will end in a usage whereby these expectant beneficiaries will remain on their clover-patches as long as the law of privilege will allow of return, while others are shut out who really ought to be favored, if the dispensing of favors could be made at all compatible with the offices of those who are chosen and ordained to the responsible "care of all the churches." But this is impossible. I maintain, fearless of contradiction, that the true work of a Methodist Bishop is only done when, with the best lights he can gather on his pathway, he distributes the preachers in view of the wants of the churches, for every one of which, as an apostolic Bishop, he was chosen to care.

It is only in a very limited and subordinate sense that a Bishop can be controlled by the personal interests and conveniences of the preachers. It has always been, and I hope always will be, the understanding of our Church that our ministers, when they voluntarily enter into our itinerancy, lay themselves as a "living sacrifice" upon the altar of suffering and service for the Church, and not that the Church is to be offered in any way as a sacrifice upon the altar of ministerial accommodation. Suppose, under our present unfortunate law of privilege, it should frequently turn out that when one of our best pastors has been two years in one of those delightful charges, and from which no one could wish to be removed, and while he is still decidedly useful there, and while the charge still desires his return until the law of privilege is utterly exhausted, the Bishop should feel compelled to remove him. Suppose, I say, that at the end of two years—the point from which we have removed our old itinerant ship in order to gain more marginal latitude—this man of God, upon whom you solemnly impose the great trust, "the care of all the churches,' should feel satisfied that the care of some of the churches demands at his hands the removal of this popular and useful pastor to some new charge where his eminent pastoral ability would yield a larger income to the Church than could be gained by his return to his late charge, what ought a Methodist Bishop, a consecrated man of God, to do in such a case?

With all our invasion of episcopal prerogative, it is still a fundamental article of faith in our economy that in all such cases the determining power is with the Bishop. But suppose the presiding elder, who in some degree stands related to his district as the Bishop does to the Conference, having his feelings unduly enlisted in behalf of this man's return, should earnestly oppose the Bishop's judgment, and insist on the preacher's return to his late field of labor at least for a third year. Perhaps most of the great jury incidentally impaneled to answer this question will say: "The Bishop ought to exercise his conscientious judgment in this case, and send this man where the interests of the Church more imperiously demand his pastoral qualifications." Very well; but if the General Conference had let the two years' term alone, and had taken the ground that all changes in this direction were of hazardous possibilities in regard to the future of Methodism, both in relation to a self-sacrificing ministry and an independent episcopacy, it would have met with an universal indorsement—unless, indeed, there should be a few preachers among us who are carried away with the vain hope that if they could get into the Discipline something like this indefinite privilege of return they could work themselves into a sort of settled pastorate under an itinerant flag. This would be the "honorary degree" in the itinerancy. Such preachers, however—if there are any such—would after all become in a ministry properly itinerants, the ignoble of the band; every such preacher urging and finally carrying such a law would increasingly embarrass every member of the Conference, doomed to desire no favors from any mere privileged grant of power to the episcopacy. The zeal of such preachers might turn out to be zeal for your places. The point I am coming to is this: If the two years' term had been left as it was, then, in the case I have supposed, the presiding Bishop would have had no difficulty in using this important preacher just as his imposed "care of all the churches" dictated he should use him. But now the fearful fact to be seen is this: Every step in this direction is a step into the wilderness. Such a preacher as our illustration has supposed might have felt aggrieved at being removed from a place of many comforts to one of few at the end of one year, seeing that the law would have allowed him two, but for the Bishop's conscientious belief that he was, by the obligations of his office, bound to consider the wants of the Church of much higher grade in moral obligation than the comparative comfort of a preacher. But whatever of discontent might arise in the former case, the extension of the pastorate from two years to four has really increased the ground of complaint and the occasions of discontent by the difference between the loss of one year and the loss of three.

Surely every practical mind will see that whatever was ever gained to Methodism by the severity of its ease-sacrificing spirit of itinerancy—while it was yet the ruling passion in the ministry to suffer hardship for the kingdom of heaven's sake—must be lost to it exactly in proportion to all the changes wrought in its working economy with any view to self-indulgence.

I am solemnly emphatic in my use of the words "with any view to self-indulgence." My postulate is that Methodism has been losing in her early aggressive spirit and energy ever since she gave up the one-year pastoral term. The change to two years was a sort of self-indulgent compromise. It had become a matter of trouble to move every year; hence, the law was changed so as to allow the Bishop to send a preacher back a second year if he thought proper. But, as was expected by the friends of this extension privilege, it soon came to be looked upon as a sort of right to stay two years on any good, fair field of ministerial labor; so much so that nothing but the well-known fact that the legal necessity to remove one man created the moral necessity to remove another. But for this the removal of a man from an easy, desirable field of labor until it had been occupied two years would lead to murmurings and disaffection fatal to a high-souled and high-toned itinerancy, and also to an episcopacy determined to use the ministers put at its disposal for the good of the Church as a whole in such fields of labor as the evident necessities of the Church might most clearly indicate to them

As to the change from one year to two, I affirm to-day it was not brought about from any clear idea that it would inure to any increase of ministerial force or success in an itinerant ministry; it was conceived of and brought into being as a measure of self-accommodation. The change from two years to four is upon the same principle. No one has dreamed that the Church will receive any fresh impulse in the way of spiritual life by this change. It is true it was pleaded for on the ground of great good to arise from longer familiarity with the same pastor. But no one believed that the chance to hear the same man four years successively would render the itinerant ministry more effective by rendering it more self-sacrificing. Nor did any one suppose that a ministry already alarmingly remiss in the exercise of discipline against disorderly walking in the Church—an evil known to be on the increase—who had already neglected this divine order in the Church under the two years' régime, would give the Church a wholesome pastoral administration under the extension to a four years' term. Therefore, I am obliged to infer the presence of a self-accommodating spirit rather than the apostolic spirit which urged on Christian ministers as the principal virtue in a man called to preach the gospel to every creature the "endurance of hardness as good soldiers of the Lord Jesus Christ." If the General Conference had provided that the Bishops might return the same man to the same work, even indefinitely, on an official request from the people of his charge on the four following grounds: (1) That his ministry was still fresh and instructive as at first; (2) that his intercourse with the people at all times was strictly ministerial and pastoral; (3) that he diligently instructed the children as required in the Discipline; (4) and especially that he faithfully executed the moral discipline of the Church against disorderly members—then I should have felt that the privilege of indefinite extension of the pastoral term was one of great promise to our Church. But in the absence of such evidences and upon the occurrence of a four years' ministration, with popular applause and a lax discipline, both our ministry and our people will inevitably degenerate. And the time will come when the fearful malediction of God, "Woe to them that are at ease in Zion!" will fall upon us.

It is likely that the world-wide commission with which Christ sent out his first preachers implies, upon the very face of it, that their successors throughout all time should feel that the desire and the will to preach to the greatest number of sinners would be an indispensable passion. Would not one-half of this great nation have been a moral waste until this day had there been no Methodist itinerancy? And have not many of these pioneers, in planting churches in this great wilderness, preached to thousands of listening sinners in their annual dispersions among the scattered inhabitants of our once Western wilds, while upon our present four-year plan, if it had been used as a rule, they would only have preached to as many hundreds? I close this section of the discourse by giving the following as my opinion: Put any preacher you have got upon a station, and keep him there four years, preaching on an average to one thousand hearers, then send him to the same class of hearers, a year at a place, with a thousand average hearers at each place, there will be twice as many souls converted out of his four thousand as out of his one thousand hearers. If this be true, then every extension of the pastoral term will be a fearful contraction of the number of souls each one of us might preach to in a common life-time. The willingness of a Methodist preacher to shut up his ministry

to the hearing of five or six hundred souls for four years
when, by a little more labor and self-sacrifice, he might
preach to five or six thousand souls in the same length of
time, is good *prima facie* evidence that in his preference he
belongs rather to a settled than to an itinerant ministry.
Herein are the reasons of my settled opposition to any extension of the pastoral term to any mere law terminus. No
one, I dare say, among all the advocates of this extension
plan will admit my conclusions; yet I maintain my position on this question to be true, or else a law in chemistry
several times instanced by St. Paul as evidently true, and
as perfectly illustrative of moral sequences, is false—to wit,
that in all these things " a little leaven leaveneth the whole
lump." Under this law of inevitable consequences it is
only necessary to ascertain whether this spirit of extension
belongs in its family associations most naturally to an actual traveling or to a substantially settled, or congregational,
ministry. For if the wish to remove all restrictions so as to
allow our episcopacy to return a man all his life to the same
pastoral charge belongs in its inherent laws to the causes
which have already tied down so many ministers to a mere
garden-spot instead of turning them loose in a world of sinners lost, as has been the case with many of this abnormal
race of preachers, who have whittled out sermons by the
week, and suffered ten times more about the literary merits
of their pulpit performance than about the wants of a large
class of their fellow-citizens, who by force of circumstances
are out of reach of the preaching-place and are cut off from
the advantages of stated preaching and church privileges,
but who might have been served by some itinerant Methodist preacher, if the good work did call him to sacrifice a
day of his selfish home-indulgences upon the altar of ministerial service, or by some settled minister if it did not call
him to risk his literary reputation by too much extempore

preaching. Now, this leaven of a settled pastorate was at work in the General Conference when a vote in favor of an indefinite extension was easily passed, and was only reconsidered and modified so as to compromise between contending parties, the prevalent spirit showing itself clearly in taking the longest term proposed.

. . . .

To me it is no small matter to know that I am in the apostolic succession. I do know that we are in this line so far as our itinerant ministry is concerned. There is no original evidences of any settled ministry in the apostolic organization of Churches. Christ himself was an itinerant preacher. The twelve apostles during their Master's lifetime did not, I apprehend, preach at all. They were called to be witnesses of their Lord and Master both to the Jews and also to the Gentiles. While Christ was among them in the flesh, they were in a process of preparation for his ministry. It was intended that they should graduate only after reaching the fullest conviction that Jesus Christ was the Son of God. (See Matt. xvi. 16, 19; John xvi. 31.) They were to constitute a grand board of commissioners on earth to represent their Great Teacher—his doctrines, his life, his death, and his resurrection. Even after his resurrection these disciples who had gone in and out before him were directed to "tarry at Jerusalem until they were indued with power from on high." While the apostles were yet with him in their preparatory course, Jesus ordained seventy others and sent them out, two and two, on their thirty-five circuits, into every city and town, whither he himself would come. For Christ never sends his ministers where he does not go with them. These seventy disciples returned flushed with success, and reported that "even the devils were subject unto them" through their Master's name. They were really sent out by divine call and appointment; but they were called and sent out as itinerant preachers. After the Pentecostal baptism the twelve and the seventy and all became itinerant preachers together. Paul the apostle, who considered himself as least and last among the apostles, but claimed apostleship by divine appointment—perhaps without any human ordination—was eminently itinerant.

This general amalgamation of these first ministers of Christ in the great itinerant system of preaching we know from the records in the Acts of the Apostles—a book written, as I believe, in order to teach the Church a clear outline of an organism best adapted to the planting of Christianity in all the earth. We know of this unity in practice by the frequent mention of the twelve among the other itinerants in this grand invasion of the empire of hoary idolatry. The beautiful and exact parallelism that appears between this apostolic itinerancy and the itinerancy of Wesleyan Methodist preachers brings us very closely into the line of apostolic succession. And unless I am much mistaken, we will come into this apostolic line just as closely in our chosen episcopacy.

What, therefore, God has evidently modeled for us let us not spoil by remodeling it to suit our selfish indulgences; but let us rather build "according to the pattern shown us" in the Acts. Itinerancy, as a system of preaching to make converts to Christ, can never be substituted by any other mode of preaching that can supply its opportunities to do good in exact accordance with God's intentions to have the gospel preached to the poor. An itinerant preacher, filled with the love of Christ and the consequent love of souls, feels like a philanthropic physician employed to heal and comfort the destitute and the afflicted. His obligation is perfect outside of any consideration as to the ability of benefici aries to reward him. So have itinerant Methodist preachers in their grand rounds labored for the good of men. They were not looking out for congregations that could feed them, but for souls that they could feed. It is as true as gospel that universal sympathy with human souls is only to be looked for in the hearts of evangelists; for their hearts, being comparatively dead to all domestic and local ties, live at ease and comfort only in the one great business of bringing sinners home to God.

But let us come, secondly, to consider the import of St. Paul's apostolic language: "*That which cometh upon me daily, the care of all the churches.*" And here, my beloved brethren in the episcopacy already, and my brethren who are now to be ordained as our episcopal pastors, let me fix your anxious minds with intense concern upon this question: "Are we henceforth to be burdened with the care of the churches?" *You are.* And it is my duty to show you that in imposing upon you this heavy burden we only follow the light shed upon our pathway by apostolic example.

The question of two or of three orders in the ministry of Christ must have a brief notice. I see not how any episcopal Church that goes beyond a mere election to some official position and adds to such election a solemn ordination, ceremonially performed with prayer and the imposition of hands, setting apart a man from among the elders to a specific work in the gospel ministry, can deny a third order in that ministry. Solemn ordination to an acknowledged ministerial function, permanently set up in Church organization, is obliged to be an order. Exactly so do I understand Methodist episcopacy. It is true our people have been wont to separate our episcopacy from the doctrine of a third order in the ministry simply because Mr. Wesley believed there was no order in the simple gospel ministry above that of a regularly constituted presbyter. So all of us believe. When an elder is promoted into a Bishop he has no more ministerial order than he had before; but he does have more ministerial rights and powers. He becomes a universal pastor within the jurisdictional limits of his episcopal diocese. And if the elders so determine in their ecclesiastical polity, no ordination can be valid only as it is done by episcopal hands—either alone, as in the ordination of deacons, or assisted by presbyters when elders are ordained. But still, as we believe, there is no merely ministerial order above that of elders. We believe, as Wesley did, that when the necessity arises elders can restore the episcopal series again. To determine upon the episcopal form of government by a distinct ordination to the office is to determine that there are three orders in the gospel ministry in the structure of that Church organization. But we do not say that a Church cannot be constructed outside of episcopal ordination, and that there is a line of episcopal order directly descended to us from apostolical ordination. We see not how what we mean by Bishops could ever have been created except by regular ministerial ascension in the way of orderly consecration for ministerial pastoral care and authority. Accordingly, we find in St. Paul's pastoral epistles, beginning with the diaconate, the following language: "They that have used the office of a deacon well purchase to themselves a good degree, and great boldness in the faith which is in Christ Jesus." This "good degree," as I understand it, is the eldership, and, if this view is correct, goes far to prove the correctness of the faith of all Episcopalians in the matter of ministerial orders above that of Presbyterians. The Episcopal Churches alone, I think, have an order of ministerial deacons. In other Churches "licentiates" are at once transformed into elders. But the text quoted from 1 Tim., chapter iii., verse 13, as also the narration of St. Luke in Acts vi., both indicate the correctness of the view here advanced. Some of these deacons were preachers, and I infer they all were preachers. Paul's salutation to the saints at Philippi —including the Bishops and deacons—places the deacons in a distinct class in the Church, separated by positive order both from the saints and the Bishops, or, as some would prefer to say, the elders. This pastoral epistle shows most clearly that the same general moral qualifications demanded in the deacons were required as positively necessary in the life of a minister called to the office of a Bishop. A Bishop is divinely intended to be a ruler in the Church of God; and the argument is that a man who does not rule his own house well cannot be intrusted with the government of the Church.

The title of Bishop is synonymous with that of overseer. But overseer really means one invested with ruling power over many persons properly subject to some great owner of the premises overseered by such legitimate agent. And here let me remind those who may come after me that the guardian authorities of our Church have not observed at all times, as was meet, this apostolic direction concerning the admission of men into holy orders. I have seen elders in our Church who did not rule their children or households as the divine appointment as to this order requires. And I will venture the remark that not one of this class ever showed any ability in taking care of the Church. Conference should guard the door to ministerial orders; the Bishops must have men who know how to care for the Church, and will do it, or else all their "care of the churches" is unavailing.

Let us look a little farther into the dignity of the episcopal office. Is it a mere agency created by a body of men who are the legislators of the Church, and incidentally electors of Bishops, of such sort that the agent can be deposed from his place by mere resolution of the body that elected him? Can such deposition proceed upon the ground of some grievance, real or fancied, without any charge against his moral character or complaint against his official acts? Do not our Bishops pass, by virtue of their consecration, into the hands of an ecclesiastical court, duly constituted for determining for what and when and how a Bishop may be deposed? If this is not the true view, and a Bishop knows his danger of degradation from his office for something like the holding of a political opinion by a mere vote of a majority of the General Conference chancing to differ from such opinion, then I have to say that a man willing to be Bishop in such a case must have but little of lofty self-respect.

We hold that the office enters into and becomes a part of the man, so that while he may forfeit his right to exercise the office by moral delinquencies, and may, upon a proper charge and after fair trial before a proper court having constitutional jurisdiction in the case, be deposed, or even excommunicated, yet he cannot be deposed upon a resolution without a charge by a simple declaration that it is the sense of General Conference that Bishop Anybody should cease to exercise the episcopal function so long, for instance, as he is connected with Freemasonry, because he knew at the time he became connected with it that we, the majority, had declared Freemasonry to be the sum of all villainies. I have used Freemasonry here in the place of another assumed disqualification for the exercise of the functions of an invested right, and I have brought in the subject here because I am preaching an ordination sermon preparatory to the ordination of four Bishops. And I do this further because multitudes of our people have always believed that the division of the Church in 1844 was wholly on the slavery question, whereas slavery was only an occasion in the premises. It might almost be affirmed, without modification, that the Church was divided on the question of the episcopal office—whether in relation to the authority of the General Conference it was like a gentleman's coat loaned in a friendly way to a friend which can be resumed again at the call of the real owner, or whether it was an invested right, like an equitable right to real estate which could only be alienated by a decree in equity showing a forfeiture of right. The majority acted on the ground that the General Conference, being the supreme legislative council in American Episcopal Methodism, had a right to depose a Bishop as an employé of the General Conference without trial or charges or specifications according to ecclesiastical laws. Thus it will be seen that the protest on which rested the justification of the minority was a protest against extrajudicial proceedings.

But, brethren now awaiting ordination, we do not so understand your relation to this General Conference. We are proud to say to you that when we confer upon you episcopal honors and power, we place you beyond the reach of our arbitrary action. You may forfeit your right to your office, and lose it in some other court, but we cannot depose you by adopting a resolution that you are "deposed from your office till you dissolve your connection with—your mustache."

From all this it will appear that we attach much higher dignity and sacredness to the episcopal office than the majority did in 1844.

. . . .

But I resumé again the question of a third order in the gospel ministry. It is true the New Testament does not speak of a third order only in the way of official title—Bishop—which, when considered as the appropriate title of an office filled by serving an interest vast in its boundary and immense in its value, rises at once into a dignity far above any that is suggested by the mere name presbyter.

Indeed, it is clear to me that the duties and responsibilities peculiar to such an episcopacy as ours, in the very nature of things, constitutes an order in the gospel ministry. You cannot graft these powers on a mere eldership; they demand a special ordination; and without formal consecration by prayer and the laying on of hands, such an officer as Bishop could not be recognized in the Church. No mere appointee from among the elders, without episcopal ordination, could ever have done the work of our Bishops. And this of itself goes a good way in proof of my opinion, which is this: that this very sense of fitness is good presumptive proof that there is such an order, because there is such an office. In the ordination service itself there is evidence of the consciousness that ordination to any distinct ministerial work, not common to all elders as elders, is the recognition of an order for that particular work. To elders we commit authority to preach and to administer the holy sacrament, while to Bishops we commit authority to "perform the office and work of a Bishop in the Church of God." His right to preach and to administer sacraments are not now committed—not even enlarged. In all this it seems to me that a Bishop is intended to superintend, to oversee the Church; to see that the under-shepherds all do their ministerial and pastoral duties faithfully. Our Bishops are not pastors in the sense of personal care of the members of the flock; they are pastors of pastors; they are to supervise the whole work of the Church, and see that its machinery is all kept in good working order.

. . . .

The glory of our episcopacy is that from the beginning till this day our Bishops, the living and the dead, have kept themselves unspotted from the world. And we feel entire confidence in you all that your future will be as praiseworthy as your past has been. You must not let your overtasking work tempt you to take any ease by substituting a care *for* all the churches in place of "the care *of* all the churches." And you must do all you can to make the care of all the churches in your more arduous fields of labor a rebuking example to us who are your under-shepherds. A little self-indulgence in you will be contagious among us. It is a remarkable notification to us from our Lord that the higher we rise in ministerial dignity the more does it become our duty to make ourselves servants to all. Nobility in the gospel ministry is increase of work.

Go, then, my brethren, unto your new fields of labor. We will not send you out without our blessing and our prayers. But the Lord's blessing is your only hope. It is for this we will pray. In your blessing and in your success we are all blessed. Go, then, and feed the flock of Christ over which the Holy Ghost hath this day made you overseers. And remember that you are more than sentinels charged with the care of an army of defense. You are this day constituted watchmen to watch against all wolves that may seek to destroy Christ's sheep. Your burden would be weighty if by this preferment you were charged with the care of all civil and social order and good behavior. But before all these interests your charge rises up into immortality in its endurance and into sacredness in its nature. You are charged with the care of the Church which God is said to have "purchased with his own blood," and whose members he keeps as the "apple of his eye." You are, therefore, the trustees of an interest too precious to be bought with silver and gold, an interest bought with the precious blood of Christ, and therefore an interest whose neglect is profane. We expect you, therefore, to address yourselves wholly to "the perfecting of the saints," to the work of the ministry, to the edifying of the body of Christ, until we all come in the unity of faith, and of the knowledge of the Son of God, unto the measure of the stature of the fullness of Christ, to whom be the glory, both now and forever. Amen.

Public Opinion.*

THE tendency of the world is to a state of society in which opinion rather than law shall dictate and control the actions of men. Nor is the issue to be deprecated. The fact indicates the comparative perfectibility of our race. The law—even the law of God in its details, its specific injunctions and prohibitions—was not made for the righteous, the good, but for the disobedient, the profane, the bad. The necessity of government originates in the lawless passions of mankind; and while recognized as a divine ordinance and as essential to internal peace and public order, and to national amity and relations, yet, under our constitutional theory, the best government is that which by any direct force governs the least. This apparent paradox, however, presupposes such an enlightenment of the people, and such an infusion of the religious element—at least so far as proper moral judgments are concerned—as shall enable the masses to know their duty and interest, and incline them to do the one and seek the other. On a simple calculation of advantages and disadvantages as to time, character, and influence, men are presumed so to apprehend the legitimate end of a true government as to obey its rules not so much from reference to their authority as from a wise estimate of personal and relative interest. The great principles of justice as they relate to persons and property prevail in this country—not because of the penal sanctions by

---

*A Commencement Address before the University of Georgia, Athens, Ga., July, 1878.—EDITOR.

which they are guarded and enforced, but from the perception of their essential rectitude, respect to public opinion, and as to many from the fear of God. The same may be affirmed of the common morals which dignify the reputable citizen. These men do right, not from a special judgment in any particular case, but from convictions which have radicated into habits, and, save when interfered with by some powerful counter-impulse, act with the force and regularity of instinct. The highest style of human character is not formed by the mechanical operations of arbitrary laws, constraining from an unwilling subject a reluctant obedience, but is the result of opinions and principles derived, it is true, from God, and supported by the spirit of grace and the retributions of eternity, yet, acting through the medium of intellect, knowledge, and conscience, in conformity with the constitutional laws of mind and heart, which if obeyed, even from lower motives and considerations, elevates man far above the unreasoning savage or the vagabond of civilization.

These views, carried out to their ultimate results, and sublimed and sanctified by Christianity, will realize the visions of prophecy on earth as the Bible ideas of heaven in eternity. The transformation of human nature into the divine image, and man's conformity to the mind and will of the Deity, will involve the regeneration—if not the abolition—of the present order of things, physical, social, political, and religious. The world and its organizations will cease to be, and the kingdom that Christ now maintains in all that is peculiar to it will be delivered up, and then, as to the unfallen angels and the saved of earth—the aborigines of heaven and the redeemed colonies from this old world—one mind will rule; not by law and the appliances of authority, but by sympathy, accord, unity of sentiment and affection. Such is the divine programme; and its consummation will be the glorification of God and the good forever.

On this general idea allow me two remarks: First, every real improvement in society is an approximation to this order; the final culmination is yet distant and invisible; nevertheless, the progress hopeful and the end attainable. Lower standards of judgment and action than those the Bible proposes may be adopted; still, if conformity to them lifts man up from his debasement to a higher plane, and thus brings him nearer to truth and under its directer ray, the whole movement is an aspiration kindled by some breathings of our ancient hope or some influence of that "light which lighteth every man that cometh into the world" It is our nature seeking the chief good under the unavowed, unsuspected inspiration of the Almighty, erring perhaps in the dimness of its light, yet struggling after freedom and perfection.

The second remark is that the power and efficiency of opinion, sentiment—whether good or bad, right or wrong, supported by the holy or the profane—is to be accounted for by the fact that in either case our nature responds to a law of our being—the law of sympathy and control, mind acting upon mind, heart upon heart, according to taste and education, morality and constitutional proclivities.

This idea, however, is not to be interpreted and understood as though there were a law so universal and controlling as to abate in the slightest measure our personal responsibility, or even to constitute an apology for errors of opinion or practice. Whatever may be said of circumstances, education, company, neither nor all together possess any compulsory power. They can at best but persuade, entice. The human will is free, sovereign in its prerogative—can decree. Every agent stands upon the foundation of his own spontaneity, and is responsible to government and to God. The fair inference from the doctrine is that it furnishes both argument and motive for circumspection amid danger and for stern resistance to evil, no matter who abets or what may follow. To stand up against a multitude, or even a class, a mere clique, is hard work—almost impossible for some people—and demands great moral courage in all. Such are the ramifications of society, and such the infirmities of human beings, that under the wisest teachings and the most imperious claims of virtue and right, melancholy examples will occur of weakness and subserviency; but these only constitute beacons to admonish, and not instances to alarm or discourage.

But the question very naturally arises, What is that subtle, mysterious, potent element we call opinion—public opinion? Is it the opinion of one or more leading minds? of a class—the rich, the great, the titled? of the majority of the people? Is the press its exponent? or does it find embodiment and expression in the sermon, the lecture, the oration? or is it the silent, unuttered conviction of the multitude, indicating its existence not by speech, but by action? Who shall answer these questions definitely, satisfactorily? Perhaps in a general discussion of the subject no direct answer can be given. If from the world of opinions a distinct selection were made and the inquiry put, an astute observer might write a biography of it, its parentage, progress, and dominion. Each opinion, like each action, has its peculiarities of circumstance, relation, and result; and he who is called on to adjudge and define must know all that qualifies the one and the other. Indeed, it is impossible to give a precise answer to a general question. In fact, what is commonly called public opinion is an exceedingly complicated affair, often doubtful in its origin, unintelligible in its combinations, and very dubious in its range. It is sometimes assumed to serve a purpose when it does not exist at all, and very often is magnified as a pretext to intimidate opposition or as a vindication of a reprobated action. It is complex as Ezekiel's vision of the wheels, but without the intelligent eyes ever looking right on to a given result—tangled in its involutions, revolving, tumultuous, indeterminate; and whether it will end in chaos or creation is the problem in process of solution. It is very often a perfect personification of demagogism, itself a weathercock, varying with every wind that blows—to one thing steady never. With the crude materials of society—the plastic, nebulous elements always abundant, and always ready for experiment—a dexterous manipulator may give them turn, shape, organization, realize any ideal, appropriate to any destiny. The easiest thing in the world is to form a public sentiment when a vice which many love to indulge is to be countenanced, or when it becomes the interest of a man or a party to put down another for particular purposes. Under the institutions of our country, and because of the diverse views of the people as to legislative policy, we sometimes have two public opinions, each rampant as a bull of Bashan; and when they meet in conflict the rage and roar, and din and dust, are terrible; and, as each side tells us, the life of the country is the guerdon of the battle. But the country survives, whichever way the battle goes. Communities, whatever their mistakes, passions, or conflicts, never destroy themselves by direct intention; and in the collision of ideas about a common interest, precious alike to all, there is enough of truth in either theory to neutralize the evils prophesied by the other. It is not, however, with party policies, national sentiments, statecraft, as these operate upon the public mind, that I propose to deal so much as with the local and social phases of the subject.

And first let me say that among the most powerful and formative specimens of opinion, as they affect individual character, and through individuals society itself, is what I will call a fireside sentiment, household notions, domestic ideas, mother's views, father's doctrines, wrought up by affinity and natural selection into systems of thought and judgment. The family is the embryo of what we call society—the first form of government, and still the fountain of authority and influence. Now, while among each class—the religious, the moral, the worldly, the profane—there may be a general correspondence of the ideas natural to the relation, yet in each one there is some modification or addition or omission which determines its family opinion and marks the character of its subjects. This view limits public opinion in its origin to a very narrow sphere, and a halfscore would be the census of its first adherents. But as the Father of Waters—disemboguing its mighty current by many mouths after its flow of several thousand miles into the Gulf of Mexico—may be traced back to a mountain-spring, so this little fountain, bubbling up in some sequestered spot, may be, often is, the head of a river of influence that may color the ocean into which it flows. Springs feed rivers, sparks kindle conflagrations, and the mightiest results have very insignificant beginnings. Sure as we live, in the homes of the people are to be found the motive-elements that give shape to character and destiny to the country. These influences are overlooked, underrated, because they are silent, retired from observation. We are struck by the public, sudden, startling occasions which seem to furnish at once motive and development to character. But the causes which produce these effects are anterior to the occasions which bring them into action. All the possibilities of life, after its kind, are contained in the seed and in the laboratory of nature; by occult processes the work of germination begins, and the outgrowth in form, flower, and fruit is but the development of unseen causes and powers below. The lightning dazzles and commands attention by its lurid flash and its rapid motion; while the blessed sunshine, because of its commonness and its quiet, noiseless descent, awakens no notice; but it is the bath which gladdens the earth with light and covers hill and dale with charms. The red bolt which cleaves the yielding air, and is followed by the booming thunder, may rend the trees of the forest and make the solid ground to quiver, but this power is incidental—is seldom exerted, and is always to be dreaded. The effect too is local. The soundless sunbeam shines everywhere, nourishing vegetation, painting the flowers, making the waters sparkle, the fruits to ripen, and filling the world with food and gladness. In like manner—remote from markets and highways, from court-yards and hustings—influences soft but mighty, gentle but creative, are always at work on minds and hearts, forming tastes, sentiments, convictions; determining modes of thought, creating standards of judgment, and organizing systems—at least in their elements—destined to disturb or bless society, and, it may be, to convulse or fraternize the world.

In the same line of thought, I may say there is a conventional opinion among all the professions, all the grades, and all the ages of society. The lawyers are a community with some peculiar ideas, professional idiosyncrasies; so with the doctors, so with the preachers, so with the representatives of each of the mechanic arts. These ideas may be right or wrong, hurtful or beneficial; nevertheless they are not restricted to the parties who avow them, but, extending outward, contribute no little to that public opinion which embraces all classes among its friends and adherents. The older people too of a village or neighborhood often have a set of notions very influential upon themselves and upon their judgment of others. Young people—and especially young men—from a variety of causes, such as equality of condition, similarity of tastes and pursuits, and especially inclinations toward the same vices—fall naturally into associations where, without formal rules or any thing like positive preconcert, opinions obtain authoritative as law, as despotic as tyranny itself. Now, all these in their respective spheres enter as elements into the composition of that very undefinable thing which, in its most comprehensive sense, we call public opinion. In other words, that thing which in all these classes is a law of action, a rule of judgment, a power or representative of a power to be feared and conciliated. As currents of water are diverted by pebbles as well as by ledges and bowlders, so influences, insignificant and incidental, come in to modify, dilute, or neutralize popular sentiment, or to change its form, direction, or result. So that, after all, opinion is the resultant of a very strange composition of forces. But as feeble, attenuated threads by combinations and by twist may form a cord, a rope, a cable, so any one of these forces may be weak as the filaments of a spider's web, but all of them in aggregation may bind the strongest in helpless bondage.

The combinations are often fortuitous. The issue might be one thing but for the modifications which come of early education, from fireside prejudices. It might be another thing but for professional interference, or something essentially different from either but for the old people or the young people. And after all, but for mutual antipathies among all these, some undefined dread, some ghostly apprehensions reciprocally acting on all the parties, they would all conspire and agree to make yet something else of it. Very often the outspoken boldness of one man arrests the drift of the public mind, revolutionizes the thoughts of a community, and constructs out of the hazy, nebulous mass of ideas a new creation. In all these cases many persons would like to see a change, but, in deference to what they consider public judgment, are afraid to say so; and when one is bold enough to take the initiative and give utterance to what he thinks, he constitutes a rallying-point around which the half-formed, chaotic convictions and sentiments of a whole community cluster and revolve. Such a man is often credited with exerting an influence which really never belonged to him. No man's private convictions are altered. Every one thought and felt in their souls as they do now under their apparent change. They all stood shivering upon one bank and wished they were upon the other side, and he, a little bolder or more adventurous, broke the ice and led the way, and in they all rushed and floundered across. Such men are important to the world—not because they are particularly great or wise or good, not because they are powerful from their position or services, but from their peculiar organization they will often do what wiser men fear to attempt. Some are gifted with a happy infirmity of the reasoning faculty, and through the pred minance of hope and the impulses of enthusiasm are blind to the real difficulties of an enterprise, and so venture and win, while the broad views and sober calculations of the timid philosopher lock him up in "masterly inactivity." The latter may reason well, and logic, precedent, and authority may all be on his side; the other, with less foresight, seeing no hazard, yields to his imaginative power and impulse, acts promptly, and success gives him eclat. Failure would have stigmatized him as a fool; and fail he would, but that every one, obeying his own convictions, under cover of a bold example, seems to adopt him as a guide. He is but a pioneer to regions where others meant to go as soon as the way was opened.

Now, this subtle, intangible, Protean something exerts an incalculable influence for weal or woe on individuals and society. It makes or repeals a law, relaxes or executes it, and sways the scepter of an absolute dominion. The embodiment of a nation's ideas, it is practical legislation. A despot, its prescriptions annul existing statutes, and, anticipating formal enactments, its decree is final and conclusive. A stupid idol, the multitude bow in reverence at its shrine. No matter whether the image on the plains of Dura be gold or brass, iron or clay, the people come with sackbut, psaltery, and harp to chant their devotions and present their festal offerings. Blind to the vanity and absurdity of this degrading domination, which fetters intellect, forestalls judgment, and exacts an unreasoning obedience, very few are brave enough to assert a manly, dignified independence. Although there is a vast difference between an ostentatious singularity, an arrogant, self-willed opposition, and a sedulous, obsequious, punctilious conformity, yet most people prefer the latter, albeit it involves the loss of self-respect, the sacrifice of individuality, and merges all that is characteristic and distinctive and personal and heroic in assimilation and subjection to this many-headed god. It is one of the evils incident to what we call a high civilization—the vaguest, most indefinite, plastic word in our language—that it has but one matrix in which to cast the endless vanities of mind, temperament, and proclivities which nature offers to her molding hand. Arbitrary, stereotyped, iron-cast in her processes, the result upon all who yield implicitly to its manipulations is a sort of social self-annihilation, and the substitution of an artificial personality, moving about in prim propriety and mechanical exactitude; pinks of perfection without freshness or fragrance; human automotons acted on by external forces; neither men nor women as God intended them to be—natural, free, individualized—but slaves in whom the will has abdicated in favor of that mythical entity called "*society*." "I must do as the world does" is a base, cowardly, unmanly, godless maxim.

Yet many avow it, and glory in their shame. Many more practically adopt it who in theory denounce and repudiate it.

"The world" is a denomination for a system of ideas, customs, modes, and fashions, sometimes immoral—often silly—but to those who recognize its dominion no discrimination is allowed. Unswerving fidelity is the condition of citizenship, and disloyalty, even in favor of truth and righteousness, the signal of expatriation. Young people of both sexes seem to cherish a sort of conscience, a religious reverence of this absurd, illegitimate authority. They dare not think for themselves any further than to study the dictates and watch the movements of this dread sovereign. In the history of tyrants there is none whose police is so universal, whose espionage is so minute, whose dominion is so perfect. He takes charge of us and ours—our wives and children, our manners and our equipage, our dress and our habitations. And strange to tell, the more ridiculous his decrees the more popular they are, and those who suffer most by his impositions are his most earnest devotees. Perhaps stranger still, fickleness in his legislation is an element of power and perpetuity. Like Proteus in his changes, and like Jupiter in his dominion, his government is strengthened by revolution and his authority consummated by debasement. At once a demagogue and a despot, he cajoles by flattery and reigns by terror. Sometimes he announces a platform and requires the faithful to swear that his most dubious terms are clear as sunbeams, and his most unmeaning generalities precise, specific, proverbial; and they obey him. Sometimes he puts forth a man as his type and representative, and then woe to the luckless wight who does not lift his beaver and do obeisance! Again, he enunciates a doctrine false, foolish, long hated, often indignantly rejected. No matter; his decree obliterates the past, confounds memory, sanctifies inconsistency, converts heresy into truth, somersaults into patriotism, and transforms treason into statesmanship.

Wearied with the affairs of empire, at another time he comes down from the cabinet of princes and the halls of legislation and goes forth to regulate the tailors and hatters, mantua-makers and milliners. At his nod fur gives place to felt or silk, and hats grow tall and hard and sleek; coats hang *in medias res*—half-way between swallow-tails and roundabouts. The precocious boy, donning man's apparel, visits the ladies as a gallant before the time of life when his father first wore shoes. Bonnets dwarf at his command, till naught is left save a tiny frame—faint memorial of things that were. Starch resigns to hoops, and the miss's sleeves grow wide as her grandmother's skirts, and all the fair sisterhood deformed by pads and puffs; bustle and Grecian-bends have become the pegs on which illicit fashion hangs in fantastic forms her wares and merchandise. But no folly disgusts, no innovation revolts. All the giddy beaux and flaunting beauties of the land vie with each other in admiration of all the silly, senseless metamorphoses of this stupid Baal. It has been said that ridicule is the test of truth. It may be; I doubt it. Certainly it seldom dethrones error or emancipates the human mind from the thralldom of fashion, whether it relates to dress or taste or opinion. The philosopher may argue, the cynic may sneer, the preacher condemn, and the wise and sober remonstrate—the devotees of the reigning order laugh at the old fogies, and rush on with their follies, rejoicing in their progress and enlightenment.

The same pernicious subjugation to this arbitrary, irresponsible power exhibits itself in the sphere of morals and social life. It is not more real in villages than in cities, but sometimes is more apparent because the field of vision is more limited. Its effects are deplorable. A vicious sentiment, if once inaugurated and allowed to form its associations, is a pestilence in darkness and a destruction at noonday. Like poisonous miasma in the atmosphere, it cannot be neutralized by dilution. To expel and purify there must be a storm of public indignation. Allowed to exist and to spread its enticements for the young, it grows cunning in its evasions of parental authority, its deceptions and hypocrisies, until, indurated in the process of depravation, it becomes bold, daring, reckless, defiant; and when the spirit of insubordination and irreverence has waxed strong, self-respect and right estimate of character decline, and then all regard for public opinion—outside of the polluted circle to which these degenerate youths belong—vanishes away, and the miserable victims of this corrupt and corrupting combination go from bad to worse, from improprieties to grave offenses, and at last from vice to crime. Betrayed by specious sentiment, encouraged by companionship, flattered by commendation, and emboldened by example, these parties to evil practices join hand in hand, sustain each other, and expedite the travel to moral ruin.

These things always go beyond the design of the original movers. The social hour, with its glad feelings, its unsuspecting confidence, is the tempter's opportunity—the festal cup the instrument, and the hilarious animation of the youthful heart the ally of the fatal foe. Under these circumstances friendships are formed, familiarity ensues, and congeniality of sentiments and pursuits engenders tastes, maxims of conduct, habits of life potent, bad, inexorable. It is a singular development in these little communities that while the members claim the largest liberty, and boast themselves of their independence, they are the veriest serfs and slaves, never daring to resist the law of the company, and, while glorifying freedom of opinion, scourge with scorn every individual of the class who ventures to think for himself. The poor fellow who, wearied with his bondage, would fain restore himself to the rights of a free agent and the dignity of a free man is mercilessly pelted with reproaches, gibes, and sneers. The only spirit in the throng brave enough to avow his respect for virtue, and his desire to return to it, is denounced by the real dastards; and he is doomed to struggle with himself and with them if he triumphs in his reformation.

All clubs and combinations for the patronage of vice should be shunned even as the upas-tree. The grave, the moral, and the good ought to set themselves against evil even in its incipiency, if they would guard the young and protect themselves. The current reputation of well-nigh every place is derived from the worst people in it, save where they are such an inconsiderable fraction as to be overawed by the public opinion of the larger and better portion. The reason for this is be found in the fact that vice is bold, brazen, intrusive; parades itself in hotels and public places, glories in notoriety. Every traveler and passing stranger sees and hears, and, reporting as he goes, blasts the place with an evil name. Parents suffer in this way by imputation. Churches are charged with inefficiency, and the public guardians, the officers of the law, and the friends of order are sometimes denounced as too base to care or too timid to interfere.

Whether, therefore, we consult our own respectability, peace, and happiness, the reputation of the place in which we live, or the security of the rising generation from the snares and gins of the profane and corrupt, from the serfdom of a bound and fettered spirit, or the wildness and debauchery of dissolute sentiments and habits—all nursed and nourished by banded companionship—let us see to it that we furnish the means of knowledge, enlightenment, and elevation; diffuse just views of character, influence, and social merit, and secure such employments, recreations, and pleasures as shall forestall the evil-thinkers and the evil-doers, and bring even them up to the nobler walks of culture, truth, and purity.

Christ and Him Crucified.

"But I determined not to know any thing among you, save Jesus Christ, and him crucified." (1 Cor. ii. 2.)

IT is a serious question what subject is best suited to an audience and an occasion like this. Is a commencement sermon a mere compliment to Christianity as a religion recognized in the principles of our Government and by the great body of our citizens? Do we by religious discourses and devotional services simply propose to dignify the exercises which are to follow? or is the reason for it to be found in the relation of man to God, and in the evident need of religious influence and divine aid in the responsible duty of education, the development of mind, the promotion of character, the preparation of the young for honorable citizenship? This, as I understand it, is not a ceremony without reverence or heart or object, but the homage of faith in God and his revelation, a formal acknowledgment of our dependence upon the principles, motives, and obligations of our holy religion for the achievements of the past, the progress of the present, and the precious hopes of the future. I have chosen a theme which contains directly or impliedly all the doctrines and precepts, the admonitions and promises, of the Bible. Christ and him crucified is the common nucleus around which gather all the truths of revealed religion—every thing distinctive and peculiar in the Christian scheme.

---

*A Commencement Sermon before the University of Georgia, Athens, Ga.—EDITOR.

Very weighty reasons must have influenced the apostle to the utterance of a resolution so decided and, in the judgment of the world, so singular. The gospel found the Corinthians immersed in vice, and devoted with an idolatrous attachment to the subtle philosophy and the artificial eloquence of the Greeks. They had their masters in each of these departments, who attracted crowds of admiring pupils, and as rivals were sustained and cheered in their competition for intellectual fame by their respective followers. Even after their professed reception of Christianity they clung with fond tenacity to the wisdom of words, valued to excess miraculous gifts, boasted of their attainments in knowledge, and sought in the preachers of the gospel the same attributes they had been accustomed to admire in their heathen teachers. Hence, there were divisions; the Church was rent with unhallowed contentions. Each party had its leader who was applauded for his proficiency in the rules of reasoning or his skill in the artifices of a studied rhetoric; and in the heat and acrimony of their debates they assumed that the success of the gospel depended upon the decorations with which it was recommended to the world. They did not object to the substance of Paul's preaching—for they were fond of new things—but to the manner. They demanded more refinement in delivery, conformity to the prevailing tastes, the popular standard. They were not averse to hearing the principles of the faith, but wished them mixed with wisdom of words. Abstruse themes, philosophic discussions—these were the fashion, the rage, the demand of the times. Paul was in a dilemma. He must yield to their taste or lose his popularity. He does not hesitate. To correct their errors and humble their pride, he reproves their party zeal, their antipathies and predilections, and teaches that the gospel achieves its success by a divine influence, and pours contempt upon those distinctions by which the hearts of the Corinthians had been inflated. Atonement for sin by the death of Christ was the apostle's great theme, and this was incapable of embellishment. It was too awful for the drapery of a gorgeous rhetoric, too simple for the arts and adornments of a dramatic oratory. This bold announcement was not the splenetic outburst of passion provoked by the folly of the people, nor the self-will of a strong man delighting in antagonism and contrariness, but was the conviction derived from revelation, experience, and his high commission to preach to the Gentiles. No other knowledge could compare in importance with this; no other knowledge was saving but this. The knowledge of Christ is the highest science, the most reliable, the most enduring.

The offense of the cross is coëval with its proclamation, and constitutes one of the anomalous phases of the human mind. A preacher may discourse of the unity of the divine nature, on God's universal providence, on the immutable distinctions of right and wrong, on the equity of the golden rule, or even on man's accountability to the God who made him, and men will listen with approbation; but the moment he speaks of atonement, of sacrifice for sin, salvation through the merit of a Mediator, the pride of intellect bristles in indignation, and the venom of the heart spouts and spits in unappeasable rage.

But let us consider the meaning of the peculiar expression, "Christ, and him crucified." We who believe in the doctrine of atonement interpret the phrase as affirming not the fact of the crucifixion, but a sacrifice for sin and faith in it as necessary to salvation. Others who deny atonement think that the apostle merely announces *the fact*—a marvelous event in the history of a nation. Yet others, who claim for themselves the high distinction of a rational Christianity, construe the passage as teaching that Christ died a witness to the truth, was a good man and a martyr. Scripture is the best interpreter of Scripture, and the apostle's own explanation determines his meaning beyond mistake. He says (1 Cor. i. 23): "We preach Christ crucified, unto the Jews a stumbling-block." Was it the fact? They did not deny it; they did not doubt it; they acknowledged it; they gloried in it; it was their boast. How, then, could they stumble at it, be offended by it? Preposterous construction! We preach Christ crucified, unto the Greeks foolishness. How? Why? Was it a strange thing with them for a moral teacher to be put to death? Had they forgotten Socrates and the hemlock? Nay, verily. Many of his disciples remained, still fond of their Master and his sayings. Many of their own great men had perished by the popular verdict. Every form of death decreed by the courts or the mob was familiar to them. There was nothing incredible in Paul's statement considered as an historic fact.

Again, on their low construction: How was the power of God manifested? When, how did Omnipotence intervene? The best of men was dying; was divine power summoned to the rescue? If yea, then it was baffled, not glorified. "Come down from the cross!" was the cry of the mob. Power was tortured, defied, laughed to scorn. The innocent, illustrious Sufferer cried: "My God! my God! why hast thou forsaken me?" Thunders of heaven, where slept you? Angels of God, where were you encamped? Power, indeed! No power here but the rage of cruel malice, the triumph of wicked conspiracy.

The wisdom of God! Did wisdom plan his escape? circumvent the subtilty of his foes? magnify itself by exploding the scheme of the Jewish council or defeating the decree of the Roman tribunal? Nay, verily. On this low plane of interpretation the death of Christ was the confounding of earth and heaven, the failure of prophecy, the eclipse of hope, the despair of the good, the triumph of Satan.

But let us try the other—the orthodox—view of the phrase, and see how the text explains its meaning. Christ crucified, or salvation by faith in him, was a stumbling-block to the Jews because they sought justification by works; they rested in the outward law, "nor knew its deep design." They misunderstood their own sacrifices—had lost all conception of their original intent, and had reduced the doctrine of atonement to the level of a symbolic ceremonial, signifying nothing. They were righteous, and despised others. Now, to be told that their works were faulty, without merit, was on offense; and, in the blindness of their rage, they stumbled. This doctrine implied the impotence of their own Scriptures—that the very doctors of the law were blind leaders of the blind. It convinced them of sin, brought them under condemnation, and classed them with the common herd of sinners. Proud of their lineage, their temple, and their sacrifice, they were startled, outraged, by a statement which ranked them with the Gentile dogs round about them.

The same doctrine was foolishness to the Greeks. For this Hebrew missionary to come to Greece with its schools, its philosophy, and its literary life, and teach that they could not be saved but by faith in a man crucified as a malefactor, rejected by his own countrymen as an impostor, was to them the very foolishness of folly. The story of the cross they heard with impatience, the monstrous draft upon their credulity well-nigh exhausted their politeness, and when Paul mentioned the resurrection they could not stand it. The assembly dissolved, declaring the speaker was a babbler. A few promised to hear him again on these matters, but never did; the rest departed, undecided whether they had been listening to the drivelings of idiocy or the ravings of a madman.

Foolishness! The Jew and the Greek still survive—stumbling, scoffing. But we preach Jesus and the cross as the vital point of the Christian religion. Take this away, and the gospel is nothing; there is nothing saving in Christianity but this; this comprehends all. It is the wisdom of God, and the power of God. Wisdom is knowledge in action, adjusting means to ends. The term implies difficulty, complication—a problem to be solved. A tremendous issue is involved. The rights of God and the interests of the human race are in conflict. How can man be just with God? No voice comes from earth or air or sky to give the answer. Abashed, confounded, is the boast of every age. Hoary learning is dumb; silence reigns in heaven. The great end to be reached is the salvation of sinners. What are the difficulties to be overcome? They originate in the moral government of God. Prerogative must not override law. This would unsettle the foundations of authority. Rectoral justice must be maintained. One attribute must not wound another. How, then, can God be just, and yet justify the ungodly? How can he condemn sin, and yet pardon the sinner? How can sin be remitted without infringing the rights and tarnishing the honor of the divine government? and how can the sinner be rescued from the wrath without a forfeiture of the divine veracity? This was the mysterious problem which all created intelligences deemed inexplicable.

See how the cross of Christ solves the problem. Never was the divine law so completely vindicated and the claims of justice so awfully asserted as when the Lawgiver offered himself as a ransom. No other possible manifestation of the malignity and the atrocity of sin, of God's utter, uncompromising abhorrence of sin, could equal the sacrifice of Calvary. Holiness and justice beam from the cross in awful splendor, while exhaustless streams of mercy and grace gush out to bless the race. "Mercy and truth have met together; righteousness and peace have kissed each other." There is no relaxation of law, no encouragement of sin, no eclipse of the divine glory, but a fuller, brighter manifestation—the light of the knowledge of the glory of God in the face of Jesus Christ. Here, then, is wisdom— the wisdom of God, infinite and infallible intelligence displayed in an efficient and wondrous arrangement to enlighten, bless, and save a fallen, guilty world.

It is "the power of God." The cross brings no accession of power to God. He was and is the Almighty, the Omnipotent, but power was restrained. The power that saves must not be mere power defying law, crushing right, unsettling the order of the universe, but power in harmony with government, with the claims of justice, the demands of holiness, the order and well-being of the universe. It is a false theology which represents the Father as vindictive, implacable, intent on punishment. Nay; God is love. Love is his name and his nature—the very essence of his being. God was willing to save, but law restrained power. The evil of sin cannot be shown save by its punishment. Rivers of oil, the cattle upon a thousand hills, a hecatomb of slaughtered angels, cannot suffice for sacrifice. The nature that sinned must suffer. The God-man—allied to both parties, representing each—comes to suffer and to die. Christ crucified solves the problem.

Divine power, long pent up, broke forth like a rushing mighty wind, and Pentecost reports three thousand converts as the first signal proof of its freedom and the harbinger of its future achievements.

'T was great to speak a world from naught;
'T was greater to redeem.

God made the world by the breath of his mouth; he redeemed it by the blood of his heart. In creation God spoke and nothing heard his voice, and the crude materials of the universe, void and without form, appeared. Power wrought chaos into cosmos. In the old creation power dealt with dead, insensible, unresisting matter; in the new it deals with a sentient nature full of active, hostile elements, passions, will, affections—all dominated by an original, ineradicable enmity. To create was Godlike, the work of the Absolute, the Infinite, the Almighty; to re-create, yet more divine. "The heavens declare the glory of God; the firmament showeth his handiwork."- But redemption reveals his loving heart drafting upon eternal power for a new creation more magnificent than the whole visible universe. The power of God in the cross is the power to save; power to illume the understanding, to awaken conscience, to subdue the will, exalt and refine the affections; power to rescue a fallen sinner, and fit him for a destiny more glorious than Eden. No wonder the apostle gloried in the cross; for "it is the power of God unto salvation to every one that believeth."

The grand proposition of the text is that there is nothing in the world, nothing even in Christianity, saving but the sacrificial death of Christ. The end proposed is the salvation of sinners; and to bring this about there must be adaptation between the means and the end. God might have filled the Bible with any other truth—scientific, political, or philosophical; but these, while they have their sphere and their use, do not touch man's moral status—his relation to God and eternity. The Eastern caravan, laden with gems and gold, the spices and perfumes of every land, faint with dust and heat and thirst, perish if water be not found. The treasure cannot save them. "The world by wisdom knew not God;" and all the wisdom of the world, hoary with antiquity and cumulative by the accretions of the ages, cannot avail to tell how God can be just and yet justify the ungodly; how man may be saved from the discouragement, the terror, the despair of guilt. We must have "the living water."

God has two ways of effecting his purposes—what we call the ordinary and extraordinary miracles, in the use of which he works by means or with means, or contrary to means, as in the case of the blind man anointed with clay and spittle; but in the gift of revelation the subject is proposed to our reason. The truth of the gospel must adapt itself to our condition. What, then, is our condition? We are fallen, corrupted. Every system of speculative unbelief denies or excuses the moral pravity of our nature, and yet undervalues and depreciates that nature itself. Any philosophy which classes all religions indiscriminately together as so many stages in the religious development of humanity overlooks the fact I have stated, and this fact is the fundamental difference between true and false religion. Those who reject Christ and atonement deny this. Let them account for the evil in the world. Vice does exist; iniquity abounds; children "go astray from the womb, speaking lies." Are these the natural outgrowth of a virtuous nature? Nay, verily. But we are told, by way of defense and explanation, all these things are the effect of example. O how, then, we retort, came these things to be universal? Surely in the long lapse of time and generations some virtuous posterity of a virtuous ancestor would have been discovered.

Do any still say that human nature is equally capable of good and evil? Why, then, we ask, the greater propensity to evil? A bad example is always more efficacious than a good one. Nature affiliates with the bad; the good antagonizes nature. To yield is easy; to resist is hard. In the one case we go with the current and the wind; in the other we must breast these formidable forces. Virtue is a struggle with self and sin, the world and the devil; vice is a pastime, a sweet morsel, an enchantress, and, though her steps take hold on hell, she strews the path with flowers.

Try any other doctrine—even of revelation—and there is a felt want, a sense of insufficiency, no foundation for confidence and hope. The religion of nature—Theism, or Deism—does not provide what we need. It is an instinct of our nature to recognize the Author of our being; but faith in God as Creator and Ruler only is not adapted to satisfy the religious wants of man, but rather to fill his bosom with profound anxieties. The moment this great truth ceases to be a pure abstraction, and is realized in the consciousness, it startles, it alarms. The thought of being in the world along with the God of the universe—absolute in authority, irresistible in power, mysterious in his attributes, purposes, and modes of dealing with his dependent creatures—becomes terrific and appalling. Consider the Almighty as the God of nature. The heavens and the earth declare his eternal power and Godhead; but these attributes are a source of terror rather than consolation. After all, inaction with its wonderful contrivances does not teach the benevolence of God. The beauties of nature, the enjoyments of life, might suggest the thought, but contradictory teachings repel the idea. Mingled with the bright, pleasant, and attractive are shadows, sorrows, and alarms. Convulsions rend the earth, famine and pestilence waste it, deserts disfigure it, and the sentient creatures suffer with anxiety, disappointment, and pain, and at last sink into death, loathsome and forgotten. The changing phases of nature leave us to pendulate between hope and fear; uncertain, bewildered, there is no rest, no satisfaction.

The phenomena of Providence are anomalous and unintelligible to mere faith in God—diverse, changeable, conflicting, contradictory, utterly confounding the distinctions of friends and foes. Whether he loves us or not, who can tell?

Even the knowledge of God as revealed in his law serves no better purpose. Nay; this view of God is most alarming of all. Nature and Providence alternate in their expression. They smile as they frown; they beam in beauty and blessing, or rule or rage in terror and destruction. We hope as well as fear; we rejoice as well as tremble; compelled to doubt, we are yet rescued from despair. But law—stern, inflexible—persists in condemnation. The menace is perpetual. The mountain burns with fire; I dare not touch it. The curse reverberates in undying echoes through every chamber of the soul. O wretched man, let not your heart despair! God in nature is God above me—dim, distant; "clouds and darkness are round about him;" whether he is friend or foe I cannot tell. God in providence is God beyond me—concealed, mysterious, doing wonders; he breathes in compassion and wastes in wrath—creates and destroys. I cannot comprehend him. God in law is God against me—revealing sin, threatening vengeance, anticipating the doom of eternity. I exceedingly fear and quake. But God in Christ is God with me, and for me, and in me—my God.

Outside of Christ and him crucified we have the moral law for our guide. Well, yes; there is more law in the New Testament than in the Old. The gospel does not teach a law less strict in its requirements; yea, the holiness of law shines here with a brighter glow. But we are corrupt, guilty, unhappy. We need grace. Go to the criminal condemned to die and offer him law, and what can you say to break the bonds of his despair? It is mercy for which he cries.

But those who deny the sacrificial death of Christ, and hold him as a martyr and a witness, point us to his example. We cannot study it too much; but this cannot save. Example is only law embodied alive in action; and when the law is unwelcome so is its exhibition. Did the Jews profit by Christ's example? They had his gracious words, and hated him the more; they witnessed his tender, forgiving spirit, and gnashed on him with their teeth. The very excellence of the example provoked hate and persecution. The law works wrath; so does its exemplification.

But the gospel has brought life and immortality to light; and here is motive to virtue, encouragement to hope, an antidote to death. Ah, it is delightful to contemplate the fact that the body shall live after death, live beyond the grave! But this is not the whole of the revelation. Heaven is the residence of the saints. But we are unholy. Yes, there is a land where the day never darkens into night, where the sky wears no cloud, where there are no griefs nor graves, and all is light and health and joy; but over the arch of the gate is written: "There entereth here nothing that defileth." O the announcement of life awakens apprehensions harder to approve than the fear of annihilation! Live forever! Under what conditions? Subject to the same infirmities, wants, tendencies, aspirations; exposed to pain, loss, disappointment, toil; surrounded by temptations, dangers, foes. O is there no better lot nor hope? Then death is better than life, and untimely birth than endless being.

The truth as it is in Jesus is the only foundation upon which a scriptural and reasonable theodicy can be built. The atonement is exhaustive of Christian doctrine. It struggles for utterance in the earliest pages of inspiration. Through all the dispensations of religion to man it was the subject of a progression and gradual revelation. The history, biographies, manifestations, and ceremonies of the law were the swaddling-bands of an immature Christianity. The entire sacrificial economy of patriarchal and Levitical times proclaimed Christ crucified. The atonement is the gospel. In it the character of God is presented in the perfection of every attribute. Truth, wisdom, justice, shine undimmed. The purity of the law is more deeply unfolded in the gospel than anywhere else, and its claims attested with thrilling emphasis in the death of Jesus. The lost condition of man stands awfully revealed in the tragic exhibition of Calvary. The remedy provided at such an inconceivable cost is the most overwhelming statement of the fearful fact. But while the gospel makes the most awful disclosures of human corruption, it provides a remedy equal to the desperate emergency. Here are the safeguards of society, the vital forces of a high civilization, the only elements of perpetuity in government. There is a philosophy which receives and lauds the gospel, but only admits it to a niche in the great temple of philosophy. It is one—but only one—subordinate idea or principle. Their religion is civilization. They only look to worldly, physical, intellectual results. They find man, society, the world, in disorder, but suppose that more skill, more wisdom, better appliances, will set all right. The great changes and reforms desired will be reached by natural agencies, the inherent forces wrapped up in human nature, or by the latent elements belonging to our modern civilization. The improvement of our legal codes, the multiplication of schools and newspapers, are prescribed as the infallible remedies for our moral and political disorders. It is a favorite maxim with our public men that when the lights of education and knowledge shall be universally enjoyed then will our liberties be founded upon a rock, and the permanence of our happy form of government secured against all the accidents of time. Alas! the normal forces of human nature are prone to evil, not to good. The tendencies of society develop corruption, not sanctification. It has been thus with every type of civilization the world over, and must be to the end of time. If history attests any fact, it is that modern civilization, with all its material aggrandizements, its conveniences of art and science, the magnitude of its architectural inventions and constructions, if divorced from an evangelical faith, will be involved in as absolute hopelessness as the proud attainments of Nineveh and Babylon, of Greece and Rome.

Paul's Charge to the Elders in Ephesus

(A CONFERENCE SERMON.)

"Take heed therefore unto yourselves, and to all the flock, over the which the Holy Ghost hath made you overseers, to feed the Church of God, which he hath purchased with his own blood." (Acts xx. 28.)

THE Christian ministry is a divine expedient for the improvement of mankind, an ordinance of God devised by his wisdom and supported by his authority. It is a vocation which, as compared with professions merely human in their origin, is marked by several distinguishing characteristics. The dignity and importance of it are to be measured—not by the glitter of its external accompaniments, but by the grandeur and duration of its consequences. He who magnifies his office by just apprehensions of its attributes, instead of exaltation and conceit, cherishes the deepest convictions of his defects and utter insufficiency.

From the remotest antiquity, among all civilized nations, there has been a class of men who devoted themselves to the preservation, increase, and transmission of knowledge. Their speculations were subtle, their arguments logical, their maxims respectable. But to whom did they address themselves? To selected friends, to admiring pupils, to privileged orders. Never did they appear in public except on special occasions, when personal vanity was to be gratified by the acquisition of fame. The gospel preacher is the herald of glad tidings to all people—people of every color, clime, and condition—

the man of the city, the field, and the woods; the poor, the sick, the desperate, the beggar, the convict, and the slave.

The priests of heathen religions were appointed to conduct the pomp of lustrations and sacrifices, to perform august and delusive ceremonies, to mutter mystic sentences and unintelligible oracles. The Christain minister is ordained for the inculcation of truth and to watch for souls as one that must give account. The authority of his message does not depend upon pedantic refinement of thought, upon subtlety of reasoning, or the turgid exaggerations of pompous eloquence. Nor does he strut before the public gaze in gorgeous vestments, holding men's persons in admiration because of advantage; or claim acceptance, prophesying smooth things, to court the favor of the vain and worldly; but like the angel of the apocalypse standing in the sun, he is hidden by the splendor of the revelations which he unfolds—the excellent glory of Him whose truth he delivers.

The disputes which have agitated the Church as the channel through which ministerial good is conveyed, the legitimate mode of vesting it—however unfortunate in misleading and corrupting many incumbents of the sacred office—may nevertheless be considered as the concurrent suffrage of ages as to the divinity of its origin and its vital relation to the highest interests of Christianity. The assumption of those who, with great swelling words of vanity, arrogate to themselves peculiar, exclusive rights and privileges, proceeds upon the monstrous idea that God transferred, parted with, all his original rights in the premises, and delegated to the so-called apostolic successors the power to perpetuate the Christian ministry. It is a suggestive fact—a fact that answers all theories—that the presumption of these pretenders to a divine prerogative have met with a signal rebuke in the failure of their efforts to achieve the great end of gospel preaching—the salvation of souls. They labor in a field concerning which God seems to have commanded the "clouds that they rain not upon it." The grace they promise to convey is no more grace. Its ancient virtue has been lost in its passage through the famous historic aqueducts along which we are told it flows; and now, diluted and neutralized, it has become another thing, and its name is humbug. Conscious of their weakness, the propagandists of this pretentious organization have turned their efforts of late into a new channel, and despairing of the conversion of sinners—the chief work of a true gospel preacher—have confined themselves to the seduction of the faithful. Entering into better people's labors, they beguile unstable souls and lead captive silly disciples with social bribes and unchristian indulgences. Not very apostolic that! It was the glory of St. Paul that he did not build upon another man's foundation, nor boast in another man's line of things made ready to his hand.

I submit to my brethren in the ministry whether the time has not come—fully come—when we should no longer tamely and silently endure the flippant charge that we are irregular, uncanonical, without ecclesiastical authority. Fidelity to souls, loyalty to our Lord and Master, demands that we speak out; that we rebuke, not with mincing words and bated breath, but boldly, sternly, without fear or favor, the arrogant exclusiveness which sets up a certain Episcopal sect as "the Church," and ranks Methodism as a "Society," without clergy or sacraments. I am disgusted with this flummery, this unmitigated nonsense.

If there be any thing in the apostolical succession, it must be because God called the apostles to preach the gospel; then every man called of God to preach is in the succession in the only sense in which there is any sense in it. Yes, brethren, our ministry is not human, but divine; not derivative, but original. It did not come from Peter or Paul, popes or bishops, Wesley or Asbury, but from God out of heaven. The Lord Jesus Christ, the great Head of the Church, "counted us worthy, putting us into the ministry." Let those who prefer it boast themselves of lineal descent, of mythical legitimacy, and canonize the shadows and relics of the dead past, the hoary treasures of the elder time. They are welcome to the tombs and bones of antiquity, to the rubbish of history afloat upon the tide of time, and all the self-complacent deceptions by which they feed their vanity and make merchandise of souls. The signature of God Almighty authenticates our ministry. A converted soul, a living faith, a working zeal, a spiritual, growing Church—these are our credentials. A revival of pure and undefiled religion, where souls are born unto God, is a more potent indorsement than the dictum of a council; the baptism of the Spirit a higher qualification than canonical robes or episcopal manipulations; a divine call, and earnest, self-denying obedience to it, is a richer endowment, a holier investiture, than all ecclesiastical warrants, adjuncts, or parchments. Without these no ministry is legitimate, and with them we may defy falsehood and persecution, the artifice of men and the malice of Satan.

These remarks have been made, not by way of assault, but defense; not to disparage others, but to rebuke their claims, their insulting, insufferable arrogance, and to exalt and confirm my fellow-laborers in the ministry in their conceptions of duty, independence, and obligation. I have followed the example of the great apostle to the Gentiles, who, in his farewell address at Miletus to the elders of Ephesus, indicated his ministry, his doctrine and practice, and sought to confirm them against the insinuations and devices of those who, after his departure, would enter among them speaking perverse things to draw away disciples after them.

As a Church, as a body of ministers, we set up no factitious claims to public confidence and favor. While with due self-respect we insist that socially we are as genteel as the best, we do not profess or desire to lead the ton and to be counted as the élite of the fashionable world. Nor do we court the giddy by patronizing their follies, but rather reprove and denounce them. Nor do we substitute worship for preaching, nor "church music" for praise, nor sacraments for conversion, nor liturgical dullness for religious solemnity. Nor do we pretend that our ministry is the only channel through which the grace of Christ will deign to flow, and that all outside of our communion are left to the unpromised, uncovenanted mercies of God as the dernier chance, the dubious, bare possibility of salvation. Separated from the world by profession (would to God that I could add by non-conformity too!), at war with its sins and sensual pleasures, with no special eclat of learning to justify pride with our association, with no architectural piles consecrated by the touch and moss of years to indulge art and sentiment, with no popular modes to satisfy the superstitious and the Pharisaic, with no periodical festivals or fasts to quell conscience and buy impunity in wrong-doing, our only alternative—if we would hold our ground and go on to prosper—is personal holiness, a sanctified ministry, and a devout, godly membership. With these prerequisites we may well abide comparison with others, and we can, without doubt or fear, stand the scrutiny of the world and the test of time.

The Church is a compound organization, made up of ministers and members—distinct yet united, their obligations reciprocal, and each essential to the integrity of the whole. The ministry is not only organic in the constitution of the Church, but it is invested by our common King and Head with executive functions, the right exercise of which is indispensable to her health, vigor, and development. The priest's lips should keep knowledge, for he is teacher; but there must be government as well as instruction; oversight, discipline, training, the assignment of every man to his place, the active circulation of every element capable of usefulness, as well as sermons, lectures, and exhortations. Preaching, I concede, is the great instrument of doing good. Its importance can hardly be exaggerated as a means for propagating truth, for winning souls and the increase of numbers; but it may be relied on too much for building up, for protection against the world, and the maintenance of a living, spiritual piety. Pardon me, my brethren, but this is the very point at which the Methodist ministry has broken down as compared with the fathers of our Zion. I have long been persuaded that the preachers are responsible for well-nigh every evil which mars the beauty or enfeebles the operations of Methodism. Judge me by what I say; I never insinuate. It is my habit to speak out. I never loved you more — nor indeed so much — as I do to-day. Your Christian manliness, your heroic endurance, your meek and self-denying labors under hardships, privations, and all the evil omens of a dark and threatening future, have enthroned you above all other men in my confidence and affection; but I say to you:

> Let Zion's watchmen all awake,
> And take the alarm they give.

We are not as holy as we ought to be. We have done the work of the Lord carelessly. We have dodged responsibilities, connived at evils in the Church, feared the rich, neglected the poor, dropped the reins of discipline, broken the rules we promised to keep; we have been timid, distrustful, faint-hearted, when we ought to have been decided, bold, unyielding; permitted the world and its friends to encamp within our territory when we should have met them at the border with waving sword and defiant banners and warned them off. By silence we have permitted people to think themselves religious who neglect all the relative and social duties of Christianity; for lack of organization and oversight suffered young converts to go astray and perish in the face of the Bible and discipline, and contrary to both; compromised with conscience, trusting that the protracted meeting would reform the drunkards, convert the dancers, settle the quarrels, smooth over all difficulties; and, when the last doubtful experiment has failed, consoled yourselves with the hope that your successor might have more nerve, wiser management, or better luck. In all those things you did not exactly mean to do wrong, but you have blundered through false ideas of personal responsibility. To save time and trouble you have sought to *lump* the work, which can only be wisely done by attention in detail. Instead of seeking to destroy these evils by numerous guns of lighter caliber, you bring one mighty columbiad to bear, fire at long range and long intervals, giving to the enemy time to repair damages, to intrench and recruit between every discharge. Big sermons and big meetings have their use; we need them; but the woods are thick with scouts and skirmishers. The emissaries of Satan and sin are not always embodied; they scatter and skulk and creep. There are spies and deserters, and traitors too. To meet and circumvent all these there must be system, discipline, obedience. There must be instruction, warning, reproof, police and courts and administration. The captain of the Lord's host must have eyes that never sleep, hands that never hang down; instant in season and out of season, he must "reprove, rebuke with all long-suffering and doctrine."

"Take heed therefore." This impressive exhortation to the elders of Ephesus is prefaced by a concise, telling report of the apostle's life and labors among them, of the doctrines he taught, the tenderness and assiduity of his zeal, and now he beseeches them to take care of the crop he had planted, to devote themselves to its culture, and to guard against the waste and ravage of enemies, whether they came from abroad or arose from within. The duty is compound—twofold—personal and relative: First, take heed to yourselves; second, take heed to the flock, all the flock over which the Holy Ghost had made them overseers; third, feed the Church of God, which he hath purchased with his own blood.

First. *Take heed to yourselves.*

The qualifications for the Christian ministry are numerous. I cannot undertake to specify them all—even by name, much less by enlargement. If we classify them as intellectual and moral, we should embody only a general truth, open to extreme and vicious error on either side. The preacher must have a deep personal experience of the truth and power of Christianity, and pray earnestly for divine illumination; but if he neglect reading, study, mental culture, and discipline, he is an enthusiast, vainly trusting that God will patronize his sloth and furnish by inspiration that which, in the order of nature and gospel too, can only come from toil. If he rely on genius, on books, on education, on compact argument, or on brilliant declamation—and there is some tendency this way—then no wonder if a jealous God dooms him to barrenness, and makes the reputation he sought the instrument of his discomfiture. To combine piety and study, knowledge and faith, preparation and dependence on the help of the Holy Ghost, is hard work—too hard for unsanctified human nature. When a man has read and thought, and written and argued, and ornamented and pruned and polished till criticism smiles approval—to think that such a trumpet may utter a powerless sound, that sensible people may be blind to such demonstrations, deaf to such appeals, is too much for the pride of opinion, the conceit of mere intellect. Then again, such is our infirmity, and so stealthy and insidious is error, that we are tempted to lean upon our long service, voice, and experience and familiar acquaintance with truth, and thus the feeling of insufficiency is diluted, if not evaporated, and in spite of convictions and experiment, and even struggles, to the contrary, we come to our work shorn of our strength, and, like Samson, we say we will arise and go forth as at other times, and wist not that the Lord has departed from us.

And now to all this add the gravity and grandeur of the work we have to do—the truth of God to be proclaimed, the world to be reconciled to Christ, sinners to be converted, the Church to be sanctified—and no wonder that the Bible lays such stress upon simple faith, upon deep humility, upon self-abnegation, upon tireless zeal. Who is sufficient for these things? Blessed be God, none need despair! Though scantily endowed by nature and education, after all the main qualification is the gift of God. Let a man do his duty; prayer can command the rest. I have seen the encampment of Israel panic-struck, down-hearted, ready to flee away; the enemies of God defiant, boastful, full of mockery; the old and strong and wise too much discouraged to preach, and the task committed to some untrained stripling, all unused to the arts of this holy war, but fresh and strong in the simple faith of his good old father's house, and before his sling and stone Goliath went down, and all his followers fled away.

I believe in study; I know the value of it, both from use and—God forgive me!—from the neglect of it; but I tell you there is no preparation for preaching like faith in God and his word.

If the Methodist ministry has lost power in the pulpit, I will not say the Church is responsible for it, but it is largely to blame for it. There was a time when our people judged a preacher by his fruits—the present, visible results of his ministry. When they spoke of a great sermon they did not refer to its intellectual power, but to the revival that followed it; they did not quote in æsthetic admiration some striking metaphor, but they told who was struck down; they did not compare brilliant passages, each according to his taste, but they commented on the consolations they had felt, upon the hopes which had been inspired. Every preacher felt that his position in the Conference depended upon his power, upon his usefulness—that he was to be measured, not by his literature, but by his sheaves; not by his oratory, but by the prosperity of his charge. Nowadays the Church wants a preacher who can attract the young people, and fill up the house; who is abreast with modern ideas, and will connive at all the innovations of those whose only idea of Church improvement is in stripping Methodism of her individuality; who will deliver short, pretty orations, and not worry people about their souls and such things as heaven and hell and a world on fire. I have noticed in all the Conferences that under this class of men—and they are in great demand—the Church regularly wilts and dwindles, prayer-meetings die out, family altars are broken down, and the good old mellow, melting love-feasts that wrapped a man's soul in an air balmy as paradise, and made him feel as rich as the gold of the New Jerusalem, are all numbered with the things that were.

Take heed to yourselves, brethren; the Church herself may corrupt you by erecting false standards of merit and tempting you to collude with her mistakes. It is your business to mold the Church, not to be molded by her. She is committed to your oversight; you are to be ensamples, shepherds, guides. Beware of the fear of man that bringeth a snare. Beware also of self-love, of man-pleasing, a morbid sensitiveness about your reputation. "We have not received the Spirit of fear, but of power, of love, and of a sound mind." These are the elements of greatness and goodness too. Cherish your inheritance. Let no man take your crown, either by threats or promises, by flattery or persecution.

Take heed to your spirit, your doctrine, your practice. Your spirit must be one of self-devotement, of deep humility. This is indispensable to personal piety, and, under the evangelical dispensation, is the essential furniture of him who serves the sanctuary. I have never known a man in our Conferences entertain the temptation, brood over the idea, that he was underrated, that his appointments are too humble and obscure for his claims, and that envy and jealousy had pushed him aside, who did not decline in religious enjoyment, lose moral power, and, in not a few instances, locate and backslide. A meek and lowly spirit does not negotiate and hint and maneuver for promotion, but rejoices that it is allowed to work at all.

Never mind yourself, brother; let yourself alone; drink in your Master's spirit; let duty absorb you. An angel sped with equal alacrity to bake a cake upon the coals for a fasting people as when God sent him to rescue Jerusalem by the slaughter of the Assyrian hosts. The honor of the mission was not in the work to be done, but in the source of the command and the obedience of the servant. Paul, pleading with exquisite address for the pardon of Onesimus, a fugitive slave, was as great—perhaps more lovely, more like his Master—as when a prisoner in chains, by the thunder of his eloquence, he made the judge tremble on his tribunal.

The grandeur and efficacy of gospel preaching depend upon the powerful exhibition of a few great truths. They must not be smothered by grouping around them philosophic speculations, nor diluted by rationalistic modifications to accommodate a carnal intellect. Announce them fearlessly; they contain in themselves the elements of defense and perpetuity. Instinct with the breath of the Almighty, they partake of his own immortality. Like Christ walking on the waters, they can stand when all else goes down, and when Peter is sinking can save him too. Preach the word. Preach Christ; preach him as though you saw him upon the cross and felt his blood gushing warm upon your soul. "Continue in them;" preach on; it is as important to you as to your race. Preach on; it is doing good, and will do more. Preach on; and thou shalt both save thyself and them that hear thee.

Second. *Take heed to your practice.*

You have persevered a long time, but do not remit your watch or dismiss your guard. O to "abstain from all appearance of evil;" to be filled with the Spirit; to give no offense to Jew or Gentile, or to the Church of God; to be "all things to all men," not by trimming, but by adaptation; to maintain the savor of piety like the holy oil on Aaron's reverend head—all this demands wisdom, watching, grace, prayer. You may not fall by scandalous sin, but you may forfeit your prestige as a preacher by vanity, by indolence, by covetousness. You may escape denunciation as a hypocrite, and yet defeat your usefulness by imprudence. You may not be chargeable with filthy conversation, and yet err by foolish talking and jesting which are not convenient. You may be popular with the young, the giddy and thoughtless, and yet sink in the confidence of the wise, the sober, and the aged. You must harmonize the companion and the preacher, the parlor and the pulpit, and be an example "in word, in conversation, in charity, in faith and purity—in all things approving yourselves as the servants of God, that the ministry be not blamed."

Third. *Take heed to yourselves and to all the flock of God.*

You are to feed and care for the flock, all the flock—the rich and the poor, the faithful and the wandering, the sheep and the lambs. They must be fed with sound doctrine; every one must have his portion in due season. We must seek to know them in their persons, to know them in their inclinations; what sins they are most in danger of, what temptations they are most in danger of, what duties they neglect. This work will demand social intercourse, private inspection, and public instruction. You are overseers divinely appointed—set apart by solemn ordination to teach and guide and govern the churches committed to your care. Most of you brethren preach often enough; some do not. Once a week in a station is far too little, either for preacher or people—a compromise to keep up reputation on the one hand and to indulge sloth on the other of more than doubtful propriety. The sheep that are limited to an acre pasture, not over juicy in its vegetation, and allowed to graze "thirty minutes by the watch," and then doomed to chew a scanty cud for a week, are not likely to fatten or to multiply.

Many of you are laborious pastors, visiting from house to house, attending Sabbath-schools, and praying with the sick; but some are sadly at fault in all these things, and their statistics tell on them. Salaries unpaid, no increase of members, meager collections, and a private letter to the Bishop begging for a change. "We want no better preacher," some of these letters say, "but we want a live man—a man who mixes with the people, and who will not break up a meeting with twenty mourners at the altar because he wants to go home."

But who is faithful in the administration of discipline? Somehow the word "discipline" is associated offensively with "arraignment," "judicial trial," "expulsion." This will not often be necessary, and these extreme cases are the most seldom neglected. This is an ultimate idea; discipline includes much more. It is admonitory, preventive, curative. Amputation is not an inevitable sequence of every wound. The health of the ship is not to be preserved by casting every patient into the sea. Every man who slips is not to be harshly denounced and summarily cut off. No, no. How reads the book? War on the unruly, comfort the feeble-minded, uphold the weak, reclaim the wandering, guard the exposed, the fallen raise, the mourner cheer. Reprove, rebuke with all long-suffering; do not threaten and abuse, scold and bluster; but in the spirit of meekness entreat and, if possible, restore. Find out what is wrong. Go talk with the delinquent; argue with him; plead with love in your heart and tears in your eyes. Be prompt; instant in season and out of season. Watch against the beginning of evil; crush the egg; stop the leak. Do not let the weeds go to seed. Incipient disease can be managed; chronic maladies are incurable. A member was absent from the prayer-meeting last night; hunt him up to-day and "stir up his pure mind by way of remembrance." The Church-meeting was poorly attended; go round, see the absentees; set the time for another; tell them you will call the roll. Study to make your meetings entertaining. Distribute work among the members; give every one something to do; 'hold them to a careful, rigid responsibility. See, yonder is a brother; he is cold, tempted; he has just quit praying with his family; his conscience is sore, his thoughts are troubled. Admonish him, encourage him, help him to rebuild the broken altar. A married man joins the Church; tell him what to do, how to do; start him right, help him along. Let them all know that we cannot, will not, after proper time and effort, allow any man to stay with us who does not pray with his family. Stewards of God's house, give an account! Overseers of the Church of Christ, what is your report? Tax your memory; look over your papers. Are you satisfied with your year's work? Have you taken care of the flock—all the flock? Has no soul for whom Christ died received hurt or hinderance by reason of your negligence? Have you never healed the hurt of the daughter of God's people slightly? Do you insist as earnestly as you ought upon simple, practical, experimental godliness? Do you teach the Church that relative duties are essential to personal piety? O brethren, exalt the standard of holy living!

Preach holiness. We must have more family religion, household piety, parents consecrated, children taught in the Lord and of the Lord. This is the great want of the times. The tabernacle of the righteous and the temple of the Most High must be energized in spirit and service. The Church in the house must coöperate with the minister in the sanctuary. The Church and the family are divine institutions—related and intended to be reciprocal, mutual helps—nursery and orchard. They flourish or decay together. The Church in the house is the well-spring; the Church in the temple is the reservoir; the water will stagnate or go dry if the fountain be sealed or the channel be clogged. When all our married Methodists, like Zachariah and Elizabeth, walk together in all the commandments and ordinances of the Lord blameless, their offspring may not be as John the Baptist, but with respect to them they will verify the Saviour's words that the "least in the kingdom of heaven is greater than he." If every father would say, "As for me and my house, we will serve the Lord;" if every mother, like Anna, would wait upon the Lord, day and night, with fastings, tears, and prayers, then the Church record would be but a transcript of the baptismal register, and the jubilant shout of our Zion would be as the voice of many waters.

Fidelity to these grave and responsible duties is enforced by three considerations.

First, we are ourselves set apart by solemn ordination to feed the Church, to guide and govern—not by constraint, but willingly; not by filthy lucre, but by a ready mind. We must not drag ourselves to our work reluctantly for fear of censure, but spring to it with alacrity because we love it and would please Him who called us. We must not measure our service by our pay, nor forget the sheep in taking care of the fleece; but though neglected, pinched, hard run, work on, not counting our lives dear if we may but finish our course with joy. We must not lord it over God's heritage in proud authority with magisterial airs, nor wrap ourselves in unapproachable dignity, but be loving, gentle, condescending to men of low estate, patient toward all men, an ensample to all the flock, that when the Chief Shepherd shall come we may receive the crown of glory that fadeth not away.

A second consideration is, The authority and excellence of Him who hath separated us unto this work, even the Holy Ghost.

It is the concurrent opinion and custom of all Christian communities that those who minister at the altar should have the warrant of Almighty God and the endowment of the Church, the body of Christ. How grand, how awful is the ministry in this light! Embassadors of heaven, mouth-piece of God to men, stars in the right-hand of the Most High, the angels of the churches, commissioned by the Lord of heaven and earth. We may be little esteemed among men, and our work be regarded as a beggarly vocation, but we hold the highest commission known to earth.

While the grave and awful functions of the ministry involve a distinct and peculiar responsibility, it is some relief to know that on this very ground we are commended to the sympathy and kind remembrance of the Church. Our duties are arduous, delicate, complex. Let the Church pray for us. Bear in mind in your private studies as well as your public performances your absolute dependence on superior aid, and let it be your stimulus and consolation that the more abundantly you appropriate the benefits of the gospel all the more bountifully will you impart them. The degree of your sanctification will be the measure of your enjoyment, and your power with God in prayer the pledge of your success with men.

Thirdly, *The mysterious declaration that the Church was bought with the blood of God.*

We will not pause now to settle the import of this peculiar expression. Our salvation is divine in its origin, its priesthood, and its powers. The price confounds the arithmetic of earth, as it emptied heaven of its richest treasure. Creation is the breath of God; redemption is his blood. The starry heavens show forth his eternal power and Godhead; the gospel reveals his heart, all tenderness and love. His tender mercies are over all his works, and his human creatures the objects of his especial regard, but the Church is his bride and his spouse. He loved her and gave himself for her.

Bishop James Osgood Andrew.*

"A good name is better than precious ointment; and the day of death than the day of one's birth." (Ecclesiastes vii. 1.)

THE service I am called upon to perform is somewhat peculiar in its demands. The discourse which is to follow is, in the regular order of exercises, the Commencement Sermon of Emory College for the year 1871; and I am requested to embody in it a memorial of Rev. Osgood Andrew, late senior Bishop in the Methodist Episcopal Church, South. Either service singly considered would be a plain duty, without embarrassment. To combine the two so as to harmonize with the interest and object of the occasion is a task of some difficulty. Several months have elapsed since our beloved and venerated friend passed away to the home of God and the good. Funeral-services have been performed by several of his colleagues in office; memorial sermons have been delivered by leading ministers in well-nigh all the Conferences; biographical sketches, delineations of his character, reminiscences of events and incidents in his varied history, have appeared in all the papers of the Church and in some of the prominent periodicals of the country. But little, if any thing, remains to be said in the ordinary form of funeral-commemoration.

It is a beautiful tribute to the memory of our venerable brother and friend that the Church continues to repeat her testimony of his worth, and seeks to perpetuate the moral

---

*A funeral-sermon delivered at the Commencement of Emory College, July 16, 1871.

influence of his life and character by sermon, by narrative, by description—thus expressing her gratitude to God for the gift of such a man, and commending his example in every stage of his career as a model, scriptural and safe, for the aged and the young. The odor of the alabaster-box of spikenard—very precious—with which Mary came to anoint her Lord did not fill the room in Simon's house till the box was broken; so till death bereaved us our admiring love did not realize the priceless treasure in its possession; but now, admonished by its loss, it inhales with delight the lingering perfume, and labors to enshrine it in everlasting remembrance. "A good name is better than precious ointment; and the day of death than the day of one's birth."
I feel aided and cheered in the work before me by the conviction, derived from my knowledge of the man, that if Bishop Andrew were present in person, while his humility would disclaim every thing I may say creditable to himself, yet in his soul he would approve the effort to start these young men aright upon the path of life, albeit the suggestions were derived from his own precepts, habits, and history.

While yet upon the earth he was my text embodied and alive. A good name was his portion; he won it; he maintained it; it survives him. The odor fills the land. The day of his death, however calamitous to the Church and to his friends, was to him better than the day of his birth. The latter introduced him to a world of labor and sorrow; the other to an immortality of being and of blessedness. His mother rejoiced when it was told her that a man-child was born into the world; the angels of God shouted his welcome when death ushered him into their society, and the Saviour of sinners gave him the promised crown.

To estimate things according to their real value is a rare achievement—a mental triumph very uncommon among men. Yet, true wisdom consists largely in sound judgment, an accurate discrimination of the comparative value of objects which stand in competition with each other; in the sober, steadfast choice of that which is most excellent, and the bestowment of proportionable care upon it; in the grand purpose which points unerringly in one direction, and always subordinates the inferior to the superior interest. Without a countervailing influence—and commonly in spite of it—the soul takes on the character of the objects with which it has voluntary intercourse. If these objects be great and inspiring, they will have the stamp of greatness; if good and ennobling, the imprint of goodness; of littleness, if they be trivial; of corruption, if they be base; "he that walketh with wise men shall be wise, and the companion of fools shall be destroyed." So likewise with the aims and objects of life. They impress the soul, fix its bent, give it shape; they determine character, conduct, and destiny. If the aims be manly and honorable, if the objects be worthy and the plans be worked out consistently, without lapse or deviation, they will never fail to command public respect and confidence. Even in the absence of Christian motive, and when the loftiest ideal proposed is simply human, there is often much to admire and to love. But, after all that civilization and society and culture can do, that which is of the earth is earthy. The loftiest ambition which bounds its enterprise and hope within the limits of time, whatever the theater of its exploits or the success of its plans, leaves its subject far below what is attainable in the way of honor and fame. *That* is most valuable which is most useful. A name, notoriety, reputation, may come from invention, eccentricity, learning, valor, illustrious actions, but the highest types of humanity are associated with Christianity, and are the exponents of its truth and power. The man of shining talents and splendid performances is like the glare of a comet, which, with its train sweeping through the heavens, will attract all eyes and fill for awhile the papers of the land; while the sun, in his regular, constant circuit, giving light to the wayfarers of earth and shedding fertility upon our gardens and our fields, shines on without note or comment; but when the flaming meteor is passed and is forgotten, the steady sun, unexhausted and inexhaustible, beams and burns, creation's light and joy.

A good name, in the sense of the text, implies wisdom, integrity, piety. These are more precious than ointment. Among Oriental nations ointments were counted among their chief treasures. Availing himself of this idea, Solomon affirms that a good name is more valuable, more desirable, than all the delights of sense, all the titles of honor, all the profits of earth. "A man's life consisteth not in the abundance of the things which he possesseth." "A good name is rather to be chosen than great riches, and loving favor rather than silver and gold." The tendency of this materialistic, utilitarian age is to direct antagonism with these precepts of Eternal Wisdom. Money is the god of this world. In the popular creed it is the chief end of man. But fortunes are not often innocently made: "He that maketh haste to be rich shall not be innocent." "They that will be rich fall into temptation and a snare, and into many foolish and hurtful lusts, which drown men in destruction and perdition." Money implies no excellence and confers none. What is wealth without character? Sumptuous misery, gilded desolation. Diligence is a duty, employment a privilege; but drudgery, the condition of accumulation, is a curse—labor and travail without fee or reward. By a law of the mind, as well as by the judgment of God, satisfaction is taken out of those things men so greedily seek; their wishes outgrow their means, and success is unfriendly to repose. "He that loveth silver shall not be satisfied with silver, nor he that loveth abundance with increase." There are times in every man's history when loving favor is better than money, and sympathy better than gold.

"The life is more than meat, and the body than raiment." Our true being is the divine life within, and the noblest work the work we do for God.

A good name is more precious than pleasure—the lust of the flesh, the lust of the eye, the pride of life. To choose the pleasures of earth as our highest good is debasing to our rational nature, subversive of all virtuous feelings and sentiments, and absolutely destructive of present and future happiness.

The distinguishing properties of our moral nature are understanding, volition, immortality. The understanding should toil and stretch after sublime ideas of God; and spiritual truths, the chief aliment of the soul in the eternal future, should be its richest treasure here. If the loftiest imagination and noblest performance of man, when he thinks and acts without reference to a future life, are but vanity, then corrupting, beyond the power of expression, must be the pursuit of sensual indulgences. Such a life is an insult to the memory of our divine original, a burial of our ancient hope in simple brutality, an absolute forfeiture of the divine property of our being. Such a life not only degrades the intellect, but pollutes the heart. The delights of sense, the ensnaring vanities of the world, more than any thing besides, exert this fatal influence. They alienate the thoughts from God, benumb conscience, obscure the light of reason, drag down the immortal spirit from the society of the good and communion with God, and compel it to be a purveyor and a vassal to a body of corruption and death. Cut off from all holy meditation and association; encumbered with impure and groveling thoughts; clotted by foul contagion, gluttony, drunkenness, and sensuality; shorn of their dignity, debauched and imbruted, these miserable sinners are a reproach to humanity and a curse to their race. They glory in their shame, die while yet they live, and rot above the ground. But the memory of the just is blessed. A good name regales the heart with choicest memories of the past, enriches the present with the testimony of a good conscience, and the conscious sense of deserved respect, and irradiates the future with the light of hope more precious than all the joys of earth.

A good name, implying as it does the favor of God, is more precious than the honor that cometh of man. A decent respect for public opinion is to be cherished; a desire of praise subordinate to truth and moral principle is not to be denounced as criminal and corrupting. But to court the applause of men by trimming and by policy, the ambition to excel for the sake of popularity and adulations, perverts and demoralizes; and even the glory fairly won—if this be proposed as the aim and end of life—forms an insuperable bar to salvation. "How can ye believe, if ye receive honor one of another?"

After all, whatever grandeur may mark the conceptions of a mind limited to a mortal range, whatever achievements of statesmanship or heroism may shed luster upon a character belonging only to the empire of time, whatever department of this little sphere may be occupied and magnified by genius, viewed in the light of an eternity which surely comes, is nothing—less than nothing.

> When fame's great trump has blown its loudest blast,
> Though long the sound, the echo sleeps at last.

"But he that doeth the will of God abideth forever." False the light on glory's plume, fickle the breath of popular applause, transient all earthly fame and power; but the honor which comes from God outlives the body, outlasts the earth, outshines the sun.

Now, let me remind you that the race is not to the swift, nor the battle to the strong, nor yet bread to men of understanding. Whatever your native endowments, your aptitudes for business, time and chance will happen to you all. Wealth may never be your portion. The chances are all against you. The best concerted schemes are vain; miscarriages, disappointments, defeats, all may come—most likely will; riches make to themselves wings and fly away.

Pleasure is short-lived. It is for a season—a moment bright, then gone forever. It is too costly for indulgence; it demands the most expensive sacrifice. To give up your soul, your God, your everlasting welfare for the delicious excitement of carnal mirth—this indeed is a woful bargain, an immortal birthright for a mess of pottage. Those who thus irrationally invert the order of things cannot be happy long. The eager, thoughtless infatuation which greedily swallows at a single draught the pleasures of life, drains the world of its last drop, will sit down by and by heart-sick with the fullness of satiety, or wail in anguish over the wreck of hope and happiness.

"Seekest thou great things unto thyself? Seek them not." They are not necessary to thy happiness. They may not come at thy call, nor will they tarry if they do. You cannot command the spirits of this vasty deep. No lordly estate may fill your exchequer, nor pleasure's dulcet voice speed the rosy hours on rapture's wings, nor trumpet voice shout your name to the winds of heaven.

But, after all, this world is of little value. All other distinctions will be swallowed up in that grand one which subsists between those who serve God and those who serve him not. You may come short of wealth or reputation, or the friendship of the great or the idolatry of the masses, but the King of heaven will guide and guard, bless and save. "Them that honor me I will honor, saith the Lord of hosts." Here is the motive which should control your choice, and the guarantee which insures success.

Now, after this running comment upon the text, I proceed with the lessons and illustrations furnished by the life and character of Bishop Andrew. First, I present him as a beautiful example of early piety. He professed conversion and joined the Church at twelve years of age; and thus the God of his father was the guide of his youth. His circumstances were humble, his parents were poor, the country was new, society rude, schools few and inferior; and in his general surroundings there was but little to inspire and elevate. In the rudiments of education his father—a plain man, whose curriculum was confined to reading, writing, and arithmetic—was his chief instructor. The domestic library was small and—as it ought to be in every good man's house—chiefly religious. It was eagerly devoured by the untutored boy, whose mental instincts reached out after knowledge as plants in dark places lean to the sun. The influence of these books on his mind and heart and character, who can tell? But by a law of nature often verified in the history of our race, he derived his intellect from his mother. By constitutional transmission and by personal influence she molded the boy for a glorious manhood. Her strong mind and gentle kindness, sanctified by pious example, sowed the seed and presided over the germination and growth of those moral qualities which made him a man and a Christian, a minister and a Bishop. While yet a boy, leaving home for his first circuit, the maternal heart, yearning with anxiety and love, reluctant to break the family circle, yet resolved to lay upon the altar of the Church her dearest, costliest sacrifice, before she printed the farewell kiss upon his brow, said: "James, if you are faithful I shall be happy." In her, grace triumphed over nature. God accepted the sacrifice and service of her faith. Her reward was glorious. She lived to see the young Samuel whom she lent to the Lord a judge in Israel—great, useful, and honored.

Let it be specially noticed that whatever his native endowments, and however propitious his domestic associations, the true foundation of his character which loomed up in future years was the fear of God, a converted heart, religious principle deeply radicated and carefully cultured. Young men of the college, let me beseech you by this eminent example to give your hearts to God, and to dedicate yourselves, soul and body, to his service. Your nature is evil, and the world is wicked, snares abound, infidelity is abroad—subtle, insidious, full of deadly poison—temptation lurks in every path, a thousand enemies lie in ambush to destroy. You need a guide, divine guardianship, an Almighty shield. Religion will save you from a thousand evils into which, without her protection, you will almost assuredly run. It is best for your health, which folly and sin will undermine and destroy. It is best for your bodies by saving them from disease, deformity, and premature decay. Many men would have lived longer if they had lived better. The sins of their youth cut short their days, and laid down with them in an early grave. It is best for your secular concerns: "Acknowledge God in all your ways, and he will direct your paths." Temperance, frugality, and integrity; faith, hope, and charity, will make you a good name, and very likely fortune too. "The blessing of it maketh rich, and addeth no sorrow with it." It is best for your worldly connections. Without experience, imprudent, rash, ignorant of the world, deceived by appearances, exposed to evil company, what is to become of you without the preserving power of religion. The force of temptation, of example, of untried circumstances, will be too much for you. Without God you are not ready for the battle of life. "He that trusteth his own heart is a fool." "It is not in man that walketh to direct his steps." I quake for my country, I tremble for the rising generation, when I look out upon the hazards of society, the infatuation of custom and pleasure, the skepticism of philosophy, the corruptions of the press, the oppositions of science—falsely so called— the loose maxims, the demoralizing sentiments which pervade commerce, politics, literature, and even infest the Churches. Who can pass the ordeal without contagion? O Lord God, some of us have traveled these slippery places when it was easier to stand than now, and were scarcely saved! We barely escaped with our garments on, when the fires of temptation burned low; now, when the furnace is seven times hotter than it was wont to be, descend thou Son of God, and walk through the flames with these children of the Church and the country!

Religion is best for the calamities of life. Man is born to trouble. Afflictions await you. Your possessions make you capable of loss; your hopes expose you to disappointment; your best affections may become the inlets of a thousand sorrows. The days of darkness may be many, and "the clouds will return after the rain." You will need "a covert from the storm and a hiding-place" from the winds of adversity. "Acquaint now thyself with God, and be at peace; thereby good shall come unto thee."

It is best for old age. "The days of our years may be threescore and ten, or by reason of strength fourscore years;" but years will bring decrepitude, dim eyes, and dullness of hearing; desire will fail, the grasshopper will be a burden; then woe to the man who is unfurnished for the world to come! But early piety maintained and matured will shed over wrinkles and ruin a hallowed radiance, and the weary pilgrim, waiting upon the banks of the river till the messenger shall come, may rejoice in the memories of the past and the hopes of the future, and sing himself away to everlasting bliss.

Bishop Andrew's good name was the crowning glory of a life of earnest, decisive, consistent, heroic piety. Wishing to avoid what myself and others have said on other occasions, and to make this discourse useful for those whose benefit it is specially intended, I beg to present these illustrations of the integrity and dominion of his Christian principles. First, his prompt obedience to the divine call to the ministry. With every man called of God, as was Aaron, this is a tremendous struggle. I know no ordeal like unto it. The awful responsibilities of the vocation, its toils, sacrifices, and discouragements; the humbling, crushing, sense of insufficiency; the reverential fear of rushing in unbidden if I go; the terrible apprehensions of God's displeasure if I stay; the doubt of acceptance from the Church if I offer; the probable failure to meet the demands upon me if authorized to try—all these on the one side; and on the other the sudden, total revolution of one's life-plan, the surrender of hope which ambition had cherished, the dissipation of the dreams in which the heart had reveled, to forego home and fortune and ease, to embrace poverty, to consent to dependence, to become a wanderer upon the earth, and to go whither we would not. O Lord, some of us know what all this means; and perhaps in this youthful throng more than one spirit is passing through this trying ordeal. O young man—my son—if the word of the Lord has come unto thee saying, "Arise, go preach the preaching I bid thee," I warn you, I beseech you, do not run with Saul to hide in the stuff, nor take ship with Jonah for Tarshish! If you hide or run, the stuff will perish; the ship will be broken. You yourself will travel the path of life a sad, disappointed, defeated man, lacerated with thorns and briers, and be saved at last, yet so as by fire; or more likely die a miserable apostate, bereft of hope, disinherited of heaven, ruined world without end.

It would be difficult to imagine a case more trying than that of James O. Andrew. Young, timid, ignorant, all unused to society—his travels limited to the neighboring mill, where the family got their bread, and the country church, where they went to sing and pray—for him to think of going out in God's name to confront the pride and pomp, the talent and culture of the world! Who can tell the tremor, the torture of his soul? But, thank God, he went! In his upheaval of thought and sensibility the moral courage of the incipient man cropped out—the index of force yet in reserve, the symbol of power, the pledge of fidelity. The love of Christ did him constrain. "Go seek the wandering souls of men." Grace triumphed over nature, the boy was merged and lost in the Christian, and the trembling itinerant rode out from his good old father's house with saddlebags, Bible, hymn-book, and Discipline, not knowing whither he went. It was a meager outfit for a glorious life. But in that sad, desponding soul there lived and reigned the faith of Abraham. In that little cloud God was forging a son of thunder. In that unopened bud there was treasured a fragrance which was to regale the Church from ocean to ocean. There rode, all unconscious of his destiny, the future successor of Asbury and McKendree, in piety and power not a whit behind the chiefest of them all.

But where are the hands that never hang down? the faith that never trembles? Elijah fled from Ahab, and begged God to let him die; and it is reported of Andrew that, conscious of his ignorance and defects, discouraged by repeated failures, he resolved to leave his circuit and abandon the ministry. On his way he met a colored man who told him he had been awakened and converted by his preaching; and, accepting the token, he rallied and resolved that if God would make him useful even to a negro slave he would resume his work and cleave to it to the end. There was the true ministerial spirit—humility, devotion, all for Christ. There was the stuff martyrs are made of. There was the self-abnegation which, in the olden times, entered the ring with infuriated beasts, drank the molten lead, handled the red fire, and played with the bickering flames for the sake of Christ and heaven.

Another remarkable instance of his devotedness to the Church and his reliance on God, and of his sagacious statesmanship in ecclesiastical policy, is found in the fact I am going to mention. For a long time after the organization of our Church no married man was found in the ranks of active itinerancy. Bishop Asbury lived and died a bachelor; so did McKendree; and many of the preachers imitated their example. The country was new, the Church was poor, the Discipline made no provision for families; and commonly the resolution to marry and locate were coincident. In this way the Church had lost and was losing her wisest, ablest, and most experienced men. The policy was wrong, though sustained by Conference opinion and distinguished example. The Church approved it, for it was economical--saved time and money. To oppose it was unpopular; to defy it was hazardous. What work will receive a married man? How is he to provide for his wife? These were grave questions, full of pith and meaning. With all our improvements in finance the support of wife and children is still an anxious question. *Then* it was the question, and unanswered save by trust in Providence. James O. Andrew and Samuel Hodges resolved *to marry and travel on*. Their wives—noble women, heroines in devotion to their husbands and faith in God—were like-minded. Mutually they determined to make the experiment and take the consequences. A new and better order of things was inaugurated. The Church has been the beneficiary of it. And out of it—for his brethren in the ministry—have come parsonages, furniture, a higher education of the people in liberality, and a less encumbered itinerancy. We are indebted to these noble men and women. They dared and suffered, but never fainted. There was the statesmanship which forecast the future, and planned to meet its demands; there the moral courage which braved the odium of an unpopular reform; there the steadfast adherence to duty at the risk of martyrdom, when more than blood might be spilled; there the faith which cleaved to God in the dark, built an altar, and inscribed upon it, "Jehovah-jireh, the Lord will provide."

The last example of the dignity and grandeur of this man which I will mention was his Christian conduct and bearing in the contest of 1844, in the General Conference at New York. Then and there fanaticism and conservatism shook hands like Herod and Pilate, and conspired to make him the victim (all innocent though they allowed him to be) of one of their great moral ideas. Arrested without accusation, judged without trial, condemned without being asked to speak for himself, deposed from his high office without law, and contrary to law, amid it all he bore himself as a man—a Christian man—without passion or recrimination. There was no bravado, no rude defiance nor sycophant whining, no lugubrious appeals to public sympathy. Calm, patient, silent, he committed his cause to God and bided his time. The Southern Church, with its self-denying ministry, its six hundred thousand members,* its papers, its institutions of learning, its revivals and glorious

---

* In 1885 about one million.—EDITOR.

progress, is the vindication of his course and the reward of his fidelity. In all the families of our wide-spread Methodism his name is a household word—their children, their colleges, their churches, are called after him. Now that he has left us, the savor of his hallowed character lingers a perfume and a benediction, reminding us of the heaven to which he has gone. He died in the Lord; his works follow him; and his influence for good survives him, and will live on beyond his own generation.

But I have said enough. The good man's life was known and read of all. I was intimate with him for forty years, and I bear witness I never knew a purer man. He lived long and he lived well. He went about doing good. His consecration was complete. He served his generation by the will of God. His youth, his manhood, and his old age were all radiant with the beauty of holiness. There is no blot upon his history. No reproach blurs his good name. He has left a heritage to his children richer than money, more desirable than lands, more precious than diamonds. To the Church his example is a legacy of instruction and encouragement, of inspiring memories and imperishable hopes. He loved the cause of Christ with undying devotion, and O brethren in the ministry, he carried us in his heart of hearts. His interceding cry for the preachers was familiar to the ear of Heaven.

He joined the Church sixty-five years ago; was an active, laborious traveling preacher twenty years, and a Bishop thirty-nine years. What scenes, what labors, what trials, what triumphs, are included in this long and honorable record! Devoted when he was little and unknown; humble when he was great and honored; faithful when he served in the ranks of his brethren; tender, forbearing, and kind when exalted to office and burdened with the most delicate responsibilities ever committed to man—I can pronounce no no higher eulogy than to say he never disappointed the hopes nor betrayed the confidence of the Church. Equal to the demands of every position, consistent in every trial, he worked diligently without complaint, endured heroically like a martyr, and triumphed like a saint.

"In age and feebleness extreme," his heart still warm with the fervor of devotion, he moved among the churches where he had preached the gospel, and from the rich stores of his own mellow experience inspired the hope of the aged and the zeal of the young, and in the spirit of benignity and love commended all to the blessing of God with the affection of a father and the faith of an apostle.

He made his last visit to the city of New Orleans, preached on Sabbath morning with more than usual vigor and zeal, addressed the Sabbath-school children—his last public act— and on Tuesday night the messenger came and smote him with paralysis, the token of his departure. He was taken to Mobile to the parsonage, where his youngest daughter lived, and there he breathed his last. He lingered for several days after his arrival. The power of articulation was sufficiently restored for him to converse. He talked of the Church, and God, and heaven. He sent messages of love to his colleagues, to the Conference, and to special friends. His soul was full of peace and hope and joy; there were no distressing doubts, no gloomy fears to shade the closing hours of his well-spent life; and the memory of his gracious words linger with us like the evening-star shining over the place where his sun went down. O it was a glorious death! The old body, trembling, tottering, worn out, lying down in dreamless slumber; the tired, weary soul, coming up from the deep, dark waters of its last baptism, and shouting back to weeping friends, "I have fought a good fight, I have finished my course, I have kept the faith." His body lies in yonder grave-yard, beside the wife of his youth. From this woodland town some years ago her ransomed soul went up to heaven. By his dying-request his remains were brought from a distant city for interment here,* and when the voice of the archangel and trump of God shall peal over sea and land they shall rise together and be forever with the Lord.

Behold, ye aged disciples, companions of the departed Andrew, the goodness, the patient kindness, the all-sufficient grace of God! Be encouraged. Your God will never leave you nor forsake you. He was with Andrew all along and to the last; and above all, at the last. You may outlive your capacity to labor, and infirmities may come upon you, and the world forget you, but he will never turn you out-of-doors. He will remember the kindness of your youth, and your hoary hairs shall glisten with the light of his benediction. When heart and flesh shall fail, the nearest, dearest friend of all will be Him who made and who will deliver you. Endure to the end. Hope on to the last. You are riding at anchor off the haven now; the next wind and tide will waft you in. And now, young men, accept this feeble tribute to the memory of a great and good man who loved you, prayed for you, pointed you to heaven and led the way. I have not intended to glorify him, but to benefit you. Let his life be your pattern and guide. Adopt his principles, imitate his habits. Devote yourselves, like him, to the service of God and man. He lived to be old; you may depart in your prime. Readiness to die is the best preparation for life. O let the voice of the living preacher to-day encourage you to love and seek and cherish the good name so gloriously illustrated in the life of the deceased, and glorified by his death, and consecrated by his grave! To you especially who are about to

---

*The body of Bishop Andrew rests in the Oxford cemetery.—Editor.

go out from college to take your places in the world, I pray you distinguish this day by the surrender of yourselves to Him who says to each of you, "My son, give me thine heart."* You are standing on the threshold of a perilous future; will you enter it without God? The question is of awful moment. Whether your Christian friends shall rejoice or be miserable, whether you shall be a bane or a blessing to society, whether you shall contribute to the safety or the perils of the country—ah! ah! whether you shall perish or be saved—all depends, perchance, upon the decision of this hour. What do you mean to do? A place is vacant in the house of God; who will fill it? A sentinel has fallen upon the watch-tower; who will be baptized for the dead? You have been born into the world. You are the pride of your fathers, the joy of your mothers, the delight of your friends; walk worthy of these blessed affections; fulfill the hope of your family; meet the demands of your country; enter upon the service of the Church; serve your generation by the will of God; so live that the day of your death may be better than the day of your birth; and while earth weeps over your departure, heaven shall rejoice in your coronation.

---

* It is said that three young men of the college settled the question of their call to preach, and dedicated themselves to the work of Christ, while listening to this sermon.—EDITOR.

The Moral Power of a Good Woman.*

BY DR. LOVICK PIERCE.

"And so will I go in unto the king, which is not according to the law; and if I perish, I perish." (Esther iv. 16.)

THE very sound as well as the sense of the text thrills our common humanity with the feeling of an agonizing sympathy. One feels as if suspended between the gloomy court of death and the bare chance of life, and yet compelled, from a sense of duty, to take the awful risk. Such precisely was the situation of Queen Esther.

Circumstances unbargained for by her had placed her in a relation to affairs fast nearing to desperate maturity. According to the iron rule of the kingdom every Jew found in it, with the women and the children, was to be massacred, and the spoil to be taken by their murderers. All this by royal decree, already sealed with the king's ring, and proclaimed by special post-riders throughout the one hundred and twenty-seven provinces over which Ahasuerus, the king, swayed his scepter of life or death. This was the state of things in relation to the Jews; they were all under a decree of extermination, and of course if this unrelenting decree went into effect Queen Esther herself must have been put to the sword.

As to her blood she was a genuine Jewess. It seems from the record that while the long course of ceremonial preceding a royal marriage was going on, and after Ahasu-

---

*A Commencement Sermon at Andrew Female College, Cuthbert, Ga., preached by Dr. Pierce, June, 1872.

erus had selected Esther to be his queen, and the installation had proceeded to crowning her, and to arraying her in royal apparel, her Jewish blood and relationships had been kept in sacred secrecy from all the officers of the king's household. This charge of secrecy was given Esther by Mordecai, who was, I think, uncle to her; at all events he had adopted her and brought her up as his own daughter. Esther was an orphan, and well did Mordecai care for her; and well did Esther requite the kindness of his love.

In this history we have one of the many instances in which we see it practically demonstrated that God does restrain the wrath of man, and make the remainder of wrath to praise him. This God does, yet leaving man's will free in all the range of its projections. Although there was vile injustice in the deposition of Queen Vashti from her queenly rights, and although there was barbarian libertinism in the course recommended by his courtiers for the selection of another queen, still you must allow me to say that I see in these strange procedures the foot-prints of the same overruling Providence that I see in the history of Joseph—his sale by his inhuman brethren and his going down into Egypt. In all these things we see how impossible it is that God should have inspired the wicked deeds of evil men, and yet we see clearly how he managed and overruled them all. In all such histories we see God remonstrating with men and warning them; yet, when man's wayward heart persists in evil, God leaves him to hellish deeds. And when God would make the "remainder of wrath" to praise him he prevents, by some providential interference, the intended evil.

In the history of Joseph we see how God shielded Joseph by a series of simple mental impressions such as determine the course of business men all the time. Whether the Ishmaelites intended to pass Dothan when they left home for

Egypt is clearly immaterial. God, to whom all our purposes are known, knew just when and how to bring the itinerant traders of the desert into conjunction with the fell design of Joseph's brethren, and, as I understand the divine methods, without any coercion of the will. Besides the simple mental impression to which allusion has been made, there are the emotional sympathies of affectionate sorrow. These God can stir at a time and in a way to arrest or change proceedings and to prevent a great evil by allowing a less. This no doubt God did in the case of Joseph. Early in the history one of Joseph's brethren began to relent, and he pleaded that, instead of assassinating him outright, they should cast him into a pit, and leave him to die alone. This was readily agreed to. Lowering him into the pit, they sat down to their noonday repast apparently dead to their brother's woes. But not so with every one; the brother's heart was still faintly alive in one bosom; and as these Ishmaelites would buy any thing that could be sold again, and as Egypt was a slave-market, it was proposed to the hard-hearted brothers that they should take Joseph from the pit and sell him to the speculators. In this way Joseph's life was saved by God's own way of restraining the wrath of man. Joseph was sold a slave in Egypt, and after many changes in the seeming misfortunes of his life, God elevated him to the highest dignity next to Pharaoh himself. This elevation of Joseph was brought about by a series of experiences and providences most interesting and instructive, but they cannot be set in order now. Of the revelation of Joseph to his brethren in Egypt, of the removal of Jacob down to Goshen, and other events in this history, I cannot now speak particularly. It is enough for all my purposes now that Joseph, after the death of Jacob, when his brethren, in fear of vengeance, referred again to their cruel treatment of him, quieted their fears by telling them that not they but God had sent him into Egypt to preserve them and much people alive.

A just sense of God's place and presence in one of these complex scenes is the welcome Ararat on which the ark of the mind rests in happy contentment after a perilous voyage through these waters seemingly so treacherous and so dimly seen by men in their ordinary thoughts. For some people to see how God does what he does not actually do in his own choice and exertion of power is strangely difficult—difficult, I think, mainly because we do not trace his footsteps in these ways as the footsteps of God. We look for him as if he must be causative wherever he is efficient. This is a grave mistake. God did send Joseph into Egypt as assuredly as if he had projected every scene in the history. For it is in him in every sense that " we live, and move, and have our being." Woe to us if God cannot so overrule what is intended by man to end only in misery so as to turn it unto the greatest good!

I speak reverently when I say I do not see how the good that came of it could have been procured to man except by a levy of this sort upon the wickedness of some men for the good of others. If Joseph had simply emigrated to Egypt, and by meritorious deeds had ingratiated himself into the favor of Pharaoh till he became the second in the kingdom, it would have availed nothing in behalf of revealed religion. It would have been looked upon by men of the world as a lucky hit. But the case was very different; he was sold into Egypt as a slave; he emerged from prison upon interpreting dreams, after having declared to all applicants that the interpretation of dreams belonged to God himself, doing this not for delay, but to open up in the Egyptian mind—and especially in the mind of the Pharaohs—a pathway to a proper appreciation of the God of the Jews. Thus, whether Joseph was working with God and for God as one engaged, or whether God was working like God through Joseph, is immaterial to the issue before us, which is that God, in all these seemingly abnormal occurrences, was working out results in proof of the great truth that there is but one true and living God, and that this God is the God of the Jews. Hence, no one but a Jew was ever used as a divine medium in the communication of the knowledge of God to man, as a God at hand and not a God afar off. Wherefore, Paul says that the greatest benefit conferred upon the Jews, in the covenants made with their fathers, was that unto them were committed the oracles of God. Upon this basis God proceeded all the time; whatever he did decidedly demonstrative of the fact that the God of the Jews was the true God he did by a Jew. He did this by a Jew—whether in Egypt by Joseph, in the court of Ahab by Elijah, in the overthrow of the altars of Baal; in the court of Nebuchadnezzar by Daniel, a captive prophet of God, in restoring to the king his lost dream with the interpretation thereof, or in deciphering for Belshazzar the mysterious handwriting upon the wall, which proved to be the knell of his departing glory. Both Nebuchadnezzar and Belshazzar loaded Daniel with honors, but the chief honor they awarded him was the declaration that Daniel's God was the true and only living God.

I have taken this range of thought because the observations made on parallel instances lead us to a far more favorable stand-point for learning the lessons which belong to Esther's elevation to the queenship and Mordecai's promotion to the premiership in the kingdom of Ahasuerus. It is especially noteworthy in reference to the Jews that God conferred upon them many distinguished honors because he was the God of Abraham. He often reminded his erring people that the blessings he was conferring upon them were not conferred on their account, but for the sake of their great fathers—Abraham, Isaac, and Jacob—or else for "his name's sake." And in all this we cannot but recognize that the covenant mercies of God are a guarantee of good to our children, well worth securing to them, if by their folly they should forfeit the best part of their inheritance. That children should be exalted in their civil and social relations here is desirable. God's dealings with the Jews as his covenant people, and his repeated use of explanatory terms in order to teach them his purposes, leave no room to doubt but that we can secure great good to our children by entering into covenant with God ourselves, and bringing our children within its ample folds upon the faith of its promises.

The fact that God's original promise to Abraham as his covenant was national as well as personal, civil as well as sacred, should never be lost sight of. The Jews in their day were to be quoted by other nations as a wise people in legislation, having laws more righteous and just than others, but especially in having a God near at hand and ready to give them whatsoever they called on him for that was good for them. On this basis it was that the petitions of the Jews marvelously answered were very generally of a national interest, and were answered because they were included in the current promises made to Abraham. Therefore, whenever an emergency arose in matters of State, there was a son of Abraham at hand, as in Joseph's case in Egypt, the Hebrew children and Daniel in Babylon, and Mordecai and Esther in the court of Ahasuerus. God always preferred one of his chosen people for the highest honors to be won and worn; all of which shows that the civilization consequent upon revealed religion is to rule the world at last.

My argument is that Vashti's deposition from her queen's state was not in order that Esther might be raised to it, but that, Vashti being deposed by unrighteous tyranny, Esther was chosen in the goodness of God for the accomplishment of gracious ends. And as I read God's providences he gave the queenship to Esther upon the scheme adopted by the enemies of Vashti for filling the vacant dignity. She was selected by the king himself upon the inspiration of a spontaneous affection. He saw Esther in nature's simple, guileless charms. Whether he would have fallen under the spell of these charms had he then known that she was a Jewess is unknown; the presumption is against it. But in unprejudiced nature to see her, and suffer the enkindling of love's pure flame upon nature's simple sensibility, was irretrievable captivity. No man is actually responsible for his captivity to unmanipulated love. And such was the captivity of Ahasuerus to the charms of Esther. He loved her as soon as he saw her. He closed his sight to see another one out of the scores yet unintroduced. From this stand-point one can see exactly why Solomon, in his estimate of Jewish matrons, should have said of the wife of him who gains his choice: "Many daughters have done virtuously, but thou excellest them all." Every satisfied husband has a peerless wife.

Let us intermit the further view of Queen Esther at this time, and attend to the case of Queen Vashti. Her deposition to appease the king's wrath against her makes it our duty to inquire into her offending. The history is that the king, Ahasuerus, in the third year of his reign, made a feast to the princes and nobility of his vast dominion, including a hundred and twenty-seven provinces. This he did that he might display the riches and glory of his kingdom, and of course of his own glorious majesty. This feast lasted one hundred and eighty days, excelling at least in duration. After this, and immediately upon its closing, he made a special feast of seven days for the princes and nobility at Shushan, the palace. The company upon this occasion was more select, embracing, as I suppose, his immediate cabinet and court. Here his gorgeous decorations were displayed in all their magnificence. The inventory tempts one even now to furnish its roll. At this feast the king's wine was quaffed from vessels of gold, the vessels being diverse one from another. The guests, as I suppose, were at liberty to drink much or little, to get drunk or keep sober. On the seventh day, when the king's heart was merry—which means generally just drunk enough to make a man an enthusiastic fool over any project upon which he might stilt himself so as to make dissent from his projects of self-glorification a personal insult—the king ordered Vashti to put on the crown royal and her royal apparel, and to come into the banquet-hall to be gazed upon by these drunken lords, because she was fair to look upon —a beautiful, well-put-up woman—not now invited in as a companion of man, or as an honored guest at a royal feast, but as a woman, whose symmetrical form as a woman is to be exhibited—at least just now—as any other well-developed animal at a fair. And this show of herself was to be to men inflamed with wine and feeling themselves at liberty to discuss her in their revelry—not as Queen Vashti, but as a well-developed and beautiful woman. This coarse order of the king the noble Vashti refused to obey. Whereupon his wrath kindled into fury so hot that it burned within him, and he appealed at once to his wanton advisers—all of course in sympathy with his offended majesty— as to what should be done. They—as corrupt politicians always do—gave advice they thought would please him; they advised him to issue his decree, sealed with his ring, and sent throughout the provinces of his realm, commanding all wives to obey the orders of their husbands in all things. This was done, as they pretended, to prevent the bad effects of Vashti's example, but really to justify the king's cruel act in the degradation of the queen; for her exclusion from his presence and court was part of the decree.

But we cannot pass away from Vashti, nor let her pass away from us, without paying to her memory a tribute of the highest regard. If we were called upon to reply to Solomon's startling inquiry, "Who can find a virtuous woman?" as soon as the preliminary question was settled as to the meaning of words, and it was agreed that by "virtuous woman" we are to understand a woman of true moral courage—moral courage enough to protect the dignity and sacred purity of her own native womanhood from all wanton public gaze for the gratification of carnal admiration—we would turn to Vashti, and say to Solomon: "Here is one who has won and who wears, with indisputable title to it, this distinguishing and distinguished honor." Vashti had courage enough to maintain the dignity of her pure womanhood even at the cost of her royal crown. To judge of what was proper to her as a woman was a gift with which God, her Creator, had endowed her, and which she nobly defended in this trying hour.

Ladies, let me say to you to-day that women do have rights, such rights as your illustrious sister, Vashti, illustrated so grandly. If any of you as Christian women should have a husband who wants to carry you where you think a Christian woman ought not to be seen, do as Vashti did—stay at home. This is a woman's right. As for those hybrid women toward the north star, who are fussing for "woman's rights," I fear they are as dull upon the rights of womanhood as they are fierce in their claim for woman's rights. It is my opinion that if a case should occur to the leaders of that faction similar to Vashti's, they will dress and go in.

Permit me to use this renowned instance of the glory of womanhood as a commendable example to your precious sex. The venturesomeness of some women into scenes and associations where the flinching nerve of native modesty recoils to go is one of the most alarming signs of the time. It operates like an unperceived rust upon the polish of a metal capable of damage by its defacing power. The enslavement of the sex to fashionable idolatry is fearfully servile.

· · · · · · · · · · ·

Vashti scorned a crown at the cost of her womanly dignity. Ahasuerus might by despotic power take from her his part of the crown royal, yet he could not take from her, as a woman, her nobler crown of purity. This was in her—part of her very self. The richest jewel that composed it was the diamond of her womanly modesty. This precious jewel God has committed into the voluntary keeping of every woman for herself; for its safe-keeping Vashti was deposed. And while the throne of Ahasuerus has crumbled into dust, and his name survives dishonored, Vashti's star still brightens, and she stands to-day a true queen of her sex. Her record is clean and good. Noble Vashti! long may Georgia's comely daughters do honor to thy memory by their disdain of exhibition for the gratification of wanton eyes!

After the king's wrath had cooled down, and the ghosts of his wine-cups had flitted away, he remembered Vashti. In what particular way he remembered her the record does not say; but from what ensued I suppose it was that under his drunken delirium he had made himself queenless, and that he now began to realize the loss of her who was the true glory of his court. But his decrees, under the law of his realm, were irreversible. As Vashti was lost to him, filling the vacancy was a desideratum of pressing magnitude. His servants, or chamberlains (and demagogues are always fruitful in expedients), advised that by special order a great company of fair virgins out of every province of his vast empire should be brought to the house of the women at the palace in Shushan, under the care of Hege, who seems to have been a sort of apothecary-commissary to furnish these women with whatever was necessary to their pretentious ceremonials of purification. All this was readily agreed to by the king; it was, as I suppose, only a more refined method of management common at this court in supplying the harem. To me it seems remarkable that in those days, when monarchs were more monarchical than in modern times, there seems to have been no care for royal blood in the marriage of kings—if marriage it was on the woman's side. Marriage in ancient monarchs was capricious; a king's wife was only his preferred woman. Hence, as in this case, the queen was not engaged, as in the sweet vows of love's courtship, but selected and taken as a gentleman nowadays would select at a fair a blooded horse.

Ladies, at the review of these things, even at this late day, my blood grows hot, old as I am, to think that there ever was a man of human rank, even in the days of Ahasuerus, who would dare to take a woman as a helpmeet for him into the semblance of a wife until he had entered into the sacred chamber of her loving heart through the portal of her elective love. If I could believe that I was preaching to a daughter of Georgia who would not infinitely prefer to be the wife of some noble swain, running a nice little farm and domiciled in a pleasant rural cottage, elected by her love alone, than to be the wife of Prince Alexis,* if she were to be taken as a maiden fair to look upon (which was the only reason Ahasuerus gave for wishing to exhibit Vashti to the gaze of his drunken lords, and the very reason why Vashti glorified her womanhood in sternly refusing to lend it to such an unhallowed use)—I say if I could believe there was a woman in Georgia who would not pre-

---

* Prince Alexis had just visited the United States.—EDITOR.

fer the rule of love in electing a husband to a rule of self-seeking vanity in gaining a prince, I would close my sermon, put on my sackcloth, and in bitter wailings in our streets would cry, "Woe, woe, to Georgia's female fame, for there has appeared a canker of leprosy on its face!" Georgia cannot afford to breed women of this animal style; the Southern climate, as our past history shows, is only suited to the production of true women who, while they must be seen in life, never seek to show themselves in plumes to wanton eyes.

Among the captives carried away from Jerusalem in the time of Jeconiah, King of Judah, was Mordecai, a notable Jew of the tribe of Benjamin. "He had brought up Hadassah—that is, Esther, his uncle's daughter; for she had neither father nor mother, and the maid was fair and beautiful; whom Mordecai, when her father and mother were dead, took for his own daughter." Under the wide door opened by the king's decree Mordecai, who knew the excellences of Esther for the vacant queenship, managed to bring her in for the chances of the succession. Her charms as a fair maiden must have been most resistless, for it seems as if the old chamberlain Hegai, keeper of the house of the women, was so enthused at the sight of her charms that he prepared for her the most choice apartments in the house and gave her the most distinguished attention, all of which no doubt even then dimly presaged her future glory.

When it came to Esther's turn to be introduced to the king, she required less in the way of pageantry than any of her predecessors. Esther was one (I hope many of Georgia's fine specimen daughters are like her) who felt that if Ahasuerus was to be won by trinkets, Ahasuerus was not worth winning. She determined to win his love on her own account or not at all. And well did she bear herself; she was no sooner seen than the conquest was made. Ahasuerus loved her on sight—loved her so naturally and so decidedly that he wanted no more of the unseen company of maidens presented. In the charms of Esther he found his utmost ideal of female beauty and loveliness realized. At once, as I understand the history, he put on her head the royal crown, and proclaimed her queen.

What a change! First an orphan of the captive Jew, next a ward in the house of Mordecai, next queen in the most magnificent court in the East. In the providence of God such a change must mean more than the accident of mere love. I venture the opinion that whatever Esther lacked in education she did not lack religious education according to the faith of the Jews. This opinion is fully justified by the course adopted by Esther to preface her bold adventure into the presence of the king in behalf of her people; for no one can doubt that prayer was added to the three days' fasting in her behalf when she as queen was to test her favor at court by the largest request a queen ever made to her loving lord. The Jews, as a people, only expected relief in answer to prayer, accompanied by fasting. It is clear to me that there was in the mind of Mordecai, in advance of open hostility, an impression that a crisis would arise in reference to the Jews out of which their deliverance would in some way come according to God's delight in them as his peculiar people. Of course if his cousin Esther should become queen at the court where these issues had to be determined, it would improve the chances of successful intercession. Subsequent events showed the wise foresight of Mordecai, and the power of Esther at the court showed that decrees gloried in as irreversible could be dissolved by the moral power of woman, when wisely exercised, as snow is dissolved by the simple presence of natural warmth.

What Queen Esther did from her more exalted position

every woman can do from her humbler position, if she will but bring into her moral enterprises the same sort of moral power. Before such a power the icebergs of man's selfishness will melt away, and by it she can overcome the obstinate unbelief of a husband whose heart could not be won to religion by other means. If I understand the meaning of the Spirit as it inspired the mind of St. Peter in his epistle to the churches, where he speaks of the adornments of Christian women, we are taught that women whose outward adorning is made up of mere show and glitter, whose costly array supports the proofs of their subjection to the lusts of the world and the pride of life, have no moral power either at home or anywhere else. And this is, I believe, as absolutely true as that a corrupt tree cannot bring forth good fruit, and for precisely the same reason.

Dear Wesleyan Methodism, how art thou mangled and mutilated in the hands of thy silly daughters who have undertaken to represent thee after the women of a fashionable, wicked world! I speak as unto wise women; judge ye what I say.

Esther was chosen queen in the seventh year of Ahasuerus. Soon afterward he made a great feast in honor of his bride that was called Esther's feast. During these days of bridal festivity the king did a great many clever things in the way of granting releases; whether of prisoners, debtors, or felons, we are not able to say—likely of all. It may not be out of place here to say that while we think Ahasuerus, in the elevation of Haman to the premiership, manifested a poor knowledge of men, we must award to him the merit of being a fine judge of women; for we do not think that any king was ever more fortunate in two queens than was Ahasuerus. As to what he made the great crime of Vashti we make it her crowning glory as a woman, and say that instead of losing a crown for her integrity it ought to have secured it to her forever. As to Esther, her immortality as a queen is secured against all loss by her record as the savior of her people.

The promotion of Haman to the highest office in the kingdom was a sad mistake. He was a haughty, bad-hearted man—a vile court intriguer. But the king had raised him up next to himself; had clothed him as the highest of the princes. Clad in the ensigns of royalty, and authorized to receive, and of course to exact, the homage of the people, he strutted forth with imperious majesty. But Mordecai, the Jew, refused to bow to Haman—for what particular reason, we are not informed. You will naturally conclude that it was from personal dislike. But I suppose it arose from his Jewish religion; he would not submit to man-worship, even at the risk of conflict with the government. At all risks Mordecai, sitting at the king's gate, persistently refused to pay honor to Haman. His friends remonstrated with him; Haman was told of it, and Haman communicated it to the king. But all to no effect as it regarded the indomitable spirit of Mordecai; to Haman he would pay no servile honors. With this began Haman's scheme of vengeance, including in its wide and deep malice the extermination of the Jewish race in the kingdom of Ahasuerus. He pleaded to the king that they were a set of nondescripts, having laws diverse from the king's people, and that they endangered the interests of the kingdom. It was a specious and artful plea, and had its effect. Haman, like a vile courtier, sought to complicate the religious laws of the Jews with the civil laws of the kingdom. He succeeded in his intrigue, and the king gave him authority for the killing of all Jews living in the provinces that together made up the kingdom. The day was fixed—the thirteenth day of the tenth month, which was the month Adar. It was a hasty as well as a murderous decree. Surely the king did not know that Esther was by her blood doomed to be one of its dishonored victims—of which, I suspect, he became bitterly apprised in after thoughts. The decree was sent by post-carriers, as I suppose, to all officers, civil and military, who were to see to its execution, and who, as a stimulus to their zeal, were authorized to take the spoil to themselves—a booty of no small gain.

This proclamation thrilled the hearts of all the Jews with horror and dread. Especially did the noble Mordecai feel the pang of its cruelty. He had before saved the king's life from the fell design of assassination by two of his chamberlains. He had proved himself to be a faithful subject, and now to be wantonly outlawed was more than his soul could quietly endure. And he rent his clothes, put on sackcloth and ashes, and took the streets of Shushan as an inconsolable mourner. In all this Mordecai may have had wise ends in view.

Now commenced the secret communications on the state of affairs between Mordecai, the queen's dearest kinsman, and the queen herself. Mordecai insisted on the queen's influence with the king as the best chance; the queen argued the difficulties in her way as dark and discouraging, pleading the stern law of the court that whoever entered the court uncalled—although the queen herself—was put to instant and certain death, unless upon the uncertain chance that the king might extend the golden scepter as a token of mercy. She pleaded, as deepening her doubt of success, the fact that she had not for thirty days been called to the king's presence. The result of the conference was that the noble queen resolved to brave all danger. She said in effect: "If this is the only alternative, I will do or die. I will go in unto the king uncalled, and take the chance of death as the end of the law or of life as the boon of the king's favor." "If I perish, I perish."

She gave orders through Mordecai to her people that they should observe three days of entire fasting; surely of prayer also. She said that she and her women would do so likewise. All this doubtless to insure the blessing of God upon her desperate mission. On the third day, while the altars where her people prayed would still be wet with the tears of their grief, she would clothe herself in royal apparel and adventure herself into the king's presence.

Immortal, peerless woman! The glory of thy queenship is eclipsed in the splendor of thy moral courage, and the greatness of thy mission itself in the magnanimity of thy self-offering in its behalf.

Upon this noble principle the queen put on her court-dress, for without it she would have been looked upon as a naughty intruder. (And it is a fit emblem of a penitent sinner preparing himself to gain audience and find acceptance at the mercy-seat. His court-dress is a broken spirit; a broken and a contrite heart God always accepts.) At an early hour of the day, as I suppose, Esther appeared before the king in her unmatched loveliness of person and character. He was moved at once to relieve her of the suspense of a venture. He hastened to hold out to her the golden scepter, the top of which she gracefully touched. The king saw, no doubt, that in her heart lay some hidden grief which she had come to pour into his ears, and he made haste to open to her a door as wide as her wants might be. He adjured her to make her requests and petition known, and pledged a response to even the half of his kingdom. The difference between "requests" and "petitions" which we find all through the course of this narrative, I suppose to be this: "requests" related to herself, "petitions" to others. The king disembarrassed her by letting her know that he would grant to her either or both. Here begins the proof that

Esther was a great as well as a good woman. Finding the king in her interest, and not finding it best to open to him the entire budget of her court business at that time, Esther very adroitly and with diplomatic skill waived her ultimate request and petition, substituting them with the request that the king and Haman, his prime-minister, would attend her banquet of wine that day, which the king very gracefully agreed to do, notifying Haman accordingly.

During the banquet the king most graciously renewed his pledge to grant the queen her requests and petitions to the half of his kingdom. He saw most clearly that having him and Haman at her banquet was not the design of her venture into his presence uncalled. But the queen, seeing no doubt that the king was more and more inwrapped in the meshes of her diplomatic net, again waived the full answer to the king's anxious inquiry. She saw that the king longed to gratify her in granting her all she asked. She therefore put him off with another request to attend her banquet of wine the following day—he and Haman only. Again, with kingly courtesy, he consents.

But between feast and feast what troubles they did meet! The king in his palace was as one on a bed of nettles, and Haman at home as one haunted by evil spirits. There was honest, refreshing sleep for neither.

But to-morrow came, and, passing over much that intervened, we meet the king and Haman again at the queen's banquet of wine. Again the king renews his inquiry after the queen's "requests and petitions," and reassures her of his complacent regards. The time having come when, in her opinion, she must take the chances, she, in terms and tones of queenly respect, made known her prayer. Here begins the unfolding of her heart troubles. Her language is exceedingly courteous; it is also well chosen and elegant. Her request and petition were, if she had found favor with the king, the reversal of a decree consigning her and her people to the sword on a certain day then near at hand. She modestly intimated that even a decree of enslavement she might have borne in silence, but the indiscriminate slaughter of her people was more than her nature could bear.

By this time the king's sympathies were all boiling over, as if he were ignorant of the real contents of Haman's decree which he had allowed him to seal with the royal ring. Hence, he inquires who had done this evil deed? The gentle queen answers firmly, "This wicked Haman." At this his wrath boiled over, and leaving the banquet-hall he walked for a time in the king's garden—as I suppose to regain self-control. While the king was gone Haman, feeling the day of retribution had come, implored the queen's intervention in his behalf; and when the king returned he found Haman, in his desperation, fallen upon the queen's bed. This only inflamed his wrath; and so it was that the revelations of the day and the culmination of the king's wrath ended in the hanging of Haman on the very gallows he had disdainfully erected for Mordecai, the hated Jew, who would not do him reverence. How fickle is fortuitous fame!

. . . .

Esther is queen and Mordecai prime-minister at the court of Ahasuerus. Esther's moral courage and moral power had saved her people from destruction.

This brings us to the sense of our chosen theme for this day's special service: the moral power of woman when well directed and when sustained by moral courage. In Queen Vashti's refusal to dishonor her sex by exhibiting her charms to roystering lords we have moral power and courage of high order; and in Queen Esther's lofty and unselfish daring of all dangers for her people we have an example of moral power and courage for the admiration of future times.

. . . .

Queen Esther, by a wise use of her moral power and courage combined, proved much more than the adage that woman is the power behind the throne. This alone could not merit immortal fame. For Jezebel and Herodias—infamous both—each exerted this power on the minds of kings; but it was diabolical power. Queen Esther's was the power before the throne. And if you, young ladies, will use the moral power God has given you over men and the children of men in a wise and well-directed way, you can save a large proportion of our race that will go to perdition if you—in the bland and beautiful period of maiden witchery—instead of using your power as women ought, only cater for them in what they call a "calico carnival;"* for, as things now stand, you have authorized the belief that you will go into any thing considered bearable if it comes in the guise of style and fashion. If any trial of this sort is ever attempted on the young ladies of Andrew Female College, hiss it into disdain. Some college, where sanctified education is a public promise, must unfurl the banner of revolt against imperious, frivolous fashion, or else our effort to enrich the world by a class of women who will think and nobly act for the honor of women is a failure, and we are doomed to sing low upon our boast of sanctified education. Its angel face will nowhere appear where its worth can be tested; great women will still be worshiping at the shrine of small things, furnishing presumptive proof that notwithstanding they have received the culture of education their minds still find delight in tinsel.

To the young ladies of the college it is meet that I should

---

*About this time in Georgia "calico balls" in the name of charity were all the rage.—EDITOR.

address a few parting words. I do it indiscriminately as to classes. As to Andrew Female College, you will be the representatives of its true merits You will be the proof-sheets of the literary and moral type-setting done here. And if you shine as brightly as the fine polish we try to put on you, you will increase the number of our matriculates—seeking the same fine polish—fifty per cent. You make us, as a faculty of instruction and as a board of trustees, dependent on you for success and renown. Beautiful catalogues and "fuss-and-feathers" puffings will only prove something outside of the real glory of a female college. Its alumnæ will seal its fortune of fame or its doom of shame.

. . . .

It is a remarkable fact that in reference to the most intimate and endearing relation of life a consistent Christian character in woman has always been looked upon by sensible men as the jewel trait in her life. This is a singular instance, in man's common sense development, of moral nature. I suppose nothing would show more desperate moral obliquity in a man than to be looking for a very irreligious woman to be the wife of his bosom and the mother of his children. Every great-hearted, truly virtuous woman in the country would loathe him as a human fungus. He would be marked as Cain was by a mark of cursed alienation from all open communion with higher human life.

All this, young ladies, shows with unmistakable certainty the great moral power with which God has endowed you as a sex. Woman was indeed intended to be a helpmeet for man in every sense of help—as well as mental and moral, as physical and social. In civilized life cut off men from a becoming respect by first-class female association and they tend backward and downward, as if by gravitation. All that society wants in order to lessen and finally arrest the tendency to deeper, darker putrefaction in the social walks of high civilization is a body of refined, educated Christian women who will refuse, on the ground of moral propriety in high and holy womanhood, to mix themselves with promiscuous assemblies, where, by universal consent, it is understood that every woman in the assembly voluntarily opens the way for any emotional effect that might become incidental to such assemblies. I say voluntarily; for whoever volunteers to be present where sensual flames, by common consent, are known to be favored, betrays the lack of moral innocence.

I do not, ladies, intend any fulsome flattery of you when I tell you you can put an end to every carnal amusement of the age if you will add moral courage enough to the moral power of womanhood to put all carnal entertainments under the ban of your withering contempt. I tell you where you refuse to give your sanction men will cease to go.

As to "carnal entertainments," all are carnal where the animus is irreligious. No woman ever lends her influence in favor of a fancy-dress ball, masquerade, common dance, skating-rink, opera, circus, or theater without announcing herself a sensualist in so far as public allowance has provided for fashionable sensualism. I beseech you, young ladies of Andrew Female College, spurn from your blessed patronage all affiliation with forbidden sociality. Then, if Heaven so decrees, the spirit of the watchful and loving old Bishop will be about your college lives as an unseen friend and guardian, rejoicing in your godly example.

But methinks I hear some of you say: "Why, if we girls of Andrew Female College were to adopt these wholesome advices, it would only be as a drop in ocean's broad monopoly." This might be true, and yet it would be true also that the spirit of reform would be evoked from its long surrender of moral rule in the halls of festivity and seated again on its own native throne—the courageous moral will of godly women. Then we could always find a Queen Esther ready to brave dangers when great moral interests are at stake.

Ladies in general, I appeal to you all. I know you are flesh and blood, fallen and much disabled in moral strength. I know it is as much our duty to stay the tide of immorality by cutting off its supplies as it is yours. And I can see very clearly that if all men would refuse to sustain these vice-breeding associations they would dry up. And social intercourse would then, like some malarial swamp, cleaned out, cleared up, and made subservient to dry and wholesome culture, be a blessing to all around it. But if my more imbruted sex refuses or fails to do this great, good work, will you, O lovely daughters of Georgia, not help save our homes and the Church from the poison of evil social customs that now reign in the fashionable world? I will, in hope, answer for my listening audience. You will say to us to-day: "Fast and pray for us, and when the time comes that all must be saved or lost that depends on us, although there may be some risks to us, if moral life depends on our taking the risk, we will screw up our courage to the daring point, and into this Thermopylæ we will throw ourselves. And if we perish, we perish." But you will not perish. Esther immediately saw the golden scepter of peace held out to her, which she gracefully touched, and saw at once the star of hope emerge from beneath a dark and angry cloud that up to that auspicious moment had concealed its radiant face.

. . . .

In conclusion, ladies of Andrew Female College, let me assure you, in behalf of your faculty, the board of trustees, and of the South Georgia Conference—under the paternity of which you derive your kinship of high affiliation with us—that, in our opinion, your intended *alma mater* cannot attain to real glory except as her daughters become illustrious patterns and patrons of every Christian virtue. We mean to make you good scholars, if you will. But we are bound to notify you all in advance that you can be no cause of glorying to us unless you win for us, and also for yourselves, the high distinctions of sanctified learning. If your higher culture is not used for a wider range of intellectual inspiration as to the ways and means of doing good—by the wise use of your moral power and by the exercise of moral courage up to the demands of well-developed womanly integrity—then you are doomed to be looked upon by wise men as a failure. And it would have been better for you to have been educated in a cotton-factory than in a Christian female college. A highly educated woman who is openly irreligious is always loathed by good men. It is our high ambition to send out from the classic halls of Andrew Female College not jeweled women, but women jewels. Shall we do it? The affirmative answer, young ladies, is with you. Say yes.

And now I commend you to God, and to the word of his grace, which is able to build you up and give you an inheritance among all them that are sanctified. Amen.

Mary's Love.*

"Then took Mary a pound of ointment of spikenard, very costly, and anointed the feet of Jesus, and wiped his feet with her hair; and the house was filled with the odor of the ointment." (John xii. 3.)

THE Bible is a wonderful book; wonderful in its revelations of God and of man. Much of its excellency lies in this, that as a book of instruction it is not a theory, a speculation, a philosophy. It does not deal in general representations, but descends to particulars—not in abstract notions, but in practical effects. The Scriptures illustrate, embody, exemplify. They present principles associated with character and conduct. The lessons we are to learn come to us not as the dry deductive inculcations of a teacher, but incarnated, alive, and in motion. The canvas on which the pictures are spread breathes, the forms are animate, and the expression is the life and language of humanity. What is the Old Testament but a narrative of great and interesting events—a book of maxims, proverbs, and imagery? What is the New Testament? A book of divinity? a system of theology? Nay; but a compilation of facts and reflections—God and Christ and humanity illustrated.

From the day of his advent through all the stages of his earthly ministry, Jesus was hated and reviled by the scribes

---

* Delivered at the Commencement of Wesleyan Female College, June, 1876. Also before the Florida Conference in 1877, and also at the rededication of Grace Church, Newark, New Jersey, in 1878.—EDITOR.

and Pharisees, the chief priests and elders of Israel. Each of these classes of chief men and rulers, under the promptings of their prejudice and passion, as occasion served, maligned his character, denied his claims to the Messiahship, and denounced his miracles as the result of diabolical collusion. Two events now conspired to precipitate a culmination of their rage. First, the resurrection of Lazarus, itself an overwhelming demonstration of Christ's divine power. "Then many of the Jews which came to Mary, and had seen the things which Jesus did, believed on him." The story and the interest it excited were likely to spread. When some of the witnesses of this transaction carried the tidings to the Pharisees, they held a council and said: "What do we? for this man doeth many miracles. If we let him thus alone, all men will believe on him." Second, the Passover—one of the great annual festivals of the Jews—was at hand. It was a national custom to execute great criminals—especially false prophets and raisers of sedition—on these occasions, because the concourse of people at Jerusalem was so great as to make the example admonitory and influential.

This recognized association seems to have suggested this as a fit time to rid themselves and the nation of the despised Nazarene. The Sanhedrim met in council and resolved to take him by subtlety and kill him. The whole thing was to be clandestine, secret; not on the feast-day, lest there might be an uproar among the people. To what stratagem they meant to resort in order to make sure of their victim, and yet avoid a possible popular tumult, we are not told. Their thoughts were private, their plans unwritten. They intended to skulk as spies, to lie in wait and take their chance by day or night.

While yet undecided but eager, fearful of miscarriage yet resolved on some desperate venture, Judas came with his foul proposition to betray Jesus. This changed their plan. They accepted his offer, and struck a speedy bargain with the vile, money-loving traitor. But mark, the crafty policy of the council and the base design of Judas were both overruled by Heaven. It was not the purpose of God that Christ should be taken off by assassination, or even by regular trial in the presence of a few witnesses to his death and the signs which accompanied it. These capital events which constitute the basis of our religion God intended should have a multitude of witnesses, that they should transpire when Jerusalem was thronged by Jews and proselytes from all parts, and that through them the accounts of the crucifixion and the resurrection should be transmitted to the most distant places. A religion destined to be the religion of the world must go forth authenticated by a great cloud of witnesses—Jews and Gentiles, friends and foes.

While the Passover commemorated a wonderful event in the history of the Israelites, it was at the same time a grand institute and type of our redemption. Hence, Christ is called "our Passover, sacrificed for us." It was eminently fit that the legal typical shadow should now cease in the presence of the true Paschal Lamb, who was about to give his life a ransom, not for the descendants of Abraham only, but for the whole world.

Bethany, though now but a small and insignificant village, was, in the days of our Saviour, a considerable place, situated on the ascent of the Mount of Olives, about two miles from Jerusalem. It is canonized in sacred story as the residence of Martha and Mary and Lazarus, and as one of the favorite retreats where Jesus sought rest and retirement from the weariness of his public labors. Of this his last visit we have three distinct accounts by the evangelists Matthew, Mark, and John. Luke reports another and distinct transaction, which has been strangely confounded with the one under consideration.

In this story Simon, the leper, gave a supper, and invited Christ and his disciples to be present. Christ, according to his custom, courteously accepted the proffered civility. The company was a remarkable one. There was Simon, the leper, healed and sound, himself a living witness of the miraculous power of Jesus. The man whom loathsome disease had made an outcast, whom no one dared to touch, had been restored to his home and family, and was now the generous host of a feast that inspiration has made historic. There was Lazarus—once dead, now alive; buried, but raised up; yesterday a disembodied spirit, to-day robed in flesh and blood—a guest with his Deliverer in the house of his neighbor, and both the beneficiaries of his grace. There was Martha in her true character as well as proper person, her individuality distinct, consistent with itself. They made him a supper, and Martha served, and the service was at once the exponent of her constitutional complexion and the expression of her loving devotion. There too was Mary, serious, devout, contemplative; rapt in the fervor of an unearthly love; subdued by the sorrows of a self-depreciating penitence, yet aglow with the ardor of adoration, oblivious of food and appetite and social festivity, intent only to lavish upon her Lord in symbolic action the unutterable tenderness of her spiritual being. Words could not respond to her emotions, and tears became the interpreters of her sensibility. She could not tell the yearnings of her soul in articulate speech, and she invoked the aroma of an ointment, costly and precious, that the sweet perfume might translate her heart. Embalming the Saviour's head in liquid odors, the fragrant memorial of her love, in token of her humility she rained tears upon his feet, and, disdaining the fabrics of an earthly loom, she wiped them with the hair which God had given her for a covering and her glory.

Now behold how this beautiful scene was marred by the unseemly indignation of the selfish and the censorious, who said: "Why was this waste of the ointment made? For it might have been sold for more than three hundred pence, and have been given to the poor. And they murmured against her." How subtle and specious the pleas of "covetousness!" Judas was the mouth-piece of this hateful vice. But other disciples sympathized with him; they had indignation within themselves. They said nothing, but accepted the language of Judas as the utterance of their thought. They looked their approval of his ill-natured censure and prudential suggestion Rebuked by the lavish generosity, the uncalculating service of this godly woman, they cloak their grudging selfishness by an affected, pretentious charity for the poor. They envied their Lord and Master, himself the poorest of the poor, the delicate and timely honor which the gentle Mary, with long self-denial, had garnered from her own scanty stores, and then seek to cover their base resentment by claiming an hypothetical benefaction for the needy. Alas! an honorable sentiment, proudly announced, is not always the promise and pledge of corresponding action.

Here the meek and lowly Jesus kindly interposes: "Let her alone; why trouble ye the woman? Why do you put her to pain? How can you so roughly wound her gentle spirit? She hath wrought a good work on me. You wholly misinterpret her conduct; even she does not fully understand the significance of her action. Taking counsel of her religious heart, her devotional sympathies, while my enemies with crafty malice plot my destruction, she has come to testify her faith and her worship. It is the custom of your country and surrounding nations to embalm the corpse before interment, nor are they wont to be parsimonious in these honors to the dead. She hath done what she could, and has come aforehand to anoint my body to the burying. The poor ye have with you always, and when ye will ye may do them good; but me ye have not always. This is the last opportunity. When my decease is accomplished there will be no time for this ceremonial. Events are about to transpire the most wonderful in the annals of time or the councils of eternity. The malice of men and the rage of Satan in fell combination are scheming for my destruction. The crisis is at hand. Yet a little while and my enemies will be jubilant over my dead body. My disciples, smitten with terror, will fall from around me and stand afar off mute with grief and wonder, helpless and voiceless in their despair. Condemned, outcast, forsaken of God and man, suspended between heaven and earth as if unfit for either, without sympathy or friend, save as dumb nature responds to my agony in her darkened sun, her rending rocks, and the graves of her dead. Yet, when all is over and my resurrection shall rally the hopes of the Church, wherever this gospel shall be preached, this shall be told for a memorial of her."

This passage is suggestive and full of instruction. The first lesson is fundamental to Christian faith, and, where it is intelligently apprehended, constitutes an anchor to the soul, sure and steadfast, holding the mind steady and secure amid change and darkness, upheaval and revolution. "The Lord reigneth, let the earth rejoice," expresses it all. Amid the seemingly casual and distressing events which take place in the world through the avarice, treachery, ambition, or impiety of mankind, it is well to advert to the determinate counsels and foreknowledge of God as bounding, directing, and overruling all for the establishment of his truth and the safety of his people. How freely men can act, and yet how subordinately! There is a divinity that shapes the means and the end, rough hew the materials as we may. There is a real but inexplicable concord between human liberty and the certainty of those events which have been foreshadowed by prophecy, or which lurk unhinted among the secret things of God. Where divine veracity is concerned there is no contingency. The Scriptures cannot be broken. Providence marches with steady steps to the completion of its plans. Good men and bad men ignorantly but unitedly conduce to its methods.

There are many devices in the heart of men and ungodly politicians, and covetous, ambitious Churchmen form their plans with profound sagacity, and conceal them with deep dissimulation, yet often contrary to their intentions and their wishes they are led to arrange or alter them in subserviency to the secret will of Him who holds all hearts and all events in the hollow of his hand. As the great law of gravitation holds the worlds in their places, and rolls these enormous masses round through all the cycles of the ages without the loss of a second of time, and remains unjostled by the concussions of battles, the shock of earthquakes, the heaving of old ocean's restless waters, the rush of the wildest storms, and, as an ultimate law, binds the most eccentric comet as well when coming from the awful immensity of space it rushes with accelerated course toward the sun as when with lingering step it turns again to its far aphelion, so in the purposes of God there can be no surprise, perplexity, or chance. The laws of matter are but his sovereign will and their operations his continual agency, and the whole universe of intellect is subject to his control. All the discordant passions, interests, and designs which dash in eternal collision the designs of men, the ministry of angels, and the enmity of fiends as well; all the activities of superior intelligences are bound, in the contexture and harmony of Providence, to bring about the result he hath ordained, and to this end every occurrence irresistibly tends.

In the history before us the chief priests who presided in all ecclesiastical affairs, the elders who were judges in civil matters, and the scribes who were doctors of the law and directors to both, were all confederate against Christ. By crafty plot they designed to kidnap and spirit him away, and thus slake their thirsty malice in his blood while yet they escaped the tumult of a possible popular indignation. In the grand purpose of Heaven, Christ came into the world to die, but not by midnight assassination. He came to suffer, "the just for the unjust," but not on conviction of crime. He came to die—not as the victim of Jewish or Romish statutes, but as a sacrifice demanded by the law of God. And hence, in spite of the cunning malice and policy of his enemies, the glorious Sufferer stands, even in the records of a criminal court, as the spotless Lamb of God. The Jewish council broke down in the effort to sustain the charge of blasphemy; and the Roman tribunal, to which they turned, even when, for fear of the people, it surrendered him to death, declared, by the mouth of Pilate, it "found no fault in him." The mysterious counsel of the Lord was fulfilled by the free agency of man, and the voluntary, vicarious offering of Christ on the cross is signalized by the singular fact that he was tried for one offense and executed for another totally distinct. Nay, more; he was not executed for the crime for which he was tried, nor tried on the charge for which he was executed. He died by the sword of the Lord, though the hand that wielded it was the hand of man.

The Bible portraits of character are drawn in facts few and simple, but full of significance. These facts are keys which unlock every chamber of the soul, even the secret closets where lie hid perhaps the unconfessed yet plastic, potent influences which make a man what he is. For as "a man thinketh in his heart, so is he."

When the devout and gentle Mary unsealed the alabaster-box and poured the fragrant ointment on the head and feet of her Lord, Judas, unaffected by the delicate, touching act of devotion, unregaled by the odor that filled the house, true to the base instincts of his nature, cried out, "Why was this waste?"

Some men are dead to taste, to sentiment, to all high, noble, and self-forgetting impulses. They have no eye for the beautiful, no ear for the concord of sweet sounds, no heart for the tender outgushings of a noble nature. They live only among figures and dividends and percentage. No book like the ledger, and no page like the column of profits. With them the only question is, Will it pay? Is there money in it? Quick in calculation, they can tell you the profit or the loss. A prize to the worthy, a present to a friend, a memorial of the dead—it is folly, extravagance, waste. A generous offering for the comfort of another, a thoughtful recognition of family affection by a timely token outside of necessary supplies, a delicate memorial of esteemed confidence, in those cases where sympathy is better than gold, and love more precious than rubies—all these are ruled out by that last, lowest affection of the human mind, the love of money. The sweet, subtle discernment of love is a lost attribute, and the dry, dark, dead soul wakes to no music but the ring of the precious metals, and inhales no fragrance like the aroma of a good bargain.

The heartless complaint of Judas was a reflection on Christ as well as Mary, for he submitted without rebuke to this lavish expenditure. The querulous, ill-natured question was very rudely interposed. It was a breach of manners, an infraction of the law of charity, implying, if not imputing, blame on both sides. It intimated that the whole transaction was an outburst of enthusiasm, an overwrought excitement, the waste of an ointment precious in its odor—more precious in its money value. It impeaches the Master for silently accepting the costly adulation of a frenzied woman.

The solution of all this is to be found in the covetous heart of the traitor, who did not grudge the Master the honor of this anointing so much as he desired that the price of the ointment should be put into the bag which he carried as the treasurer of the disciples. The ugliest feature of his detestable sin was the assignment of an honorable reason for his unseemly interruption—a specious pretense for grasping avarice, and a bad, base affection wrapping itself in the cover of an ostentatious philanthropy. O the deceitfulness of sin, the stratagems of hypocrisy, the blinding, infatuating delusions of covetousness!

Our Saviour detects and exposes the sophistry of this self-complacent pleader, and forestalls forever the plausible but deceptious plea which declines a present, positive duty by the verbal, sentimental recognition of another, future and contingent. He teaches that works of mercy are not to be superseded by works of piety, nor works of piety to be declined under color of works of charity.

Judas is not the only man who declines or reprobates a generous act by alleging what ought to be done for the poor, rather than what he has done or proposes to do. Many a man withholds from a present claim both needy and worthy more than is meet by fanciful conjectures of what may be demanded by some possible but very unlikely event in the future. This miserable self-deception may rid them of the importunity of application, but the equivocal pretext debauches the conscience, defiles the heart, and entails upon them the guilt of mocking God by the imposition they have practiced upon themselves and others. The man who saves his money by cheating his own integrity drives a bad bargain where the gain is loss. Judas sought to have his bag replenished that he might pilfer without detection, inspiring his brethren to believe that out of a tender heart he had lavished the treasure upon the poor. He bartered his conscience for a chance to steal, and when balked in his scheme resolved to betray his Master. His hungry, short-sighted avarice, commanding the position and able to dictate the terms, surrendered its advantage, and accepted thirty pieces of silver as the price of his soul and the pay of his treason. Such are the contrarieties, the inconsistencies, the self-deceptions of human nature.

Some lean on alms without prayer, others on prayer without alms. I have known men, liberal to the Church, who left their aged parents in want and suffering. I have known some who, when generous in their gifts, would reimburse themselves in keeping back by fraud the hire of their laborers. I have known many wonderfully pious in their talk wofully deficient in action. "I hear the voice of the words of this people. They have well said all that they have spoken. O that there were such a heart in them, that they would perform and keep all my commandments always, that it might be well with them and their children forever."

The answer of our Lord in vindicating Mary reveals this great principle in religion: that God is entitled to the best we have and the most we can do. In all the statutes regulating the services and sacrifices of his ancient people the Almighty required the first-fruits of the vineyard and the field, the best lamb in the flock; and every offering was to be without blemish and without spot. Nor was this arbitrary, the jealous exaction of absolute power, but the reasonable demand of the universal Creator upon the beneficiaries of his bounteous providence. When in the progress of time and the decay of piety the Jews, still recognizing the law of demand upon their property, sought to commute with conscience by offering the sick and the blind and the lame, thus maintaining the show of piety while they economized their gifts, a prophet was sent to denounce, in awful rebuke, their miserable mockery, their egregious trifling with conscience and duty, with God and devotion. They infracted a great principle, trespassed on the rights of God, in a mean effort to conserve their own. Alas! in the services we render to Christ, and the gifts we lay upon his altar, a subtle casuistry presides over our determinations and regulates our measure. The cool, calculating spirit that controls us indicates that what we do and what we give is not the gushing oblation of a loving heart, but the tardy, reluctant, stinted obedience to the imperious exactions of law. It may be well to have systematic plans of beneficence, to give by rule, and yet a man may be too methodical in his charities, and acquit himself of obligation when he has barely fulfilled a contract.

Put a guard upon your expenses; reckon your givings by your income. I admire and commend the man who gives the tenth, yet more the man who gives a fifth, and most of all the man who, when he has given all, feels that he has not done enough. The man who is always master of himself, and counts his benefactions with slow and steady enumerations, careful not to exceed the stipulated limit, may be a helper at a dead lift in a church-collection, but he is too slow for the emergencies of humanity, and too calculating for the fervor of Christian consecration. Love —generous love—has its ardors and its transports, and, oblivious of self, and swept along by the tide of its emotions and inspirations, breaks over all the dikes and levees of a prudential policy, and leaves the loom of its treasures as the memorial of its passage.

Mary did not uncork the alabaster-vial and distill the precious ointment drop by drop, as if fearful of overdoing, but she broke the vessel, enlarged the outlet, and poured the contents with lavish affection upon the head and feet of Jesus. And now, when stingy economy and worldly thrift cried out in angry remonstrance, "Enthusiasm, extravagance, waste!" Jesus said: "Let her alone; she hath done a good work" —good for me, for she hath embalmed me for my coming burial; good for her—her aching, grateful, groaning heart has found vent in this act of adoration, and her lavish love, unexhausted by this costly outlay, when I am crucified, shall be to her hallowed memory more precious than the ottar of a thousand roses. "She hath done what she could." Not much as men count values, but as a testimony of her gratitude, love, and worship, it shall smell to heaven and blossom in the dust. When the gospel is preached, this that Mary did shall be told for a memorial of her—bound up in the immortality of the imperishable record in which it shall be communicated.

It is the fate of many good works to be misunderstood and undervalued, and Mary shared in this common lot. Once before when Jesus visited the humble home at Bethany, and she sat at Jesus' feet, bathing her sweet spirit in the soft sunshine of the Saviour's love, her heart throbbing and pulsing as his voice rose and fell in divine instruction, her sister Martha broke in upon the heaven of her enjoyment with harsh complaint of alleged neglect. Now, Martha and Mary were both good women; but they differed in constitutional complexion, and the same principles in each wrought not in opposition but in distinct lines, and neither should have sat in adverse judgment upon the other. Martha's work was necessary and proper, but Mary's choice was wiser and, all things considered, most approved; and the one would not have been rebuked but for her complaint of the other. Let not the bold judge the timid, nor the active the quiet and retiring. The unseen violet, nestling in its hidden retreat, scents the passing breeze as certainly, perhaps more sweetly, than the gorgeous rose lifting itself in conspicuous observation. The gentle piety which sheds about the humble homestead the odor of a meek and quiet spirit is as dear to Christ as the public demonstrations of more sanguine and active natures. The dew-drop, trembling in the morning light upon the waving grass, is as much the work of God as the star that beams and burns in the heaven above us.

Under her sister's fretful rebuke Mary remained silent—said not a word. Conscious of her integrity and purity of motive, satisfied that Jesus would rather break to her hungry heart the bread of life than regale himself with the dainties furnished by deft and dexterous hands, she sat at his feet and heard his word. The appeal against her was made to Christ, and to him she referred the matter, content to abide his award. Jesus sustained her choice, and applauded the wisdom of it. "But one thing is needful, and Mary hath chosen that good part which shall not be taken from her." O that my hearers, one and all—especially the young ladies of the college—would imitate her example! Religion is the good part—no blessing like it. It is good, wise, needful. It is good in itself, and wiser than all besides; indispensable to every character and allotment of human life. Choose the service of God for your business, the favor of God for your happiness, and an interest in Christ as necessary to both.

From this example and the one in the text let us learn two great lessons: First, not to condemn the pious zeal of any, lest we have Christ against us; and second, not to be cast down if our pious zeal be censured, because we have Christ for us.

Indulge me in one more comment upon this lovely picture

of simple, elevated piety. I do not think it is generally appreciated in its design, motives, or beautiful expression. Mary's heart was stirred to its profoundest depths by mingled emotions of gratitude, love, and fear. She knew the bitter hostility of the authorities of her people toward her gracious benefactor. She had heard their vindictive threats, and her mind was shadowed and tossed with the vague, ill-defined terror of coming evil. The presentiment of even a darker sorrow than ever yet had visited her home or heart hung heavy upon her spirits. And now, in the fullness of her grateful love, she designed a special honor in attestation of her faith in him as the true Messiah and in humble, expressive acknowledgment of the spiritual benefit she had received. Often before her soul had slaked its thirst at this fountain of living waters, and she longed for another draught, sweet and deep and full. Her dead brother had been brought back from the grave by the word of Jesus, and her broken heart-strings, though reknit, were tender still from the rude touch of recent sorrow, and vibrated keenly under the harsh words and threatened violence of her Saviour's enemies. The happy consciousness that she and her brother and sister had a warm place in the affections of her adorable Lord roused her soul to courage as the shadow of Christ's destiny deepened and darkened around him. She wanted him to know that while the nation despised and rejected him one meek and gentle heart clung to him in confidence and sympathy. She wanted him to feel that though Church and State, Jew and Roman, cast him off as unfit to live there was one sad, bruised but heroic, devoted woman who thought nothing too good nor good enough to bestow upon him. In thoughtful, delicate kindness she planned her testimonial, and with womanly instinct seized upon the fittest opportunity to present it.

When Christ fainted in the agony of the garden, an angel came from the skies to strengthen him. Who shall say what comfort and satisfaction filled his soul, in prospect of pain, ignominy, and desertion, when this angel of earth, in testimony of her faith and love, mingled the perfume of her ointment and the incense of her adoration in heart-felt worship at this feet? Christ's own estimate of its value we learn from the immortality with which he has endowed it. John, in vision, saw an angel flying in the midst of heaven having the everlasting gospel to preach to them that dwell on the earth. To-day I show you the everlasting gospel still going about upon the earth with the alabaster-box of precious ointment in its arms—a memorial of Mary's faith and worship, a type and a lesson to the Church in all the ages present and to come.

The Inadequacy of Secular Learning.*

"We will not hide them from their children, showing to the generation to come the praises of the Lord, and his strength, and his wonderful works that he hath done." (Psalm lxxviii. 4.)

THE majestic exordium to this pathetic and instructive discourse demands for it, alike from the aged and the young, a reverent welcome. "Give ear, O my people, to my law; incline your ears to the words of my mouth." The term "law" is used in the sense of doctrine, instruction. Solemn attention is challenged on the ground of its intrinsic excellence, its divine authority, its infallible truth. The lesson taught is denominated "law" because of its commanding force in itself, and because every great truth received in the light and love of it has the power of law upon the conscience. Founding his instruction on this grand basis, the psalmist proceeds to group around it certain weighty considerations by way of enforcement. "I will open my mouth in a parable; I will utter dark sayings of old."

Among the Orientals the parable has always been a popular vehicle of thought and wisdom. With them the Eastern princes were accustomed to try each other's wit and ingenuity. It was a courtly pastime. In them the learned men embodied their wisdom, and rested their reputation on these dexterous compositions. I suppose parables come under the head of "dark sayings"—not because they are obscure, sub-

---

*Commencement Sermon, at Emory College, Oxford, Ga., July, 1876.—EDITOR.

tle, hard to understand, but because the meaning does not lie upon the surface, is not to be comprehended at a glance, but must be carefully looked into in order to bring its treasures to the light. In the great diamond-fields of the world the precious jewels do not lie scattered upon the ground, but imbedded in the earth they await the skill and implements of the miner, who must dig and delve for their discovery. So here the sublime truths wrapped up in these mystic words must be pondered and pored over with the assiduity of a student's attention and toil; and when by searching we cannot find the bottom we must sit down at the brink and adore the depth. Such examinations will reveal much that we did not know, much which, on account of former feeble and indistinct conceptions, we did not appreciate, and open up a world for exploration that will exhaust and repay the labors of a life-time.

"Which we have heard and know, and our fathers have told us." Three reasons are stated here for giving ear and heed to these words. *We have heard them.* They are not novelties, new revelations, but consecrated transactions, household lessons. We have heard and *know them.* These things are of undoubted certainty; there is no occasion or room for dispute. They are first principles, uncontroverted axioms. It would be an insult to God to deny them—an outrage on humanity to neglect them. They are our life and the salvation of our offspring. We have heard and known them, and *our fathers have told us.* They come to us not only as original principles settled in and by the law of nature, traditional ideas hoary with antiquity, but demanding honor, reverence, and regard on the ground of their ancestral indorsements. "Our fathers have told us." These utterances come to us invested not only with the sanctity of venerable age, but the commanding obligations of parental authority.

The Israelites were frequently instructed to render their children by every means familiarly acquainted with the works and commandments of God; and now, as the psalmist and his contemporaries had derived the benefits of this most useful information from their progenitors, he was determined for himself to induce others to transmit the same great facts and truths to the next generation, and thus successively to the end of time. This natural order was and is the divine plan for the transmission, diffusion, and perpetuity of truth in the world. Infidelity to this high trust had brought the judgment of God upon the nation; and to rescue the people from the sin and curse of rebellion, unbelief, and ungodliness, there must be a restoration of the ancient régime of religious instruction and training.

It is a remarkable fact that on the subject of general education the Bible is absolutely silent. Assuming that the necessities of the race, the desire of knowledge, the promptings of ambition, the demands of citizenship, would regulate this great interest, it has been left open as one of the prudential economies to be adopted, modified, and accommodated to the changing phases of a progressive civilization. "The school question," as we call it, is now one of the great topics of popular discussion. Connecting itself, as it does, with the fortunes of the family, with our social relations and influences, with politics and government, it has long been one of the problems of statesmanship. The essential grade of scholarship, how to provide for it, how to reach the masses with it, whether it should be left to parental responsibility or assumed as one of the proper, if not necessary, functions of the State, are all mooted questions, debatable and unsettled.

The drift of public opinion, in my judgment, is in the wrong direction. I will not say that the value of education, considered as a personal endowment, is exaggerated, nor that intelligence is not a necessary qualification of worthy citizenship, nor that the right of suffrage is not a perilous franchise in the hands of the ignorant and the stupid, but I do say that the system of education that eliminates the religious element is a Trojan horse, full of evil agencies, armed for treason, stratagem, and spoils; and further, that taxation by legislative power, without the consent of the people, for compulsory education is an outrage on the rights of the citizen and an invasion of the domestic sanctuary utterly indefensible. As well establish sumptuary laws regulating the food, apparel, and furniture of the household, as to determine by an arbitrary, indiscriminate law the teacher, scholarship, and associations of a parent's child. His rights are sacred and inviolable. No judicatory, voluntary, self-constituted, or governmental, under cover of a speculative theory reputed wise and philanthropic, may assume to control in this one of life's most precious interests. This would be one of the "oppressions which make a wise man mad."

The education of the child, I grant and maintain, is a parental duty. It is the entail of fatherhood. It is the right of the child. It is an obligation of the social compact; a contribution due to the community of interest. It is demanded by the possible future relations and duties of the child, personal, social, and political. There is no precept written by the finger of God on the tables of stone, but by his ordination it is an instinct of humanity—a common, social law—which all men feel more or less, and to which, with rare exceptions, they respond as circumstances allow. After all the lamentations of some sentimental enthusiasts on this subject, after all the formidable statistics they parade to rouse our fears and recommend their plans, I venture the remark that the world—that this country at least—is not likely to be damaged much by any thing like general neglect at this point. The State and the Church are both at work; local communities have their projects; private enterprise is busy; the public mind is aroused, and nothing hinders but causes against which no legislative system can provide. The vital force of this great cause is not spent nor tending to exhaustion. It is cumulative, gathering momentum by every revolution, achieving its own triumphs, multiplying its victories, and pushing on to universal empire. But education without religion, when the conquest is gained, will wield a barren scepter, and the reign of universal knowledge will be the reign of universal corruption. The culmination of the arts and philosophy, of poetry, painting, and sculpture, in the history of Greece and Rome, was the date of their decline and fall. Their boasted civilization was the carnival of crime and the sepulcher of their national greatness.

The point I wish to make is that, while our great Father in heaven has given no precept, furnished no rule, his very silence, rightly interpreted in the light of what he did say, rebukes the conceited philosophy of those who propose to develop intellect, reform manners, elevate society, conserve the Government, by mere secular education. The divine idea seems to be that timely religious instruction is indispensable to the formation of right character, that prevention is easier than restoration, and that the antagonisms of error are to be neutralized by the preöccupancy of the mind with divine truth. Let me add that one of the agencies on which God proposes to levy for the more certain bringing about of the desired result has been overlooked, and that this neglect has been not only the loss of power on the right side, but the array of active, hostile elements of influence on the other. While the duty devolves first of all upon parents for obvious reasons, the obligation to coöperate reaches every conscience, levies upon every tongue, appropriates every appliance, interdicts all adverse interference, all lapse, all intermission. There must be line upon line—not divergent, not parallel, but in the same groove and in the same direction—precept on precept, uniform, harmonious, identical in authority and motive. "Here a little and there a little"—not a work to be lumped and dispatched by a single service; not one great exhaustive effort and then a long interval of silence and inaction, but a prudent, intelligent repetition; now a set, formal task—anon a pleasant interjection among the events of household history. And this law of the homestead is the law of the Church, the law of the school, the law of society, the law of all the generations of man. There is to be no parenthesis, no antagonisms, no neutrality.

Alas for the modern American heresy that religion is to be taught at home, and that the school has nothing to do with it! No, sirs; religion is to be taught everywhere, by everybody. The school-house must echo the lessons of the fireside, the teacher duplicate the father, and every day repeat the instructions of the Sabbath. Religion is not an incident, a circumstance, a fraction, but a continuity, a life, an entirety. It claims the freedom of earth and air. It is not recluse, robed in unique vestments, rarely seen by the public eye, shut up in cells, lingering about altars to mutter the gibberish of superstition, but a free denizen of the field, the garden and the forest, the city and the country—everywhere at home. Religion came, sent on a mission of love and mercy, and God gave her the freedom of the world. She claims every man and woman and child for her service. Every house is her home, every heart her temple. I mean hers by right; and every effort to limit her range, or abridge her rights, or stint her claims, is a usurpation, a calamity to the people, a wrong to our race.

The political theory which seeks to separate the scholastic training of the rising race from the Bible and prayer and the name of Christ, and to subordinate the rights of God, the laws of personal piety, and the responsibilities of parents to the prejudices of Jews and Catholics and infidels—you may call it republicanism or democracy, but, in the name of God, I pronounce it a damnable heresy, fraught with disaster, a shame to our civilization, and a curse to our liberties. I verily believe that any school system managed by the State is a grievous blunder, false in policy, demoralizing in its sentiment, and mischievous—not to say fatal—in its results. The complications which surround this subject with so many embarrassments are not inherent in the subject itself, but grow out of the nature and principles of our Government and the impartial relation of the Government to the whole people. The argument based on economy is powerless when we remember that that is a very expensive economy which saves at the sacrifice of a great moral duty. The policy cannot be right which necessitates for its maintenance the doing of a wrong thing. When Uzzah put forth his sacrilegious hand to steady the ark, imperiled by the stumbling oxen, God smote him in anger, and he died. What shall we say of the presumption of the nation that, under pretense of relegating religion to better hands, heaves the ark overboard, and, for the sake of progress, drives the empty cart along? The State cannot do my work as a parent, and ought not to try upon a plan which subordinates as secondary and out of place that which I have taught as primary and paramount and of universal obligation.

Now, let us see how, by a simple adherence to God's word, we avoid all difficulties and conserve all interests. We who insist upon the inseparable union of religion and education are apt to be understood as desiring to propagate sectarian ideas, denominational tenets, ecclesiastical dogmas, and the metaphysics of theology. Nay, verily; but simply to fulfill a duty grafted by the Almighty upon the parental relation, the obligations of citizenship, and the ties and interests of a kindred race. The text is clear on these four points: First, the things to be taught; second, the time and mode of communication; third, the persons and parties who are to teach; fourth, the gracious results which will follow.

Of course I cannot particularize. I state general propositions. The first great fact is the grand Bible announcement that in the beginning God created the heaven and the earth, with all which they contain; that when nothing existed besides himself, worlds, angels, men, animals, came into being at his command. This fact is the basis of all science and all theology. It is a primal truth, the starting-point of all rational investigation, the key to all the arcana of nature, furnishing to a finite mind a reasonable account of what it fails to explain by referring to the inscrutable possibilities of an infinite power. Modern science travails in agony to get rid of God; and while not quite bold enough to deny him altogether, yet teaches doctrines which make him expletive and unnecessary, saying that matter is creative, that life is the result of certain physical conditions, and that she is the universal mother from whose womb all things proceed. To forestall the rival claims of idols, false gods, and all the cunning craftiness of infidel philosophy, the Bible reveals the Almighty as Creator, Upholder, Preserver; appeals to this fact as the ground of human confidence and the inspiration of human faith.

. . . .

O ye fathers and mothers of the land, ye are mortal, passing away! Teach your children while you may that they have a Father in heaven who made them and loves them, so that when you lie down in the grave you may be saved from the crushing sorrow of an absolute and universal orphanage. O ye presidents and professors and teachers, save, O save the rising race from the loneliness of an unfathered world, from the gloomy horrors of an atheistic life, and the rottenness of a grave where the pulse of life beats no more!

Connected with the great primary doctrine of God the Creator, teach your children that he governs what he has made; that all events, the vast and the minute, are under his control; and that the laws of nature are but the fixed modes of his operation. So teach them that God's providence shall be as real to their faith as the external creation is real to their senses.

. . . .

But in teaching our children the "law" and wisdom of God great stress must be laid on the work of redemption. This is the work of works, the wisdom of God, and the power of God. Tell your children the story of the "Word made flesh." Tell it all; go back to the beginning; expound the dispensations which are part of the record of God manifest in the flesh; show how God prepared the Church and the world for the coming of his Son; begin with the first enigmatic promise—the dim, misty twilight of the coming day; the first intimation of deliverance, a faint streak of light amid the gloom of fallen, blighted Eden. Long time the light struggled with the darkness; ray was added to ray as time rolled on, till by and by it broke forth a burning star, beaming upon the vision of dying Jacob. The once nebulous mist assumes shape and puts on its radiant garment, and from the horizon whence its earliest beams shone aslant begins to climb the sky; and patriarchs read in brighter line the hope of Israel, and successive prophets along the march of time strike their harps with bolder hand, till at last earth's expectant ear is startled by the voice of one crying from the wilderness, "Behold the Lamb of God, which taketh away the sin of the world!" Tell the story of his life—his wondrous works, his more wondrous words, the death he died for the sins of the world. Tell of his resurrection, his ascension, his mediation. Tell them the whole story of Jesus till they know him as their Redeemer and their all.

. . . .

And now, to the youth of this assembly let me say it is your duty to receive with eagerness and delight the religious instruction which is offered you. As the earth drinketh in the rain which cometh oft upon it, so let your minds absorb religious ideas and principles, and then, as in nature's chemistry the moisture drawn by the solar ray comes up to nourish the roots and mature the plant, these sacred deposits of truth will feed your virtues, array your character in the bloom and beauty of holiness, and ripen your soul for the garner of the skies. This institution was designed to be the exponent of the Church's convictions and the instrument of her usefulness to the youth of the land. Emory, like Joseph, has been a bough by the well whose branches run over the wall, and the benediction of Heaven has rested upon it, soft and pleasant as the morning dews that fell on "Zion's hill." Your trustees, your faculty, your preacher to-day, will all pass off the stage; age comes on apace; disease and death are reaping the field of life. You must take our places; there comes a new generation whom it will be your duty to instruct. Qualify yourselves now for your task; get ready for your work. Remember your Creator now; become religious at once. Learn to love, admire, and to adore God. Set your hope in God; no other anchorage will hold when the floods beat vehemently and the waves rush and war around you. Be steadfast—walking with God. Ballast your character with truth, and you may ride the waves of time and chance and revolution fearless of wreck and sure of the haven. Resolve to be good, and as a help and security labor to do good. The leading characteristic of a Christian is not enjoyment, but beneficence.

. . . .

My soul stands erect, rejoicing in the light of a great hope, as I look down the future and contemplate the glory of the Church. I believe we are on the eve of grand events. Light is breaking upon the pagan world; the crescent pales before the light of coming day; Mohammedan power feels the paralysis of coming dissolution. The papal throne is rocking upon its base; the shadows of that stupendous imposture which wrapped the nations in darkness for a thousand years are rolling and breaking as in the light of free thought and national freedom the people are getting ready to shout that Babylon is fallen!

[The preacher closed with a clear and eloquent statement of the great enterprises of the Church, her home and foreign missions, the great societies that are scattering Bibles over the world, the Sunday-school and its manifold activities, and drew a rapturous picture of the ever-increasing glory of Israel. The manuscript stops abruptly as shown above.—EDITOR.]

Friendship with the World Enmity with God.*

"Ye adulterers and adulteresses, know ye not that the friendship of the world is enmity with God? Whosoever therefore will be a friend of the world is the enemy of God." (James iv. 4.)

THE Epistle of James is general, addressed to the twelve tribes scattered throughout the world. Among them was great diversity of moral character and condition. There were stout, inveterate unbelievers, full of prejudice, and active in their hostility to the gospel of Christ. Some were true Christians, poor and persecuted, needing the consolations which the apostle administers. Others were mere nominal believers, united with the Church but corrupting it by their hypocrisy and worldliness. These are specially characterized and condemned in the language of the text.

The Church has never been entirely pure. The gospel-net, when thrown, gathers in the good and the bad. The time of separation is not yet. The work of judgment is divine. It belongs to God to discern between the righteous and the wicked. The ministry sow the seed—good seed, the seed of the kingdom. In unguarded hours and in covert ways an enemy—the great adversary—scatters tares. "Let both grow together till the harvest," is the Master's command. Meanwhile, although despairing of universal success, the ministry must so address the judgment and conscience of all and of each as to increase the number of the

---

*Preached in the Methodist church in Sparta, Ga., Aug. 10, 1879. The sermon raised a great stir among Church-people who crave the world's liberty.—EDITOR.

pure and the faithful. The state of the Church as a collective body is a subject full of interest, and of vast importance as to its saving power among men and as to final issues; but the question of our individual salvation is yet more vital and absorbing.

The Bible makes a broad distinction between the Church and the world, the flesh and the spirit. These "are contrary the one to the other." They cannot be reconciled. The antagonism is radical and immutable. Yet the vain, wicked, and corrupting experiment of harmonizing the two goes on, perhaps in no age of the Church more boldly and with less disguise than now. Men and women, for the sake of interest and pleasure, and in the spirit of a cowardly conformity, are adopting the maxims and methods of the world, and so obliterating the lines of demarkation as to confirm the world in its follies and to demoralize the Church in its opinions and practices.

"The world" is a term of frequent occurrence in the New Testament, and always of significant import. We are not to understand by it the outward frame of things, the visible heavens and earth, but the inhabitants—what we call society, with its imperious fashions, its giddy dissipations, its manifold follies. The apostle John, while he warns us and sets up an infallible test of judgment, at the same time defines the word in the following language: "Love not the world, neither the things that are in the world. If any man love the world, the love of the Father is not in him." These affections are unlike. They are opposed. They cannot dwell together. The expulsive power of either excludes the other. If the love of the world dominates, the love of the Father is cast out; for all that is in the world—the lust of the flesh, the lust of the eye, and the pride of life—is not of the Father but of the world. In the same line of thought our Saviour used the term: "If the world hate you, ye know that it hated me before it hated you. If ye were of the world, the world would love his own; but because ye are not of the world, but I have chosen you out of the world, therefore the world hateth you." At another time he said to the Jews: "Ye are from beneath, I am from above; ye are of this world, I am not of this world"—not in sympathy with its tastes or principles, its aims or ends. Now, these are strong declarations. Their meaning cannot be mistaken. They discriminate sharply between the religion of Christ and the world, with its things and its ways.

The text implies that the world—the vain, vicious world—is to be found within the pale of the Church. Some have made a treacherous, profane, and unholy alliance with it, and the epithets employed to characterize them sound harsh and revolting, but milder ones would utterly fail to express the enormity of the sin condemned. In the language of the Scripture, idolatry is adultery. The friendship of the world is in the same category. The relation of the Church to God is often referred to under the idea of a marriage-covenant. He is the husband, she the bride. So Paul, writing to the Corinthians, said: "For I am jealous over you with godly jealousy; for I have espoused you to one husband, that I may present you as a chaste virgin to Christ." If we can comprehend and appreciate this image as the true exponent of the delicate relations betwixt God and the Church, no professor of religion can fail to see in how many ways purity may be compromised, and with what diligent circumspection he must avoid the very appearance of evil.

It is a melancholy fact that there are many in the Church utterly oblivious of these great facts and principles. There are some vain, giddy people, not vicious perhaps, but carnal; not immoral, nevertheless irreligious. They have no fixed habits, or purposes, or principles. They float with the current, are carried about with every wind that blows—light, frivolous, unstable. They are "of the earth, earthy."

There is another class. They have low conceptions of duty, large ideas of personal rights and liberties. They see no harm in many things against which the Church, in every age, has borne the strongest kind of testimony. Their "senses" have not been "exercised to discern good or evil." They walk in darkness and indifference. The truth is, they have never been converted, and as natural men and women they do not discern the things of the Spirit.

Then, too, there are formalists, with vague notions about the Church and ordinances. These talk glibly of baptism and communion—pious enough for "forty" days to lay up a surplus and purchase indulgence the rest of the year. These are they who tithe mint and anise and cummin, and neglect the weightier matters of the law—judgment, mercy, and faith. They lavish their sensibilities on the outward—the non-essentials—until they have no heart left for self-denial or painstaking duty.

Besides all these are those who cherish a liberal theology. They hold very accommodating doctrines, and their morals are molded not by the pattern shown us in the gospel, but by the conventional notions of the social life to which they belong. With them the sentiments of "our set" are of far higher authority than the deliverances of Sinai or Calvary.

All such people as have been described in these statements indicate their moral status in various ways, and at all times, by taking their stand against scriptural and Christlike fidelity to conscience and in favor of worldly conformity. If duty exposes to reproach, if difficulty makes obedience a task, a tax upon the will and Christian independence and faithfulness are to be maintained at a loss, why then they say in their hearts: "Adherence to right would be an unreasonable exaction. God is not such a tyrant as to demand it. The Church that insists upon it is puritanical, superstitious, ultra, overrighteous." They do not believe in straight-jackets, arbitrary rules, or that unrelaxing rigor which drives a man along a given line in the face of a burning furnace or a den of lions. Their theory of religion is flexible, consults flesh and blood, and allows fleshly wisdom to legislate for them—legalizing every compliance with worldly ways that would shun a cross or gratify the desires of a carnal nature. What is fashionable is a more controlling question than what is right. The friendship of the world is not to be jeoparded by intruding the claims of a Christian profession. Martyrdom for truth and righteousness did very well in the Dark Ages—the "old fogy times" —but would be a folly in our advanced civilization. At any rate, these people who are courting the world do not intend to forestall the marriage by magnifying the trifles of religion into consequence enough to disgust the liberal, the respectable, and the refined.

Of course these people who live in the sunshine of the world's friendship never take rank among the witnesses of Jesus. If truth be derided, spiritual religion laughed at, they join with the mockers. If error becomes presumptuous and defiant, assailing all that is pure and of good report, they lift no voice in rebuke. Whatever their private faith and convictions may be, the circle of their chosen friends is not to be disturbed by thrusting the verities of Christianity upon their unwilling ears. They do not confess Christ before men. They would rather give up their place in the Church of God than to lose caste among the devotees of fashion by self-denial—by coming out from the usages of the world, and standing squarely up to the teachings of Christ. In the conflict of conscience with inclination, pleasure, honor, and profit carry the day. These are not dead to sin, not crucified to the world. The flesh, with its affections and lusts, dominates taste, choice, and action. A mess of pottage will bribe their conscience. The excitements, sensations, and dissipations of society interest and absorb them. They know more about amateur theatricals than about missions, enjoy festal concerts and suppers more than revivals. They will pay more for an excursion than to build a church; wonderfully active in getting up tableaux, rehearsing for a musical entertainment—"working for the Church," they call it—but they never attend a Church Conference or a prayer-meeting; never speak in love-feast or exhort a sinner to flee from the wrath to come. Poor souls! they work upon the ark, but never enter in. They are counted with the Church, but live in the world and for the world.

There is hardly a sin so gross or an evil so corrupting but that the world has something to say in its defense. Plausible pleas are made for suicide, duelling, gambling, horse-racing, prostitution, houses of ill-fame, the liquor traffic. If it were possible, they would deceive the very elect. The milder expressions of human depravity are not only defended but advocated—highly commended—and to censure them is well-nigh a personal insult. Such is the sophistry of passion, the deceitfulness of sin, that through obsequiousness to sentiments and maxims of the world, the Church is relaxing her discipline, and the card-table, the theater, and the dancing-saloon find friends and advocates among the professed disciples of Jesus Christ; and he who bought the Church with his blood is shamed and wounded in the house of those who call themselves his friends.

The unfaithful wife is universally condemned. For her there is neither pity nor pardon. But the gay, fast, fashionable woman, who, forgetful of the proprieties of wedlock, flirts promiscuously with men, and parades her sensuous charms for public admiration, while she may be the subject of sharp criticism, is nevertheless tolerated, and holds her place in "society." So in the Church. Scandalous sin will exclude from membership, yet the doubtful compliances with the follies and demands of the world, now so frequent, are allowed—an ominous impurity. In Christian morals it must be remembered that to infringe upon principle to do a doubtful act is not merely an impropriety, but a sin. "He that doubteth is damned if he eat." "Whatsoever is not of faith is sin." He that sacrifices an honest doubt comes into condemnation for more reasons than one. He consents under a slight temptation to offend God to please himself, showing that under more powerful temptation he would yield to unquestioned transgression. His eye is not single. He does not aim to please God. The Divine will is no bar to self-gratification. His duty to God, his relations to others, the influence of example, are all subordinate to passion, to temptation, the impulse, the whim of the hour. Like the wanton wife, who trifles with her sacred obligations, these worldly people make light of their vows and covenants with the Church, and recklessly wound their Saviour in the house of his friends. These friends of the world are corrupting the Church, mortifying their pastors, and giving occasion to the enemies of Christ to blaspheme. The process of amalgamation goes on almost without let or hinderance.

This discourse is intended as a caveat. Having stated the principles of the text and the characteristic features of those who are condemned by it, I propose to make an application of all to a single popular amusement—*dancing*. I select dancing as the more common, popular, the least defensible, and in some respects the most demoralizing. In the cities other expressions of the worldly spirit occur and abound. They are in the same condemnation. Dancing is common to town and country. The evil is ubiquitous, pervading all places and all grades of society. It identifies itself with evil by its effect on mind, character, and society. Whatever its form, from the simplest to the most complex, round or square, private or public, my observation is that in spirit and tendency and effect it is inimical to every element of genuine religion. It is death to spiritual life. It is a profane intruder upon the sanctity of the Church. A dancing community is not religious; will not be; cannot be. Bishop McIlvain told the truth—asserted an unquestionable maxim in religion—when a lady asked him, "Is it any harm for a Christian to dance?" and he answered, "My sister, a Christian never wants to dance." He, she has no heart for it. It is a forbidden thing—unsuitable, incongruous, out of character. The desire for it is proof either that we never were "renewed in the spirit of our minds" or that we have forfeited the grace of God, and are backslidden. To patronize it, to defend it, to advocate it, is to take side with the world against Christ. Nobody ever knew a very religious person to engage in it.

I confess that I have no patience with it, no toleration of it. I think it is the silliest, most nonsensical amusement that rational beings, so called, ever engaged in. It is heathenish in its origin—a pastime of savages. It is a part of idolatrous worship—lewd, sensual, obscene. This is its history. It appeals to the lowest instincts of humanity, and is the chosen sport of the vilest, most imbruted of our race. The slum of society everywhere revel in it. It is wicked, vile in its origin, yet worse in its lower associations, and most of all in its last analysis. It has been refined, polished I grant, but it cannot be dignified nor elevated. The venom of the serpent is in it. The taint of its birth, the virus of its constitution is ineradicable. It is evil, only evil, and that continually.

No one claims for it a place among the agencies for *promoting piety*. No one has ever been made better by it; it is not so designed or expected. It is a carnal enjoyment, simple and uncompounded. The public estimate of all Church-members who engage in it is lowered. Take any man noted for his piety, any saintly woman. Introduce them in a dancing-saloon, and let them " trip the light, fantastic toe." The sight would be a shock even to the bad. Everybody would feel that there had been a fall, a sad decline of integrity, a disgraceful betrayal of the Church and of Christianity. For some people to do this would excite no surprise—nothing was expected of them; but for those of real Christian reputation to mingle in these follies would be in the Church, and among the decent sinners of the land, an occasion of sorrow, regret, and shame. The universal feeling would be that religion had been outraged and sound morals damaged by the unfortunate example.

There is nothing intellectual about it to redeem it. A dog, an elephant, a monkey can learn it. The fact is, take away the glamour of fashion—the countenance which men and women of culture give it—the whole thing would be contemptible, and would go into desuetude in all respectable society. I confess to no little humiliation that our weddings, dinners, suppers, picnics, levees, entertainments for friends and visitors, are so many of them degraded by this heathenish, idolatrous, barbarian pastime. It is a reflection upon our intelligence—as if we could not be polite and entertaining without a "hop." What a name for an adult amusement! Come, we have exhausted refreshments for the body and topics for thought and talk, let us be children, play the fool, and "hop." Alas! to think that the Church of Christ is represented on these occasions. Inconsistency is the softest word the truth allows in speaking of the shameful treatment of a holy profession.

It is to be admitted that there are differences as to time, place, and company. I am told that there is a difference, as the names imply, between round and square dances; so also between the simple cotillion and the intricate and voluptuous waltz, between parlor dancing and the masque ball. But the truth is, they are all related—blood kin. The family is one. Private dancing is the prelude and preparation for public dancing. The simple leads to the complex, and the delicate to the gross. The passion grows by indulgence. For this reason I include those parents who teach their children to dance in the same condemnation with the more open transgressors, who misrepresent their Saviour, outrage the moral sentiment of the Church, and herd promiscuously with the world of the ungodly. The knowledge of the art involves the temptation to indulge it. Indeed, this schooling is a preparation for it—a provision for the flesh to fulfill the lusts thereof. The girl whose agility and grace are admired in the circle of private friends will long to display her charming accomplishments in public. Would a thoughtful parent commit the manners and morals of his children to some strolling, transient master of mazes and positions if he did not desire and intend them to shine with eclat in the giddy throng of the vain, frivolous, and worldly? Expecting them to love the world and its follies, they insure this morally disastrous result by a training that leads naturally to it. The friendship of the world is too precious a boon to be foregone, though the price of it be the loss of divine favor and the enmity with God; for whoever will be the friend of the world is the enemy of God.

Now, bearing in mind that the Church stands related to Christ as the spouse to her husband, what shall we say of the license and freedom with which so many of her members mingle with the world? How indelicate! how suspicious! what occasion for sneer and criticism and damaging rumor! As the wife, by the wantonness of her behavior, reproaches her husband and smirches herself, even when she has not descended to absolute infidelity, so these loose members discount Christianity and mar Christian fellowship. When they joined the Church they promised to "renounce the devil and all his works, the vain pomp and glory of the world, . . . so that they would not follow or be led by them." Into this solemn covenant they entered voluntarily, understandingly. It was an oath, in substance, binding the conscience. The Church accepted the pledge and promise, and enrolled them as disciples. In the sight of God and in the presence of witnesses the betrothal was made, the formula having sacramental sanctity and force.

"O foolish Galatians, who hath bewitched you that ye should not obey the truth?"—fulfill your obligations, redeem your promises? These world-courting, pleasure-seeking professors of religion, who esteem the favor, friendship, and praise of men above fidelity to Christ, are in a painful dilemma at the bar of conscience. If they were insincere when they took these holy vows before God and his people, then they deceived the Church, played the hypocrite, lied to the Holy Ghost. Their sin is aggravated. Their very profession is a falsehood. If they were honest—meant what they said—then their friendship with the world is perfidy to Christ. They have denied their Lord and Master and gone into strange alliance with his enemies.

The moral character of all the association which the text and the sermon condemns is determined by the fact that they who go into them intended to conform to fashionable society, to court the world, to gratify the flesh. They did not design to honor Christ, to glorify God, to promote their own salvation. These things were not in all their thoughts. Their motives were secular and selfish; their policy is carnal. They consented to sacrifice their honest doubts, to break over the rules of the Church, to grieve the Spirit, in order to please ungodly friends and to gratify the lusts of the flesh, the lust of the eye, and the pride of life. These things cannot be defended, and ought not to be tolerated. No use to argue or deny—they are inconsistent, unscriptural, and corrupting. No Christian society can long survive their allowance. In prophetic imagery, the earth will swallow the woman instead of the flood. The distinction which God ordained between the Church and the world will be obliterated, and the tide of ungodliness will sweep on, burying the hope of the good, and bearing the world farther from God and salvation.

The Portrait of a Friend and Helper.*

DR. BASS: At the request of the trustees I rise to respond to your remarks, and to accept in their name the gift you propose to commit to their keeping. I should be embarrassed if I did not feel and believe that but little is expected of me, and that but little is necessary.

That unveiled portrait itself responds to the eyes of all this audience. Look at it. What benignity of expression! What firmness and decision in those lines and features! How candid and transparent the working of the brains that lie behind that open brow! How warm, generous, and loving the heart which beams from that radiant face! That face is the revelation of the man. I do not know him personally. It has never been my privilege to meet him. I only know him from his local reputation and his multiplied acts of liberality. That face, however, is legible. The veriest tyro in physiognomy can read his character. Every line attests the justice of the popular verdict. He is a man of simple, unaffected piety, of sterling integrity, of incorruptible purity in private and public life. A man of wonderful business acumen, broad-minded, well-balanced, large-hearted, conscious of his responsibility, he lives and works and gives under the great Task-master's eye. With that sagacity which characterizes his business methods he selects

---

* In response to the remarks of Rev. W. C. Bass, D.D., President of Wesleyan Female College, upon the unveiling of the portrait of Mr. George I. Seney, of Brooklyn, New York, a princely friend and munificent helper of Christian education. The ceremony occurred during the Commencement exercises, June, 1881.—EDITOR.

his own beneficiaries, and dispenses his gifts with wonderful frequency and abundance. He seems resolved to be his own executor. He does not toil to accumulate, piling thousands on thousands, adding fortune to fortune, waiting till death relaxes his power to hoard or to hold, and then seek posthumous reputation by testamentary bequests always liable to misapplication and abuse. While yet living he distributes his bounty. He sows his seed with a liberal hand, and like an honest husbandman waits hopefully and patiently for his harvest.

Allow me now to make a remark on my own responsibility. I know not how you or others may receive it. It may pass at best as my tribute of respect to a worthy name and a noble man.

I have always deplored the necessity which constrained us to drop our original title—*Georgia Female College*. I liked that. It was broad, popular, appealed to the public spirit of our entire citizenship. When under pressure of financial difficulties the trustees changed the charter and the name, I was grieved in spirit. I am an intense Methodist, a Hebrew of the Hebrews, but I never fancied the cognomen *Wesleyan Female College*. Mr. Wesley I honor and revere. He does not need this recognition to perpetuate his renown. He belongs to history. His is one of the few immortal names which were not born to die. As an instrument of Providence, I regard him as the foremost man of all ages. "Wesleyan" is too common; it is not "distinctive." We have a dozen Wesleyan male and female colleges, institutes, and seminaries in our broad territory. Withal it smacks of sectarianism. It is narrow, a little too specific, a bid to prejudice on one side and a bar to patronage on the other. It is suggestive of denominational aims—aims which I approve, and which I would not ignore or disguise. Making Methodists is a very good work;

but I would not state this as an objective end. We have a higher purpose. We propose to sanctify education, to permeate our civilization with the gospel element, to bring the heart and conscience and sentiment and imagination of womanhood into harmony with the spirit and plans and kingdom of Christ.

I come neither to "praise" nor "bury" Mr. Seney, but I desire to honor him worthily and permanently. He is, I learn, a plain, direct, practical man—has no heart for form and pageantry. I doubt if he would enjoy the ceremonial through which we are passing now. I speak only for myself; I know the partiality of memory and association, and the reluctance to change, but I would be glad when yonder architectural pile shall be reconstructed, adorned, and beautified by the princely gift of our friend, to see emblazoned in bold letters on marble tablet, high upon the front, *Seney Female College.* If you cling to the old and honored familiar name, then endow the president's chair, and call it the "Seney Professorship." Either would be a compliment worth something. It would endure when yonder portrait has faded into invisibility, and when your resolutions of thanks "have gone glimmering through the dream of things that were."

This occasion suggests several things. Indulge me in a brief comment on two only.

The war left our colleges fearfully impoverished. They have had a struggle for life. Apprehension has dominated the public mind as to the possibilities of the future. It was feared that competition, debt, and the poverty of the people would break us down. If we asked for money, men felt that it would be wasted and lost; that it would go into a sinking fund—not for the payment of debt, but merely to eke out a doomed existence. Mr. Seney's gift has reïnspired the hopes of the strong and the brave, dismissed the fears of the timid and the despondent, and tranquilized the public mind with a feeling of confidence and security. He did not say, "Be ye warmed and filled," but he has put us on our feet and made us capable of self-support. He has rescued us from the waves where we were likely to perish, and brought us safely to the shore. Now the whole land lies before us. May we have grace to go up and possess it!

In these latter years we have heard a good deal of *fraternity*. It is a choice word and a good thing. The term has been upon the lips of the politician and the Churchman. Long since war's loud alarm has been hushed to silence extreme men North and South have sought to keep up sectional strife. Some of you know that I have never taken much stock in what has been called "formal fraternity." I have looked upon it as a sham and a fraud. I do not believe in that fraternity begotten of a motion in a private caucus or public assembly, negotiated through commissioners by compromise, contract, and covenant, and indorsed by legislative enactment. I believe in that fraternity which is spontaneous, the outgrowth of the heart, born of love—love to Christ, his Church, and humanity. I feel assured of my religion because I love all who love the Lord Jesus. I mean nothing invidious by the remark. I simply state an historic fact. The masses of the North have been grossly ignorant of the South, her people, and her institutions. They do not come to see us, they do not read our papers, and they have been deceived and betrayed by vindictive, malignant men, who have slandered us for the vilest partisan purpose. But we are in the early twilight of a better day. Various Northern men, representing Church and State, have visited our section, seen our public men, mingled with us in social life, seen and heard for themselves, and they have written some clever things about us, and assuaged the asperity of prejudice, modified public opinion, inaugurated a revolution of ideas. One of our own men, by speech and pen, has given more rapid motion to the wheel of reform. But Mr. Seney, like the widow in the gospel, has done more than they all. His spontaneous, unsolicited, munificent contribution to education in the South has bridged—I will not say the "bloody chasm," but the chasm of mutual alienation and prejudice and distrust which yawned between the sections. His bridge is no pontoon affair for temporary use—a frail, transient, portable, movable thing—but a solid structure, with sturdy buttresses and ample span and graceful arches; and the people on either side may come and go, assured of a welcome, home, and fellowship.

And now, sir, let me say we will guard your gift, photograph that portrait on our memories, enshrine Mr. Seney in our hearts and our prayers, and if he will come to see us—as I trust he will—lavish upon him, out of honest love, all the attention and kindness which a refined propriety will allow, and make him feel that the recipients of his bounty, if not deserving, at least are grateful.

Moral Principles the Only Safeguard.*

"He that walketh uprightly walketh surely." (Prov. x. 9.)

TO a preacher it is a serious question what subject is best suited to an audience and an occasion like this. Is a commencement sermon a mere compliment to Christianity as a religion recognized in the principles of our Government and by the great body of our citizens? Do we by religious discourse and devotional exercises simply mean to dignify the exercises which are to follow? or is the reason for it to be found in the relation of man to God and in the evident need of religious influence and divine aid in the responsible work of education, the development of mind, the formation of character, the preparation of the young for honorable citizenship? This service, as I understand it, is not a ceremony without reverence or heart or object, but the homage of faith in God and his revelation, a formal acknowledgment of our dependence upon the principles, motives, and obligations of our holy religion for the achievements of the past, the progress of the present, and all the precious hopes of the future. It is nevertheless a painful discount upon the interest of the hour that most people stress the style, the elocution, the oratory of the speaker far more than the appropriateness of the subject, the fitness of the truth delivered, or the moral results that may follow. They are more eager for literary entertainment than for a religious banquet; more concerned for the eclat of a splendid sermon than for the enlightenment of con-

---

*A Commencement Sermon, delivered at Wofford College, June 8, 1884.—EDITOR.

science or the furniture of a holy life. Even the Christian people of an audience like this at such a time come together without desire or expectation, forget to pray, and are content with a respectable discourse on almost any theme. Hence, special sermons are an embarrassment to me. Accustomed to follow my impressions in the selection of a text, it is not pleasant to rely upon a dry judgment of what is simply fit, appropriate. Besides, I miss the sustaining sympathy of a spiritually-minded congregation in communion with God, looking and longing for revival power. God is witness I never did prostitute the pulpit to any selfish, carnal, personal end. I am too old now to waste time in making reputation or courting praise. I propose a simple, practical discourse. If I cannot inaugurate a revival, I desire to furnish rules and motives for high, honorable, safe moral action. The Lord help us to plow close and deep, break up the fallow-ground, sow with a liberal hand well-chosen seed, assured that the reaping-time will come.

Upright is a strong word. It is of frequent occurrence, and always of high and interesting import, in the sacred Scriptures. It is synonymous with the strongest terms, descriptive of high, pure moral character. "Mark the perfect man, and behold the upright; for the end of that man is peace." Perfect and upright—the terms are interchangeable and mutually explanatory. To realize the force of the word in its full meaning and comprehension we must remember that man is a fallen being. Naturally humanity lies prostrate—prone in the dust. To be upright a man must rise and stand upon his feet, perpendicular, looking upward. The Greek word *"anthropos"* describes a being whose eyes are turned heavenward. The native majesty of man in his physical structure—erect and gazing into the sky—is but a faint symbol of a soul just, honest, pure. Adherence to justice in social dealings, conformity to rectitude as between man and man, both in principle and conduct, may be predicable even of the unregenerate sometimes; but in its highest intent and aim, in its widest scope and purest application, we must consider the term "upright" as including the enthronement of God's law as the rule of right over conscience and will, the sanctity of motives deriving their inspiration from the desire to please God, an integrity of purpose and action which looks for its ultimate reward in the approval of the final Judge and the associations of the blessed in heaven.

"He that walketh uprightly." Walking takes in the whole of our conversation or conduct. It is not an action simply, but a course of action; not an incident but a habit. To say that a man walks in pride is to say that he is full of it. It is his spirit, his way, his element; he is wholly under the influence of it. It inspires, dominates, controls him. So here walking uprightly implies settled convictions, well-defined principles; a steady, invincible purpose; a single aim, undivided; turning neither to the right nor the left, looking right on to the chosen goal. My observation is that this is the weak point in modern society—the absence of plan, purpose, principle. The people seem adrift, without chart or compass, driven by the winds, tossed by the waves, floating with the current; creatures of circumstance, company, custom; molded by fashion, manipulated into any shape by accident; without self-government, pliable, venal—on the market, advertised for sale. These people are not wicked by direct choice; they do not prefer to do wrong; but they are irresolute, undecided; traitors to their own high, self-determining power, they have never resolved to do right. They live promiscuously. Like a vessel at sea, steering for no port, who can tell whether the winds are favorable or unfavorable? If a man travels at random, he may move, but he does not journey; it makes no difference whether he draws back or turns aside, he makes no real progress unless he advances toward some particular place which he wishes to reach.

To be rational, manly, Christian, a man must have a fixed, governing aim, regulated by the fear of God, the love of virtue, and the hope of eternal reward. This will simplify his conduct, arrange his actions, and give every thing a relation. This will give unity to character and conduct, economize time and power, prevent waste and loss. Paul said, "This *one* thing I do." He did not mean oneness of exertion— for he did a thousand things—but a oneness of purpose which combined them all and gave them the same direction. If a man depart from the course prescribed by righteousness on any account, if he infracts his rules of moral living at any time for any reason, if he infringes upon principle to carry out any calculation of interest or honor or pleasure, then come distraction, perplexity, confusion. The foundations are unsettled, the building totters, and, most likely, great will be the fall of it. The consent to reconsider the principles, rules, and methods of an upright life is the surrender of the fort. Readjustment is always maladjustment. "Their heart is divided," said Hosea, "now shall they be found faulty." "A double-minded man is unstable in all his ways," said an apostle. "No man can serve two masters." So said Jesus. Integrity, stability, uprightness there must be, or there can be no excellency, no character; for character is the effect and force of habit, and habit is produced by constancy, consistency, persistence on a given line. "Those that be planted in the house of the Lord shall flourish in the courts of our God." A tree often transplanted, even to more congenial soil and position, will be fruitless—nay, will droop and wither and die. Better be obstinate than versatile—the one may be guided and will go on; in the other there is nothing to guide and nothing to expect. You may build upon a rock, but what can you do with a mound of sand? Let me say to those who are beginning the career of life, it is indispensable to lay down the principles on which we are to form our general conduct. If we set out without principles of any kind, there can be no regular plan of life, nor any firmness or consistency of conduct. No person can know where they are to find us, nor on what phase of our character they are to depend. These are clouds without rain, wells without water—deceitful and disappointing. So if the principles which we adopt be of a variable nature—such as popular opinion, reputation, or worldly interest, as these are often shifting and changing—they can give no assurance of steadiness; nay, rather they make provision for vacillation and instability. Equally unfortunate and exposed, if not criminal, are they who, with great swelling words of vanity, rely on a sense of honor, on the beauty and excellence of virtue, and the dignity of human nature. These are plausible words; fallacious sentiments, they sound well; seem to exalt and ennoble; but they are meretricious and delusive, the oily utterances of hypocrisy, the artful covering spread over the pitfalls of vice. To the currents of passion they are dikes of sand, temporary checks serving only to accumulate volume and power for a more desperate plunge when the obstruction gives way. The conservative influence of simply human, prudential—ay, honorable—ideas is too slight a ligature to bind one to virtue when appetite clamors, and habits urge, and the easily besetting sin pleads for indulgence.

I must not blink the statement—nay, I wish I could stamp it in ineffaceable letters upon every conscience—that the only sure principles for regulating our life must be founded upon the Christian religion, taken in its whole compass of authority, motive, and sanction. The religion that is to keep us and save us must not be eclectic, fragmentary, select, patch-work æsthetically arranged like a "missionary quilt of a thousand pieces," but an entirety, a unit, like the Saviour's garment without seam from top to bottom. Not periodical, limited to particular acts of devotion, or the mere moralities of social behavior, but pervading the whole of our conduct toward God and man. It must sanctify the heart and the home, permeate the fellowship of the community and the responsibilities of citizenship; must accompany to the court-house as well as the prayer-meeting, direct at the ballot-box as at the communion-table; there must be Christian voting as well as Christian giving, and life's daily toil be as moral and religious as the Sunday rest and the Sunday worship. The fear of God must preside in awful magistracy over our public walks and our private ways. The foundation must be laid in Christ as the Saviour of the world, and that faith justified by good works. The love of God must be supreme, dominant, subordinating all other affections, and around it must cling as the ivy to the tree the love of our neighbor. In a word, "he that walketh uprightly" must have a religion that is an inseparable element of character incorporated with all his habits of thinking, feeling, and acting, moving him all the while with the force and accuracy of instinct.

Now, let us consider some of the advantages indicated by the expression "walketh surely." First: An upright walker is sure of finding his way. It requires no reach of wit, no acumen of judgment or depth or breadth of inquiry, no plodding study, to discern what is just, to determine what is right. A man has only to open his eyes and there lies open to his view the plain, strict, obvious road of duty; on his sign-board, in legible characters, he may read the way to which Reason's index-finger points unerringly.

The ways of craft and iniquity and all ill designs are always obscure, perplexed, and intricate; they are infinitely various and utterly uncertain, so that to pick among them is a puzzle which confounds society and turns us over to the perilous hazards of the merest chance. They deny us the poor advantage of choosing the least of the evils; and where all are wrong and bad, the worst is apt to be selected. But the ways of truth, of right, of virtue are simple and uniform, easy to find, free from obstructions—"a wayfaring man, though a fool, need not err therein." Divine wisdom has engineered these routes of moral travel—not for the great, the experienced, the subtle, but for the common people—the lowest capacity, being designed to "make wise the simple," to give "the young men knowledge and discretion." The right way is an air-line without curves or grades, a highway, "a way of holiness." Hence, in the Scriptures bad ways are called dark, rough, crooked, slippery. The way of transgressors is hard, rocky, thorny, full of trouble and sorrow; it begins in perplexity and misgiving, is attended with apprehension, doubt, and fear, and ends in disappointment and galling regret. But "the path of the upright is as a shining light;" "his foot standeth in an even place." The law of his God is in his heart; none of his steps shall slide. An upright man hardly needs any counsel outside of his own honesty. He is self-adjusted. "The integrity of the upright shall preserve him, and the righteousness of the perfect shall direct his way."

Second: He that walketh uprightly treads on firm ground; he walks steadily, steps with confidence, because on this line there are no treacherous quagmires, no devouring quicksands, no Serbonian bogs to swallow him up. He stands on safe, approved, well-tried principles, and, satisfied of the correctness of his chart and the rectitude of his plan, he abides by his resolutions, holds on to his main course without flinching or wavering. Like a ship, tight and strong, his integrity is well ballasted, and sits firmly poised upon its keel, so that the waves of temptation dashing upon him do not cause him to roll in uncertainty or topple over into unworthy practices. Lust, passion, humor, interest, are all variable, chopping all around the compass; their miserable devotees are many-minded, unstable in all their ways; "they reel to and fro like drunken men," and are at their wits' end. But the man guided by conscience and principle, fortified by habit, remains even and composed in all the circumstances of time and all the vicissitudes of fortune. Such a man in every case and condition is the same man, and goeth the same way. The contingencies of life do not unhinge him from his purposes nor divert his foot from the right course. Let the weather be fair or foul, let the world smile or frown, let him gain or lose, let him be commended or reproached, he will do what duty requires. The external state of things does not alter the moral reason of things with him. He verifies that sublime utterance of Job: "I hold fast my integrity; my heart shall not reproach me so long as I live."

In such a life there are no inequalities or contradictions, no clashing with himself, no collision with others. He never deludes or disappoints in his dealings, and escapes all the inconveniences and censures which issue from unfairness and deception. It is a great mistake, young gentlemen, to imagine that craft and dexterity are the best defense against the perils of life. No calculation of probabilities can insure the safety of a man who is acting a deceitful part. Amid the unforeseen events of the future he has to fear not only the miscarriage of his plots, but the miseries which the disclosure of his fallacies may bring upon his head. Take an extensive survey of human affairs; inquire who are the men on the different lines of life that have gone through the world with most success. We shall find that men of probity and honor fill up the most considerable part of the list. Nay, that men of plain understanding, acting with fair and direct views, have outstripped in the long run those of the deepest policy who have been devoid of principle. How few persons lose their fortunes who have made them by steady industry, by fidelity, worth, and rigid adherence to duty! But how numerous and frequent the overthrow of those who make haste to be rich, who gamble in stocks, trade in "futures," make "corners" on the necessaries of life! The whole coast of illegitimate speculation is strewn with the wrecks of reputed millionaires; the bones of "bulls and bears" mingle in an ignoble, undistinguished pile. But he that hath clean hands and a pure heart shall wax stronger and stronger (perhaps financially, though that is a question of providence) in character, hope, and comfort.

Third: He that walketh uprightly has adopted the surest way for the dispatch of business, and the shortest cut to the execution of any good purpose. As in geometry, of all lines and surfaces contained within given bounds, the straight line and the plain surface are the shortest, so in morality. The just view, the direct aim, the well-defined purpose—these are the easiest and quickest way to a chosen end. On this plain platform there are no bewildering intrigues and mazes, no crooked windings and turnings, no dancing hither and thither, skipping backward and forward, doing and undoing; these are all irksome and tedious delays which waste time, hinder business, and defeat successful execution. The man who acts fairly and justly has an open, direct road before him, and has no occasion for retreat, excursion, or deflection on either hand.

Human life to be successful is very much like building a house. To begin right you must have plan and specifications, and these must be carried out in detail as the duty of every day requires. Changes waste lumber, embarrass workmen, delay progress, and mar the harmonious adjustment of parts. Loose and thriftless habits demoralize the whole man. I know men busy as bees, who work like beavers, but never accomplish any thing. They are fitful, irregular, desultory. They are not prompt to begin, nor patient to hold on, nor determined to succeed. Energy is exhausted by spasms rather than work. They piddle with the trivial parts and leave the main chance to wait their pleasure. In the meantime the hard work grows heavier, and at last is never done at all. To be upright, perfect, we must economize time, gather up the fragments, systematize business, study method, make conscience of all promises and obligations, great and small.

In these respects a man must learn to be considerate of others as well as himself. Punctuality deserves a place among the cardinal virtues. It is a wonderful economist of time—your own and that of others; the latter you certainly have no right to waste. It is a conservator of temper, patience, equanimity. It inspires confidence, promotes fellowship, fosters self-respect, protects the nerves from worry, and soothes even a peevish nature into gentleness and amenity.

Fourth: He that walketh uprightly is secure as to his honor and credit. Judged by his own apprehensions of himself or by the estimation of others, he does not blush at what he is doing nor reproach himself for what he has done. Consciousness and reputation alike defend his proceeding from blemish or blame. The past, the present, and the future—memory, experience, and hope—all bless him. Meaning right in every thing, there is no check or struggling in his mind, no sting in his heart; being satisfied with what he is about, his judgment approving, his will acquiescing, he feels that his course is worthy of himself, agreeable to reason, and conformed to duty. The guidance of uprightness is easily understood, and it is a great consolation that both character and happiness depend upon simple integrity much more than on extent of capacity. Plans of worldly policy are deep and intricate, and experience shows how often the ablest persons are mistaken in the measures they adopt for carrying them on.

For the most part, the first impression which strikes a good man as to what he ought or ought not to do is the right, the soundest one, and suggests the best and wisest counsel. If he hesitates and begins to think how far his duty or his honor can be reconciled to what seems his interest, he is on the point of diverging into a dangerous path. It is in one issue only that the man who acts from worldly interest can enjoy satisfaction; that is when his designs have succeeded according to his wish. It is the immense advantage of the upright that in any event there is something to comfort him. If success fails him, he has the consolation of having done his duty, and studied to approve himself unto God.

We all know that other views are popular and are at work in the business world. But the schemes and hopes of the eager and hasty, however well devised and however fascinating in promise, and though successful for a spell, are yet freighted with mischief and trouble. To clamber over fences of duty, to break through the hedges of right, to trespass on hallowed inclosures, may seem the most compendious way of reaching an end, but these adventurers and speculators forget that he who diggeth a pit to snare his neighbor shall fall into it himself, and he that breaketh a hedge a serpent shall bite him. The greed of gain—making haste to be rich, piling up colossal fortunes—is the sin and curse of our country. But to accumulate by fraud, corruption, extortion, oppression, overreaching, and supplanting may be the shortest cut, the most expeditious way, yet these gains are subject to several awful discounts. What a man thus makes is not his own. It is plunder, rapine, robbery, all glossed with milder names current in the world of trade; yet the eye of Eternal Justice pierces through all the webs and veils, and God, in providence, pours the malediction of his righteous judgment upon all these evil-doers and their ill-gotten spoil. It is written that "wealth gotten by vanity shall surely be diminished," and he that oppresseth to increase his riches shall surely come to want. Again it is said: "He that increaseth riches and not by right shall leave them in the midst of his days, and at his end shall be a fool." Believe me, the plain way of simple, honest industry is the best way to thrive. "A little that a righteous man hath is better than the riches of many wicked." It lasts longer, has more enjoyment in it; there is no disgorging to do at the end of the law or of a good conscience. It is a heritage that will go down to children and children's children.

Fifth: He that walketh uprightly hath perfect security as to final results. This remark applies to this world and the world to come. The upright shall not be baffled in his expectations and desires. If prosperity consists in satisfaction of mind concerning events, his success is sure. What! will he gain the victory in every battle? make money in every bargain? reap bountifully wherever he sows? Probably yes, perhaps no; and yet, according to the true notion of prosperity, he shall prosper. To a man of broad views, of high, honorable impulses, of settled convictions of right, of holy aims, failure in inferior, subordinate matters is not defeat in the main thing. With such a man the principle design, the great end, is to please God and procure his favor, to satisfy his own mind and discharge his conscience, to promote his spiritual interests and save his soul, to do good by charity to mankind, serving the public in every legitimate way, and furnishing to the world a virtuous example—all these he can most surely accomplish. What shall obstruct him in the prosecution, what debar him in the execution, of his noble resolve? In spite of all the world, by the succor grace affords, he will achieve his divinely ordained task. With regard to secular interests, he does not aim at success, except under conditions and with the reservation, "If the Lord will." Experience will teach him that it is good luck to have his projects blasted, and that missing is better than getting, if divine wisdom so determine. "The Lord taketh pleasure in the prosperity of his servants." That cannot be bad which he deems expedient and for the best. That cannot be considered as a disappointment nor counted as a misfortune which, on the plan of life and trust in Providence, we are prepared to accept with satisfaction and complacence. A wise man will always esteem that as best and most happy which secures interests incomparably more precious than worldly gain, producing fruits more wholesome and savory than all earthly products, exercising and maturing the divinest virtues—virtues worth all the wealth, all the preferment, all that is desirable in the world.

Finally: The infinite advantage, the crowning glory, of uprightness is that at the last, when all deceits are laid bare, all the glamour of pretense seen through, all perverse intrigues unraveled, all base designs stripped of the coverings which now infold them; when the engineers of mischief, the experts in fraud shall be put to shame; when all things shall be accurately tried and impartially decided—then shall the righteousness of the upright come forth as the light, and his judgment as the noonday. Then what he has done shall be approved, what he has suffered shall be repaired.

And now, young gentlemen, a final word direct to you.

I am no pessimist, but it is not to be denied that there are facts, omens, and tendencies in American society alarming to the patriot and discouraging to the Christian philanthropist. Corruption seems to be epidemic. Nothing escapes its unhallowed touch. It sweeps like a flood through the high places of the Government, and seeps and trickles through all the crevices of domestic and commercial life. The malaria of loose and vicious sentiment and of a licentious literature spreads and perpetuates the infection. To say nothing now of the violence and outrage in the form of incendiarism, rape, and murder, the rage for money is undermining all the foundations of morality, of personal honor, and public integrity. It is potent in the bribery of elections. The ballot-box, once the safeguard of public liberty, is no longer a security for our institutions. Candidates, the press, leading men, talk openly of the use of money in a Presidential campaign, as if this demoralizing prostitution of it were a regular part of the machinery of the Government. Sound policy, principles, measures, no longer determine the issue. Venal votes, bought and sold like sheep in the market, hold in their hands the destinies of the country. The intelligence and virtue of the land, revolted by the arts of the demagogue, disgusted with the tricks of the politicians, and shrinking from the contact of the vicious and the vile, have largely withdrawn from public affairs, and left the country to drift as it may under the propulsion of the malign forces at work in the midst of it. We must look largely to the young men of Christian education to reform this state of things.

We see the corruption of which I speak in the spirit of reckless speculation which prevails in every department of business. Speculation pure and simple—I use the word in its worst popular sense—in my judgment contravenes the laws of nature and providence, brings about an abnormal state of things, complicates in its results the vexed question of the relations of capital and labor, disturbs and unsettles the finances of the nation, and precipitates a panic upon the people, either by its legerdemain or its inevitable outcome. Perhaps no country in the world ever furnished such a theater for its action as our own. The vastness of our territory, the growth of our cities, the location of new towns, the building of railroads, the issue of stocks and bonds and mortgages, have all furnished the opportunity and the temptation. The mania for quick, sudden fortune has swept thousands into the snare, and in the whirl and frenzy of excitement they have projected their schemes into every line of trade and every species of enterprise, from a corner on the bread of the hungry down to the planting of an orange-tree. Ay, these bold, desperate adventurers, not content with the abounding material the numerous chances of the present afford, have stretched into the future and trade upon things that are not as though they were. This wild hunt for fortune, apart from all plans of productive industry, is the bane of our social life and a formidable bar to general prosperity. The evils are direct and indirect. On the parties themselves the stimulus, the infatuation of extravagant desires and boundless hopes, obscure all ideas of right, of honor, of relative obligation, and resolve life and character into odious, supreme selfishness. On the other hand, the toiling millions grow weary, restless, discontented with their slow accumulations, and in the ferment of thought and passion are brewed the turbulent elements which threaten social order and the stability of our institutions. Honest, productive labor of hand or brain is the law of permanent wealth, of personal virtue, of usefulness and safety.

Other evils demand mention because of their pestiferous influence on life, property, character, marriage, and domestic purity. Their long, silent toleration is one of the marvels of our history; but they are doomed to discussion, legislation, and, I trust, utter abolition. I mean the liquor traffic—manufacture, sale, license. These fountains of evil must be stanched. These sources of taxation and temptation, and plunder and corruption, and sin and shame must be relegated to the past, and human life made safer and purer by their absence. The adulteration of food now so common must be ranked by statute among the felonies of the criminal calendar, and the guilty culprits who poison the blood of the people with their filthy drugs and chemical cheats consigned to the halter or the penitentiary. This wicked tampering by mercenary manufacturers, for the sake of gain, with the life and health of the people is one of the gigantic crimes of the century, and one of the saddest developments of American genius for invention and enterprise.

Let me catalogue one other, the farthest-reaching, the most soul-destroying, God-defying of all. I refer to the lax laws of divorce as found in all the States. Human legislatures, in all their rules and regulations on this subject, outside of the divine word, have transcended their authority, and the country is reaping the woful harvest of their impious presumption. Marriage is a divine institution. It was first in the order of time. God ordained it as the fountain-head of the family, the government, and the race, and his law defines and regulates it. By divine statute wedlock is permanent and indissoluble save by the infidelity of the parties or the act of God. Any loosening of the bond on any other account impairs the sacredness of the contract and jeopards all that is vital in the institution. God made them male and female, and declared that they twain should be one flesh; but the latitude of our laws and the loose administration of them suggest and encourage separation for light and trivial causes. The result is: marriage for a limited time, divorce on expiration of contract; in other cases discord, divisions, then appeal to the courts, then remarriage of one or both; the consummation—lust, bigamy, and legalized crime.

This is a shocking representation, I know; but the facts justify me, and I make the statement here and now to array the intelligence and religion of the country on the right side of all these questions. Especially do I desire to enlist these educated young men—the pride of our families, the friends and the hope of the Church, and the future guardians of the State—as the champions of right and virtue, of reform in politics and business, of the true scriptural, inviolable relations of men and women in wedded life.

The real protection of society is in individual character. If you are personally pure and upright, however quiet and retired your life, you will be an accretion to the moral force by which the needed revolution is to be wrought. But you ought not to be merely latent, negative, passive. You must be active co-workers in every good word and work. You must not put your candle under a bushel, nor bury your talent in the earth. From this time onward the responsibilities of manhood are upon you. Assert yourselves; fill your place; take position. Ally yourselves with all that is honorable, noble, useful, and of good report. Let the people know where to find you, what to expect of you, and feel that they can trust you. These thoughts apply at every stage and turn of life, but they will grow in significance as you grow older and opportunities multiply and obligations increase. Get ready for whatever may betide you. The State needs incorruptible men to fill her offices, wise men to mold her legislation, upright men to administer her laws, men of "understanding who know what Israel ought to do." The Church, education, the college, the

Sunday-school, all need men—active, earnest, full of vim and enthusiasm — consecrated men, for the work of the present and the future. We who are passing off the stage turn our eyes with longing, prayerful interest to the youth of the land. We must decrease, you may increase.

And now I commend you to God and the word of his grace. May you live to fulfill all parental hopes, honor your *alma mater*, work for your country with credit and usefulness, stand as witnesses for Jesus and the truth, serve your generation by the will of God, and realize all the rewards of uprightness in time and eternity.

Character and Work of a Gospel Minister.*

"Till I come, give attendance to reading, to exhortation, to doctrine. Neglect not the gift that is in thee, which was given thee by prophecy, with the laying on of the hands of the presbytery. Meditate upon these things; give thyself wholly to them; that thy profiting may appear to all. Take heed unto thyself and unto the doctrine; continue in them; for in doing this thou shalt both save thyself, and them that hear thee." (1 Tim. iv. 13–16.)

TO a man familiar with the phases of modern thought, the tendencies of society, and the moral developments of the age, it is positively startling to read the descriptions of them contained in the Bible. How fresh and minute they are! how apposite! how exact! Many passages seem like a morning chronicle of yesterday's history and experience. This fact ought to take prominent rank among the internal evidences which authenticate the book as divine. These accounts of what will be—express statements uttered and recorded long centuries ago of that subtle thing we call thought; the mystery of iniquity working under a mask—are too definite and life-like to have been the mere elaborations of a sagacious human mind. It is God speaking beforehand for the warning and instruction of the Church, and especially for the furniture and equipment of the ministry.

The object seems to be threefold. First, to conserve the

---

*A discourse delivered before the ordination of deacons at the Holston Conference of the Methodist Episcopal Church, South, in Abingdon, Va., Sunday morning, Oct. 26, 1879.—EDITOR.

faith of the ministry, by timely notice, from the shock of these alarming disclosures; second, that they should keep the Church in remembrance of these things, and thus guard her from corruption and apostasy; third, to impress both parties with this great truth: that heresy with regard to any of the fundamental articles of the Christian faith tends inevitably to degeneracy—social, political, and moral. The truth of this proposition is to be found in the account of those perilous times which the apostle predicts in the future history of the Church. The access to the human mind of seducing spirits, the doctrine of devils, diabolical sentiments, the tolerance of falsehood and the defense of hypocrisy, the abolition of social ties, decrying the marriage-covenant as a despotism and a nuisance, substituting abstinence from meats for self-denial and godly sorrow, are all sequences of what the apostle calls "departing from the faith"—a serious error either in reference to the things which are to be believed or the things which are to be done. Heretical interpretations of doctrines or morals are fraught with untold, unutterable mischief. It is a leak that will sink the ship. It is a drop of virus that will gangrene the body. Let go your hold upon the faith once delivered to the saints, and you are unmoored and adrift. The winds and the currents will bear you surely and swiftly to destruction.

Keeping these points in mind (they will be useful in the sequel), let us come up to the subject from another standpoint.

Paul and Barnabas, in their first missionary journey among the Gentiles, came to Lystra, where, though resisted and persecuted, they preached the gospel with considerable success. Among the converts were Lois, the mother, and Eunice, the daughter, who had married a Gentile. The husband, it is likely, was now dead; but Timothy, the only child, was living, and became, while yet very young, the subject of gracious influences. Whether his conversion was the outgrowth of maternal instruction and example or the fruit of apostolic preaching, it is perhaps impossible to determine. If Paul sowed the seed, Lois and Eunice prepared the soil. If Paul gathered the fruit, his mother planted the tree. The faith of his maternal ancestors was inculcated if not transmitted: "The unfeigned faith which dwelt first in thy grandmother, Lois, and then in thy mother, Eunice, and I am persuaded in thee also." If this be not the law of heredity working by statute and promise to a given result (and this I neither affirm nor believe), yet is it the benediction of God descending through three generations as the seal of his approval upon household piety. In natural order, as well as gracious covenant and design, instruction precedes conversion. From a child Timothy knew the Holy Scriptures, and by them was made wise unto salvation through faith which is in Christ Jesus. To be trained from infancy in the fear of God is a great blessing, and a truly religious education is of infinite worth; but parents, ministers, and teachers of every grade must understand that to save the soul conversion must follow. The truth, "Ye must be born again," is irrespective of age. General knowledge, orthodoxy, discipline, may be auxiliaries; they never can be proxies. Graduating into religion by merely educational processes, in view of the general ignorance and imperfect capacities of mankind, is a dubious experiment in any case, and never can be of general application. Some very imprudent and misleading declarations are made now and then in these days upon this subject by some earnest Sunday-school workers and some semi-Pelagian preachers. The necessity of the new birth cannot be anticipated and superseded by any form of moral training or any measure of intellectual development. The pulpit of this day, if faithful to Christ and human salvation, must bear strong testimony against the popular tendency to substitute spiritual religion—to displace realities by similitudes. I tell you, to repeat the Lord's Prayer and the Ten Commandments and the Apostles' Creed, to get the catechism by heart and sing beautiful songs, and to receive baptism and confirmation and communion in regular succession as to time and order, is, after all, a very mild type of religion. I prefer and insist upon that form where head and heart, principles and affections, conscience and will, life and character, are all melted, mingled, and molded by divine power, and stand forth at last in the bright, beautiful image and superscription of Him who came to forgive and save.

When Paul made his second visit to Lystra he found Timothy a member of the Church, and in high repute among the people as a sober, devout young man. On the ground of former acquaintance, his family relationships, his spiritual-mindedness, his kindred sympathies in gospel-work, his natural talents and adaptations, there soon grew up between them a loving intimacy. Through mutual affection they stood in the relation of father and son, and under God the younger was largely developed by the elder.

I have often observed that the common judgment of the Church that a young man ought to preach is pretty strong presumptive evidence, outside of any impression upon his own consciousness, of a call to the ministry. By itself it would not answer, I concede, as a law of action. Nevertheless, great respect is due to it as corroborating evidence. The common opinion that there was a prediction concerning the future destiny and usefulness of Timothy may find its solution in the popular judgment of the Church that he was a person eminently fit for a high and holy calling. No prophecy, in the sense of a divine revelation, is anywhere recorded of him; and the prevailing views of the brethren, harmonizing with his own convictions of duty, may constitute the designation—the "setting apart"—which the apostle calls a prophecy, and which justified his ordination.

To come a little nearer to ourselves, it is a solemn view of the responsibilities of the Christian ministry that, whatever a man's native gifts or incidental endowments, however truly called of God and hopefully indorsed by the Church, his future is contingent, both as to his personal safety and his relative usefulness. The gospel is a charge, a sacred deposit, committed to the ministry. We are ministers of Christ and stewards of the mysteries of God. Moreover, it is required of a steward that a man be found faithful, trustworthy. These terms are significant, suggestive. In his general directions the apostle stresses three points:

First. What and how we are to teach. We must teach sound doctrine—must sow the wheat of God's truth, not the chaff of human inventions, not the myths of a vain imagination, but the unqualified verities of the holy word. We are to speak with authority, because we speak by authority. We must *testify* "repentance toward God and faith toward our Lord Jesus Christ." The spirit of the teacher must be tender but the mode of instruction dogmatic. "These things command and teach."

The second point is personal purity. "Be thou an example of the believers in word, in conversation, in charity, in spirit, in faith, in purity."

The third point is, he must be to the brethren a faithful monitor. "If thou put the brethren in remembrance of these things, thou shalt be a good minister of the Lord Jesus, nourished up in the words of faith and good doctrine."

To these high standards Timothy had already attained, and now that there might be no collapse, no loss of influence, no forfeiture of public interest, but rather accumulated knowledge, richer furniture of mind, a broader preparation for usefulness, "till I come, give attendance to reading, to exhortation, to doctrine."

The apostle doubtless refers mainly, if not exclusively, to the Old Testament Scriptures. At that period books were not numerous, and very few, if any, would have been of much value to a gospel preacher. One leading function of the early ministry was to convince or confound the Jews. To be thoroughly furnished for this work, they must equip themselves from that divine armory. They must know the promises, the prophecies, the events of the divine administration, their order and relation, and the fulfillment and harmony of them in the person and history of Christ. Preaching, at first, was emphatically a simple proclamation of the great facts of Christianity. These were the staple of every discourse. To testify of Jesus was the sole occupation of the preacher. From the days of Ezra all along, it was customary to read the law and the prophets in every synagogue, and now doubtless in every Christian assembly; and as Ezra read the law and gave the sense thereof, in after times regular officers were appointed to read the Scriptures and append suitable paraphrases and comments. Such was the origin of what we call preaching. The injunction of the text may be regarded not simply as the recognition of a prevailing custom, but an apostolic indorsement of the free reading of the Holy Book as an important part of public worship in every congregation.

"Give attendance to reading." Timothy was to read alone. His public addresses were to be the fruit of his private study. He was to imbue his mind with the light and spirit of the Bible. In it he was to find his intellectual animation and spiritual vigor. From it he was to derive the materials of his argument and the inspiration of his oratory. In this element of wonders are the treasures of wisdom and knowledge. Here are the safeguards of social order, the vital forces of a true civilization, the only elements of perpetuity in government. Read the Bible, Timothy; read it in your closet; read it in your churches; fill your head with its truth; let its revelations set your heart on fire; enrich, adorn the Church with its gems and jewels; thrill your congregations with its disclosures of the eternal future. O brethren, you need not rack your poor invention for topics, arguments, novelties! The freshest, newest, most rousing, thrilling thing in the world is the gospel of Jesus Christ. Above all other men, it is the glory of the Christian preacher that his materials are furnished by the opulence of infinite wisdom. A way of salvation for our fallen race; the recovery of the favor and image of our Maker; the divinity, incarnation, death, and resurrection of the Son of God; the empire of the Church; the prospect of glory—these are our themes. Into them the prophets searched diligently as long as they lived, and when they went to heaven found the angels bending with unsated curiosity over the same immortal wonders. In these contemplations the apostles lived, labored, and rejoiced. Out of them came their sermons, epistles, and triumphs. Compared with these, the speculations and reasonings of men are but as the toys of childhood. Our subjects never wear out or grow stale. Exhaustless in depth and variety, earth is too narrow to contain and time too short to display them. "Draw all your cares and studies this way." Beware of human glosses—the tincture of a deceitful philosophy with its distinctions and refinements. Stick to your text. Neither add nor subtract. It is the word of God, and partakes of his own power and immortality.

But we may give the text a broader range. At present the world abounds with books. "Of making many books there is no end." What to read is now a difficult question, and ought to be a question of conscience with every man, especially a preacher. Many books in high repute are well calculated to undermine faith and principle; others to defile the imagination, debauch the taste; and yet others to demoralize both life and character. Solomon said, "Cease, my son, to hear the instruction that causeth to err from the words of knowledge." The tendency is to a very large liberty in the wrong direction. If, however, we give ourselves wholly to the functions and objects of our ministry, a sound discrimination will save us from any grievous departure. I sometimes fear that newspapers have largely displaced books, and that much of our reading is recreative and desultory—a mere knitting up of the odds and ends of current history. If this be occasional, it may be allowed. If this be all, it is dissipation—it is the napkin in which we wrap the talents we bury. Our reading, brethren, should be chiefly grave, solid, religious—furnishing pabulum for thought—brain-food, with variety enough to give bone and muscle and sinew and flesh and skin and bloom to the whole mental man, so that our sermons shall not be dry, ghastly skeletons, without even decent grave-clothes, but living forms instinct with energy, throbbing with emotion, breathing inspiration, and troubling the hearts of the people like the angel which came down upon the pool of Bethesda. Read, read, gather in, lay up—not for private capital, but for public use and benefit; circulate your treasures, edify the believers, confirm the disciples, preach many things in your exhortation, let doctrinal truth be the substratum of all your deliverances. Call me fogy if you will, yet I am free to say if we had more doctrine and less speculation, more facts from experience and less of argument for defense, fewer expounders and more exhorters, it would be better for the Church and religion. Many of us, brethren, will never write commentaries or preach big sermons, but we can tell our experience, when we were awakened; what we thought, felt, and feared; our doubts, struggles, and temptations; and by the time we reach the point where God converted us, if our own tears will let us see, we shall find the audience weeping too.

"Neglect not the gift that is in thee, which was given thee by prophecy, with the laying on of the hands of the presbytery." The term *gift* is indefinite, and is differently construed by those who have disputed concerning the channel through which ministerial grace is conveyed. The prelatical idea of virtue, transmitted by successional contact through a long line of episcopal ordinations, certainly finds no support in this text. If we allow a modicum of truth in the assumption, the gift came through the hands of the presbytery, and not from popes or bishops. But the fact is, the Church was more indebted to the gift than the gift to the Church. Whether we interpret the word to mean natural talent, or gracious endowment, or ministerial office, or disciplinary authority, two things are plain—first, that the action of the presbytery was a formal recognition and indorsement of Timothy's divine call; and second, that the purpose and plan of God were largely dependent upon his fidelity to the obligations imposed. The office of the ministry is the *gift* of Christ, and the gift is made not to magnify us, but for the benefit of others. What a motive to zeal, self-denial, and consecration! Even the extraordinary gifts conferred by the laying on of the apostle's hands were to be stirred up as fire under the embers, and fresh fuel laid on. The great law of increase holds here in all its force. Use gifts and have gifts. "To him that hath shall be given." A man's ministry ought to be cumulative in power and usefulness. The light that is in him should shine more and more till the sun of life melts away in the light of heaven.

"Meditate upon these things." It is not what we eat that

makes us strong, but what we digest. It is not what we gain that makes us rich, but what we save. It is not what we read that makes us wise, but what we remember, understand, and are able to appropriate. As the miner smelts the ore to separate the metal from extraneous substances, so do you fuse the thoughts of other men in your own furnace, and mold them in the mint of your own invention. Classify, systematize, keep all you know at command, ready for use. Avoid reveries, idle, aimless musings. Do not turn your thoughts loose to gambol like lambs in a pasture, but put them in harness and train them for service. Cultivate the power of attention. Let your will dominate all your mental forces, so that by your pleasure they shall fall into line like well-drilled soldiers at the word of command. "*Meditate* on these things." Revolve them frequently in your mind. Review the nature, reasons, and motives of your ministry. Never permit your labors to become mechanical and perfunctory. Bear in mind whose you are and whom you serve. Remember your conversion, your call to preach, your solemn covenant with Christ and the Church. Let the vows you utter this day survive the occasion, living echoes pealing over the solitude of your soul like the chimes of eternity. Make full proof of your ministry; let it be exhaustive of your utmost capacity for usefulness. Amid all the discouragements of your work, nerve and nourish your soul with thoughts of eternity and heaven. In the light of the world to come, the palace dwarfs into a hovel compared with the Church you serve, and the pulpit in which you stand is grander than the throne of empires. To us as preachers belongs the preëminence of being fellow-laborers with God Almighty in the work he most delights to do.

"Give thyself wholly to them." The work of the ministry is enough for any one man to do. Here are subjects to tax the mightiest intellect. Here are interests to fill the largest heart. Here are duties to appropriate every moment of time. Our Discipline says: "Be diligent, never be unemployed, never be triflingly employed." Keep your heart and conscience in the work. Seek your enjoyment in your duties. Do not pule and whine about *your* hardships and sacrifices. I confess to no little disgust with those men who are forever claiming the honors of martyrdom while eating the fat of the land—provided at the expense of others—receiving on every side the respect and homage of the people, and all forsooth because they are required to travel and preach the gospel. Ah! beloved, if we were stripped of the honors and emoluments of the ministry, the most of us would be poor indeed. There are inconveniences and discomforts, and so in every lot. I have seen lawyers without brief or client, doctors without fees or patients, merchants without trade or cash, farmers with blighted crops and blasted hopes. We have this advantage above all other men: that while our work is heavy and hard to do, like Jonathan's rod, there is honey at the end of it. "Go thou thy way till the end be, for thou shalt rest, and stand in thy lot at the end of the days."

"That thy profiting may appear to all." While I would enforce this clause with all the vigor of my convictions and my conscience, yet I think it right to interject a caution. In these days, when the rage for education is so active and universal, I think our young preachers are in danger of adopting false views and wrong methods on the pretext of better preparation for their work. Whatever may be expedient beforehand and as a preliminary, when a man has attained his majority, and joined Conference, and traveled usefully three or four years or more, he ought not to stop to go to college. Better struggle on where he is. Study and practice, books and preaching, and pastoral fidelity, will achieve grander results, both mental and ministerial, than the training of the schools.

After all, brethren, our great preachers—popularly so called—are not our most useful men. "Gaining knowledge is a good thing—saving souls is better." Reputation is often a hinderance rather than a help to the great ends of the ministry. Bishop Soule, addressing the Georgia Conference once, said: "Thank God, I never was a *popular* preacher!" Bascom told me that fame ruined him—that his life was a failure. In a solemn, trying hour, Munsey uttered the same sentiment in a conversation with me. It is safer to abide in your calling, and do the best you can under your circumstances. If God will, the ram's horn is more effective than the silver trumpet. Yet, with single eye to the work and its end, study to show yourselves approved *unto God*, and let your profiting appear in *all things*, as the margin has it. Let it be apparent to yourself as well as to others, and especially to others as well as yourself. Let it be so conspicuous that all the people shall see it, and bless God for it. A preacher who cannot teach and will not learn ought to be cashiered. A preacher who conceits that he is a genius, smart enough, and does not read, will not study, will soon gravitate to a level far below his estimate of himself. Then comes mortification and trouble. A preacher who culminates in his improvement by the time he is an elder, and then, year after year, deals out his old moldy, musty bread to the hungry people, is too lazy to be good and too worthless to be employed. Read, think, study, pray, work, improve. Bring out of your treasury things new and old. Carry your sermons in your heart rather than your memory. Fruit mellowed on its native stem, in the genial sunshine, is far more luscious than when prematurely pulled and made to ripen in the shade. Yonder artificial reservoir holds water, but the earth around is dry and dusty; no verdure springs; the element within stagnates, grows putrid, unfit for use. The bubbling spring wells up its crystal drops in unceasing flow, and as the living stream murmurs along, beauty and bloom mark its passage. Keep your mind at work, your invention active. Strive to be always fresh, if not new. With such a text-book as we have, there ought to be neither sterility nor sameness. "Take heed unto thyself, and unto the doctrine."

Take heed to thy spirit and character, thy experience and practice. Personal purity is indispensable to power, both with God and men. Learn to be thoughtful, lest impulse betray you to imprudence and miscarriage. In innumerable ways a minister may neutralize himself, degrade his holy office, and utterly forestall the great ends of his calling. Let every man "watch unto prayer." "Ye are my witnesses," said Jesus; "walk worthy of the vocation wherewith ye are called." Beware of pride and envy, jealousy and ambition. Hold yourself—your personal convenience and your worldly interest—in rigid subordination to the claims of Christ upon you. Preach a pure and spiritual religion, and illustrate it in your life and conversation, "giving no offense in any thing, that the ministry be not blamed."

"Take heed unto thyself, and unto the doctrine." This association of thoughts is not incidental, nor the mere outcome of previous teaching, but was suggested by the vital relation between right living and right faith. Personal purity in thought, word, and deed largely determines the soundness of a man's doctrinal views. Character and faith act and react upon each other. Timothy, as a minister, must mind what he taught the people. There must be neither overstatement nor hiding of the truth. The salvation of the people was no less dependent upon sound doctrine than his own upon fidelity in the delivery of it. By doctrine we are not to understand a single truth, but the whole system of truth as revealed, and the preacher must give to each the importance, the stress which belongs to it, in the order of divine teaching. Depravity, redemption, justification by faith, the witness of the Spirit, the new birth, holiness of heart and life, eternal life and eternal death—these, with all that they imply and involve as collateral—conviction for sin, repentance, faith, absolute submission, universal consecration to Christ—these must all be taught. They stand or fall together. They are all vitally related. There is an interdependence among them, and all together they make up the "word of faith" which we are to preach, "that we may present every man perfect in Christ Jesus."

"Continue in them." *Preach nothing else.* All other themes belong to the lecture-room, the platform. The pulpit is sacred to Christ and his religion. Begin your ministry with the truth as it is in Jesus. Let this be the staple and the burden of every discourse. Continue to proclaim him as the Lamb for sinners slain; know nothing but Christ and him crucified. "Preach him to all, and cry, in death, Behold the Lamb!" For in doing this, "thou shalt both save thyself and them that hear thee." O glorious consummation! happy end of toil and self-denial! vast recompense of reward for faithfulness to Christ and his people! What more can we ask? This is abounding grace. O Jesus, bring us to heaven with our families, our churches, and our people!

Revival Needed.*

NUMBER ONE.

NOW, brethren, as we have entered upon a new year, let us have, in the name of the Lord Jesus, a *revival* year—an epochal revival, wide deep, abiding. This is the supreme need of the times. Such revivals have occurred in the history of the Church. Our own country has been favored with them again and again. They rescued us from the flood of French infidelity in the beginning of this century. They determined the type of civilization as the tide of population rolled westward. The society, the tone, the sentiment, the institutions of every State have been molded by their power or marred by their absence. We are now in a crisis, socially and politically, where nothing but the power of God embodied and manifested in a general revival of religion can control and eliminate the elements of evil. The moral atmosphere is full of malaria. We need a Pentecostal revival—mighty, rushing—to purify it. Mere human agencies may modify, abate the trouble, and thus postpone the disastrous issue, but they cannot reform and redeem the nation. The catastrophe will come. Neither education nor legislation nor administration can do the needed work. They can help, coöperate, but they cannot rule the sea and stay its tidal-waves. We must have the

---

*These articles appeared in the *Wesleyan Christian Advocate* in the spring of 1883. They were also published in pamphlet form by the editor, the Rev. W. H. Potter, D.D. They express Bishop Pierce's views, feelings, and personal attitude on the important subject they discuss.—EDITOR.

power from on high. Local religious excitements will not meet the exigency. They are not to be ignored or underrated. They have done good and will do good. Like showers here and there in a general dry season, they save the land from a universal drought. Still, as a rule, the crops are a failure; there is scarcity and distress. So in the Church, a few conversions now and then, in this place and that, prevent utter stagnation, yet leave the great mass of the Church inert and unfruitful. Our cities, towns, counties, stations, and circuits all need a moral upheaval, a work of thorough regeneration. The Church itself needs purification, not so much by the expulsion of the disorderly (though this may be necessary) as by a higher standard of ethics in business, in personal habits, in social life, and a daily, conscious experience of the grace of God in the heart.

Dearly beloved, I am not croaking. I am not taking gloomy views of things. I am not a panic-maker. But I address myself to a felt want, to patent facts, to what every thinking man who loves his race knows as well as I. Any, every system of theology or morals which leaves the heart unchanged is a failure, a fraud, a snare. I believe in the Christian religion as the wisdom and power of God, the great salvation provided for all people. I believe in prayer and effort, faith and works. I believe a great revival of pure and undefiled religion is according to the will of God as revealed in the Scriptures, and that God will respond in power to the cry of faith and the agony of prayer.

Now, then, I beseech the preachers to set their hearts upon this general baptism of the Spirit. Arrange all your plans to this end. Adapt your sermons to this result. Enlist the laity in the activities of the Church. Give the women something to do for Christ and human salvation. Interest the children, and make the Sunday-schools auxiliary to the work. Do not be content with good meetings and partial, scanty results. Aim at great things, ask for great things, expect great things. "Open thy mouth wide," says the Lord, "and I will fill it." Jesus is able and willing, mighty to save. When Christ went down to heal the ruler's daughter he wrought a famous miracle on the way, but he rested not till he reached his destination. You, my brethren, are doing good in many ways, but this is incidental, a work by the way. Your first, chief business is the conversion of sinners. Let not the erection of churches divide your mind or delay your steps. The parsonage ought to be built, the collections all taken, every duty done, but do not stop short of a revival among your people. Good salary, comfortable surroundings, pleasant society—these are all desirable, yet they cannot compensate you for a barren ministry. Let nothing satisfy you but success. "Make full proof of your ministry." "Do the work of an evangelist." Travail in soul for those for whom Christ died. Hunt the lost sheep. Persuade the prodigal to return to his father's house. Pluck the brand from the burning. Be instant in season, out of season. By all means save some.

Let us all pray and work for another Pentecost. O that we too may count our converts by the thousand! Why not double our membership this year? Is this extravagant, presumptuous, absurd? Why so? You never saw the like? never read of it? never heard of it? Well, well, is that the measure of your faith? Are your hopes bounded by what you have seen, read, and heard? Is there nothing better? Are we to live forever at this poor, dying rate? God forbid! Is the Lord's ear heavy that he cannot hear? Is his hand shortened that he cannot save? His promise is given, let us prove him. His power is sufficient, let us test it. O that Zion may travail! Let every member go into his chamber and pray three times a day, "Thy kingdom come." Let every preacher ascend Mount Carmel, and pray till the little cloud rises from the sea, and then in the spirit of prophecy announce to the Church that he hears the sound of *abundance* of rain.

NUMBER TWO.

LET us stick to the text. I do not mean to disparage any plan or appliance for good. I bid them all Godspeed. But all human schemes and agencies, however wise and active, are slow in their effects. Time is a great element in their operation. There must be patience, repetition, long, hopeful waiting. These moral revolutions accumulate power gradually. One individual is brought over now, and then another, and for a spell—often a long one—the accession of force is scarcely appreciable. In most cases public sentiment is of tardy growth; and yet without its backing law is feeble, admininistration hampered; wisdom utters her voice—even cries aloud in the streets—but rallies no audience; truth itinerates, seeking help and finding none; men are afraid of each other; and society waits to see the drift. Education might help to more intelligent voting, but this will be a small gain as long as bribery can speculate on human corruption. Illiteracy is a sad thing, greatly to be deplored, and depravity in high places may cajole and betray its unfortunate subjects, to the great damage of the country; but if there were a school in every house, and every man, woman, and child could read and write, yet without the restraints of faith and conscience, the fear of God and the dread of eternal retribution, I doubt if our social and political condition would be at all improved. Masses of people, to do right, must have religion—ay, not to mince the truth, I mean the religion of the gospel of Jesus. No other system has power to conquer, convert, renew.

Now, the point is this: The world is dying, we are all passing away, we cannot afford to wait on the slow processes of amelioration. Culture, enlightenment, civilization, social amenities may make the world better-looking—may veneer depravity, hide many ugly spots—but refinement is not regeneration. We must be born again—remolded by the Power that created us, and which alone can raise us from the death of sin or the bondage of the grave. What we want is a general revival—a great religious excitement—which shall suddenly and powerfully arrest a whole community of people, and graciously convert a great multitude in a very few days. I have seen thousands subdued into reverence and awe, even when they refused to yield to God. I have seen the moral character of a county reformed by a single camp-meeting. I have seen a solemn spell descend and abide upon a city population for days together. Stores were closed, the hammer was laid down, saloons without a customer, diversions and amusements all forgotten, and the Church and religion occupied every mind, engaged every tongue, and appropriated all the time. The Lord added daily to the Church, so mightily grew the word of God and prevailed. All of our cities and towns need the shock of one of these moral earthquakes to startle the guilty and send them affrighted and penitent to the altar of God. Every Church in the land needs a stirring up, a more genial current of life, a freer, more vigorous action. We hear a great deal about the resources and capabilities of the country, and there is a cry for capital and enterprise to develop our industries.

I sympathize with these ideas of work and progress. There are elements of latent power in the Church. These concern me still more. Indeed, a general awakening in both directions would be a blessing. The two might harmonize and mutually serve each other Diligent in business, fervent in spirit. They are not incompatible; the union of the two is the divine order—serving the Lord in both.

We hear much nowadays about "intense farming." I like the phrase. It is suggestive of thorough work, of high fertilization, of immense results. The planters generally have relied on superficial plowing in an impoverished soil with homeopathic manuring. They cover a large area, and with great labor reap an imperfect and scanty crop. One acre rightly managed would produce as much as ten the way things go on. Just so in the Church. We are expending a world of work and realizing a very partial income of souls. We multiply our prayers, but there is an awful disproportion between their numbers and the answers we get. We hold protracted services, and solace ourselves with a very few conversions out of large congregations. We talk of prosperous years, when the only evidence of life and growth is in the churches built or repaired, parsonages bought or refurnished, better pay, and larger collections. These things are useful, desirable, and take rank among what we call good works; but they fall far short of the great ends of the gospel ministry and of Church organization. Sure as we live, there is something wrong among us, something wanting. Our ideas need to be rectified, enlarged; our methods relieved of their monotony, and made more inspiring. Our faith must take a stronger grasp on the promises and power of God. Our zeal for the salvation of souls, instead of laying in our hearts like embers burned in ashes, must become a consuming fire. We must pile on fuel by thought and faith, and desire and prayers, till the zeal of God's house shall eat us up. We must muse on these things till the fire kindles, and our spirits are all ablaze, and our very bones crackle in the flame. Get out of the old ruts, brethren; they are full of holes, and you must needs go slow. There is smooth, hard ground on either side. If not room to travel on parallel lines, do as in driving in buggies—straddle the hinderances, and make better time and easier work. *Intense religion* is the desideratum now—a holy, consecrated ministry, a spiritual membership, and all praying, working, and looking for the conversion of the world. Our Lord's vineyard has been yielding a very slender revenue—hardly paying expenses—especially in Christian lands. We must prune the vines, dig about the roots, enrich, spade deep, do thorough work, and trust God for the early and the latter rains. May he grant us this year a vintage of the grapes of Eschol!

NUMBER THREE.

The more I think and pray, and the more I hear from the presiding elders and preachers as to the general outlook among the churches, the more hopeful I grow. The signs are glowing; the clouds are big with mercy; the winter is over and gone; the birds are singing, the trees are budding. All nature is reviving. Let the slumbering churches all awake. Let every preacher become an evangelist. Stir up all the elements of spiritual life. We need activity in every department—more faith, more prayer, more zeal for souls, an enlarged liberality. Do not wait for the season of protracted services. Begin at once. "The set time to favor Zion" is now. Right views and sympathies and affections, all embodied in proper effort, will determine the event, its power and duration.

But let us thoroughly understand what we are about, what we propose to accomplish. I heard my father once in a sermon make a distinction between a religious revival and a revival of religion. I do not mean to philosophize by way of explaining, but simply state facts with which we are all,

alas! too familiar. There may be an excitement gotten up
by manipulation, by sensational oratory, by dramatic scenes
glowingly described; and for a time the people seem to be
all tenderness and sensibility. There may be tears and
shouts and ecstasies, a weeping congregation, a crowded
altar, and many accessions to the membership; yet it turns
out to have been a mere church festival, pleasant enough,
but unprofitable—like a fine shower in a droughty season
followed by a dry, hot wind. The ground was too hard to
absorb, and the surface moisture was all swept away by the
heat and the wind. In these revivals, so called, conviction
was superficial, repentance shallow, and reformation partial
and short-lived. There was no improvement in the Church
itself. The apparent life—so full of promise as to recovery
—health, and vigor was simply a galvanic result; machinery at work on an automaton—no blood or pulse or heart;
mechanical force mimicking vital power. I have seen the
"very elect" deceived by it. A genuine revival contains
in itself and manifests intrinsic evidence of its divine origin; but the true test of its moral value is in the future
conduct and character of its subjects. This "tree is known
by its fruits." I steadfastly believe a Christian man may
fall from grace; but I have great confidence that a true
convert will not. People may be impressed, but not decided; convinced, but not converted; reformed, but not renewed; in the Church, but out of Christ; profess religion,
but love the world as fondly, passionately as the gayest dev-
otee or the covetous idolater. A profession of religion ought
to be the guarantee of all that is true, pure, honest, lovely,
and of good report—the highest type of citizenship, the
bond and pledge of patriotism, philanthropy, fidelity to
God and man. We hear of great prosperity in the Church
now and then—many additions here and there—but the
missionary treasury is not the beneficiary of these swelling

numbers. Nothing is helped but the annual census. The local churches are not improved in tone, habits, or attention to duty. The family altar lies waste, without sacrifice or fire.

The man returns not from business or festal ceremony to "bless his household." The woman forgets her closet and her children in her pursuit of pleasure and diversion. The preacher tries to be happy if, at long intervals, he may interject a *good* meeting anywhere in a series of dry, dull, insipid services. This "poor, dying rate" holds on. Hosannas languish, and the dreary, barren Church mourns not. This order of living is accepted as inseparable from our imperfect state, and the only hope of relief is that another religious picnic will come round after awhile. Like those churches that observe Lent—religious by canon and rubric once a year for a few days, all the rest surrendered to the world, the flesh, and the devil; "Lent" a sham, and a snare, and a delusion to those who dance and dissipate up to midnight before it begins, and resume by sunrise when it ends—so we Methodists, I am sorry to say, seem to be very earnest and active and happy during a "religious revival;" but the "morning cloud" and the "early dew" tell the rest of the story.

I do not want to be misunderstood. I am working for a *revival of religion:* a religion that converts people, renews them in the spirit of their minds, creates them anew in Christ Jesus, delivers from the bondage of sin, injects new ideas—purer, better than the old—brings them out of the world, and separates them unto Christ; a religion that redeems a man from all sin, and sets him on holy living, on self-denial, painstaking, circumspection, and prayer; that imbues his spirit with love, seasons his conversation with grace, and makes him a witness for the truth as it is in Jesus—an example, a model, an Israelite without guile or hypocrisy or wavering. In a word, let us have in the name of the Lord a revival (there is some of it in the Church visible to all—much that is latent, smothered, needing air) of pure and undefiled religion—a sin-killing, sin-hating, sin-forsaking, debt-paying, God-serving, man-loving religion; a religion that makes the Church liberal; that lifts up the fallen drunkard, sets him upright on his feet, makes and keeps him sober; that crucifies the pride of life, the lust of the eye, and the lust of the flesh; roots out the love of the world, and fills the soul with the love of the Father; a consistent, steadfast, uncompromising religion, always abounding in the work of the Lord.

The strength of the Church is not to be determined by a *per capita* count, but by experience and practice, character, and social and business reputation. Do not make haste, brethren, to receive into full fellowship. Abide by the Discipline. Heed its instructions. Large, hasty, undiscriminating accessions may give you eclat as a revivalist, but the "falling away" will discount your ministry, and wring your heart with mortification. Let every member be an increment of moral force—one not only to be counted, but relied upon; a palm-tree, tall and fruitful; a cedar of Lebanon, strong, ever green, fat, and flourishing even down to old age. O for a soul-saving revival of the Christian religion! a pure, consecrated ministry! a holy, spiritual Church, without spot, or wrinkle, or any such thing! The Bridegroom cometh, let the virgin bride make herself ready; and may we all be worthy to go in to the marriage of the Lamb!

NUMBER FOUR.

In a faithful, spiritual Church a revival is the natural order, the appropriate and habitual moral condition. Every gathering together of the people in religious service ought to be signalized by some special token of the divine presence and blessing—sometimes the spirit of praise and rejoicing among them that believe; sometimes awakening, convicting power among the irreligious; sometimes the conversion of one or more penitents. Again, all of these events concur; the Church is happy, sinners tremble and yield, and mourners pass out of darkness into marvelous light. These results characterized Methodism for well-nigh a century. The preacher and the people expected something to be done every time they met in worship. God honored their faith in the communications of his grace. Past history would be repeated on a larger, grander scale in these days if the Church travailed in spirit as once she did. My conviction is that if the Church could be rallied in her desires and efforts, believed in prophecy and promise as she ought, would rise above the limitations of her own experience—the facts that oppose and discourage present large expectations—revivals would be more frequent, numerous, powerful, and rapid in issues than ever before. I verily believe these displays of divine grace will increase till a general revival sweeps over the habitable globe. Pentecost was more than a fact; it was a type and a model. May I say it reverently, a specimen of what God could do by the preaching of the word and of the way he proposed to work. The Church, all along, has unfortunately pared down her expectations to a much smaller scale. Let us enlarge our ideas, and look abroad upon the whole valley of dry bones, and in response to the skeptical question, "Can these dry bones live?" cry in the fullness of faith: "O ye dry bones, hear the word of the Lord, Come from the four winds, O breath, and breathe upon these slain, that they may live!" Our God has infinite resources. O that the Church would trust him and "prove him!" God of grace, confound the philosophy of men, surprise the faith of the Church, reveal thy glory in human salvation.

The Spirit of God is not bound by methods. The wind bloweth where it listeth. I have seen revivals of several types, and yet, judged by their fruits, all genuine. There was a revival in Augusta in 1832, beginning in May and running through the year. It was not a sweeping flood, but a steady rain. It had power enough to work and hold the congregation all the time. The regular order of service was maintained. Only one extra prayer-meeting was set up, and that upon a vacant night. Rarely more than fifteen penitents at the altar. These were invited to all the social meetings, and conversions occurred at every service, private and public. The interest never flagged. At the winding up of the year the Church-record showed a gain of two hundred. Some of them remain to this day; some have fallen asleep; very few fell away. In 1837 an old dead church in Hancock by special effort was raised to life again. A great revival ensued. Out of it there sprung up a new church seven miles distant, which was in a state of revival for years. Though enfeebled by deaths and removals, it still lives, a strong appointment. I have just read that in Harrison county, Kentucky, a revival has been going on for two years, and shows no signs of exhaustion or decline. Such cases might be multiplied—ought to be, and, I devoutly pray, will be.

I will state another case for encouragement and for example. In 1846 Rev. C. W. Key was on the Sparta Circuit. It was a year of very general prosperity in the Conference. Revival power came down and rested upon every appointment. Brother Key had no ministerial help except when I got home from the district to *rest* a day or two. The whole circuit was on fire. The preacher divided himself out as best he could, but with all his zeal he could be only in one place at a time. Now, then, what? Close up? Send the people away? Drive the doves from the windows? No, no! Each church took charge of itself. The brethren went to work, and lay labor was blessed along with the clerical. No neighborhood suffered for lack of service. My brother and comrade has gone, but I hope to meet him again, and talk over the very things about which I am writing.

I am sorry that revivals, as a rule, have become exceptional phases of Church life. I believe in special seasons—periodical meetings, if you like—and think them scriptural, but prefer an abiding, aggressive spirit, full of faith in the Holy Ghost, working in hope, and reaching results in every service. The thing is possible; it can be done; I have seen it. The recital of just such facts makes up a long, large paragraph in our Church history. A Church thus alive, thus at work, "prepares the way of the Lord." When he comes there is no confusion or surprise, no girding of the loins or trimming of lamps. All are ready. The army is in line of battle, fully equipped, thoroughly furnished, eager for fight, and confident of victory. O what wonders we would achieve! "They that know the Lord shall be strong and do exploits." True, the work to be done is difficult. The world is wicked and defiant, the Church is largely drowsy and inert; but moral power is not to be measured by numbers. The faithful few may win like Gideon's three hundred. Faith in God and truth may substitute a host. Cease to argue and speculate and theorize. These moods of thought engender doubt. They repress courage, forestall enterprise, let slip opportunity, and multiply the very difficulties in the presence of which you stand discouraged. Never mind the past or the present, "only believe." Pray and trust.

> Something yet can do the deed,
> And that blessed something much we need.

The Spirit, the rushing wind, the earthquake, the fire, and then "the still small voice;" conviction, alarm terror, the pains of hell—all these are needed. The Spirit can bring them about. God, in a certain sense, may not be in them, but they herald his approach and make him welcome when he comes. These still, solemn, tearless, voiceless meetings I confess I do not prefer. I like the rocking of the battlements, the groundswell, the sea and the waves roaring, the Church in awe and travail, sinners confounded, and all waiting in breathless terror and hope for Jesus to wake and speak, "Peace, be still." I like the calm that follows.

NUMBER FIVE.

HAVING assurances that these letters have done good and will continue to operate on many minds and hearts, I send you another.

There are three things indispensable to the great end I am aiming at—the revival of the Church and the salvation of the country; ay, let us stretch our desires and our faith to the Bible measure, the conversion of the world.

First, a more thorough, active, earnest consecration of the ministry. I write freely to my brethren, because I know them and love them. I know their virtues and their faults, and am fully persuaded that comparatively few of them realize their responsibilities and functions. They mean right, behave well, and would be unspeakably happy if the pleasure of the Lord prospered in their hands; but the short-coming is, they are not unspeakably miserable when the Church is stagnant, and there is no aggression upon the world. They are not indifferent; by no means. They see and regret their inefficiency; but their hearts do not break with grief, their heads are not a fountain of waters, their eyes are not red with weeping. A year's labor has been barren of results. It is very, very sad, but they manage to bear it. There is no special humiliation. They have failed to cast the devil out, but there is no more fasting and prayer in preparation for another encounter. Nay, they undertake to explain away the failure so as to exculpate themselves. They offset utter defeat in the main enterprise by magnifying some little incidental success. Nobody was converted, but they bought an organ. There was no increase, but they left the Church in peace. There was no revival, but they brought up the collections. O brethren, brethren, this will never do! These things are no proof of your apostleship. You were called to convert sinners. This first, last, paramount. All other things are mere accompaniments—good, proper, well enough in their place and order, but to a right-minded minister a very inadequate substitute for the conversion of sinners. I have seen a preacher conscious of failure, and deeply deploring it, casting about for some alleviation of the painful fact. Like the woman who lost the piece of silver, he would sweep the house and sift the pile to find some crumb of comfort. The tendency of such a mood of mind is, in self-defense, to magnify subordinate things, and of course to put the main thing comparatively in the background. False standards are set up, and the reasonings and conclusions of the man are unsafe and misleading. I fear that the trend of the whole Church is in the wrong direction. Well satisfied, as we all are, that we are lacking in spirituality and power, yet to gratify denominational pride, and parade our progress and resources, we are laying great stress on statistics. Our glory is not good. The Church is not intended to represent coin, but souls. What though our wealth increases? the very knowledge of it may prove a snare. What though we outstrip all competitors in architecture, taste, money, position, power, if we have not religion enough to rid us of vanity and self-conceit, and to crucify us unto the world?

Now and then I meet with a preacher who seems lubricated with delight. His face glows, he rubs his hands with satisfaction, his tongue is as the pen of a ready writer as he tells of the new house of worship or the reconstructed old one, or the best parsonage in the Conference. "My people are generous, liberal. O we are having a good time!" "Well, brother, have you had a revival among your people?" The inspiration is all gone, and a reluctant "No" drawls from his unwilling lips. "Any conversions?" "No; but the Sunday-school is full." "Do your people pray in their families? Do they attend your social meetings? Can the grace of God be seen in their lives?" "Well, no; but they are clever and kind; and our Sunday congregations are fine, especially in the morning." So it goes. Like priest, like people; like people, like priest—deceiving and being deceived. All working on the human line rather than the divine. Now, mind, I do not say these works of which you brag, on which you lean, are wrong. Not at all. They may be; that depends on motive. I hope for the best, but much fear that many enterprises are projected, much money lavished, not to glorify God, not to promote religion, but in the spirit of rivalry to outstrip others, to indulge social pride, or to dignify our town. Let that pass. We will not judge. Of this I am sure: they are, or ought to be, very insufficient sources of comfort to a consecrated minister or a spiritual member. The plain truth is, your Church is not in good condition, not doing well, is not realizing her privilege, fulfilling her mission, unless it can be said of her—frequently, commonly—this and that man was born in her.

Now, brother preacher, I am dealing with you. I have great faith in you: great hopes of you. Your heart is right, but you are often under trial, through stress of weather liable to go off on a tangent. These catch-words, *new departure*, may well make us pause. There is no magic in them, and where they fetch up neither you nor I can tell.

Let us stick to the landmarks. Inquire "for the old paths, and walk therein." You are called of God to preach; to enlighten, convince, persuade men to be reconciled to God; to seek and save the lost; to turn people from the error of their ways to the wisdom of the just; to edify the Church, and to add to her "such as shall be saved." Look steadily to this end, and work for it. Get your mind and heart saturated with the idea, the conviction, that your sole business is to save men. Let this be your aim, rule, and goal. There must be a definite object in order to intense zeal. Vague ideas, loose plans, will evaporate all your enthusiasm. Your earnestness will be a fitful, transient paroxysm unless you keep in view the grandeur and glory of your calling. Think often of standing in the presence of the Master, surrounded by a multitude of the redeemed whom you persuaded to go with you to heaven, and let the vision inspire you, give tenacity to your purpose and wings to your zeal. Go forth weeping. Tears become you, and grief is just, bearing precious seed. Sow in the morning, and in the evening hold not thy hand; sow on the highway, where thorns and thistles grow; on the barren rocks; in season, out of season. The germ of life is in every grain; the harvest will come, and you will return bringing your sheaves with you. Travail in sympathy with Christ, and cry for souls. You never got religion while you felt that you could live without it; and you will never have a great revival till your heart breaks with longing. "Give me Scotland, or I die!" said Knox to God. "Lord, save my people, or *I* perish!" must be your prayer morning, noon, and night. O ye servants of the Most High, agonize, agonize!

NUMBER SIX.

In my last letter I stated that as preliminary to a great awakening three things were indispensable. First, a more thorough consecration of the ministry to the one special work of saving souls. Now I come to the consideration of the second prerequisite—the outpouring of the Spirit upon the churches. This, of itself, would be, in its proper primary sense, a revival. The Church needs this on her own account. She is not filled with the Spirit as she ought to be, and must be to realize the gospel ideal as to character and experience, and to carry out her mission to the world. Many members of the Church have never been converted at all. They know nothing, experimentally, of a sin-pardoning God. A new heart is to them a vague, mystic term. They have never received "the white stone" with the name written thereon which no man can read but he to whom it is given. There are secrets in religion revealed only in personal consciousness. There is no other medium through which even the Spirit can interpret. To all this inner life and its sweet private communion with God many bearing the Saviour's name are utter strangers. To bring all these outer-court worshipers into the holiest of all by the new and living way would relieve the friction of our machinery, take off the brakes, diminish the dead load, and add immensely to the propelling power—if not by the accretion of force, certainly by freedom of motion. I have seen an overloaded engine on a railroad, on an up-grade, of a frosty morning revolve its driving-wheels with tremendous rapidity, and yet make no progress. The power was there, but the conditions were unfavorable. Time is lost, steam wasted, before momentum can come in as a factor in the difficulty. There is a vast deal of power in the Church, not latent exactly, but embarrassed. There is so much *vis inertiæ*, dead weight, indisposition to move or to be moved—so much worldliness to overcome—that time and labor are lost in making a start. And then, the movement is not natural—life acting of itself—but artificial, forced, always ready and willing to stop. Thus many of our protracted meetings exhaust preacher and people before there is a tear or sigh, a shout or an amen, to inspire hope or cheer the workers to further trial. As a pastor, I always relied on the regular services, and noticed the signs. When the angel of the covenant came down and troubled the waters, when the breath of the Lord swept over the valley, when the hopeful shower fell upon the fallow ground which I had scratched over, then I put in special effort, plowed deeper, and rallied the Church for the sowing and the reaping.

And here I make two remarks—the conclusions reached from a varied experience and close observation. First, I have not much faith in those revivals that are "gotten up." "Get up a revival" is a phrase I do not like, and never use. Brethren appoint "revival meetings." If this were the language of faith and assurance, and not of hope and experiment, very well. Nevertheless, better say, "If the Lord will." You certainly cannot command it; and if it do not "come down" from the Lord, what you "get up" will be more or less, to you and the people, a delusion and a snare. Do not try to regulate the meeting by an iron-clad programme. "Dare not set your God a time." Leave the Spirit free. Do not draw your watch on him, and tell him to suspend, "for the time is out." Without the Spirit you can do nothing; and remember that you are neither his counselor nor guide. Honor and glorify the Spirit even as you do the Son and the Father.

The second remark is that when the spirit of self-inspection and inquiry is among the people, when they that fear the Lord speak one to another, when the congregation grows attentive and serious and tender, and the more spiritual yearn and fast and pray more fervently than usual, then is the time. God signals the Church to arise and march to glorious victory. Now, do not dishonor God's grace and power, his heart or his hand, by any form or measure of distrust. Rely upon him, and go forward. Do not send off for any human help. Let the revivalists alone. Do your own work. God and you and the Church can perform the duty of the hour. Do not divide public attention by bringing in a strange preacher. Do not dilute the faith of the Church by the suggestion of any other help than the divine. Hold the public mind to one line of thought and action. Rule out all division and diversion. Be sober, reverent; obey the Spirit. Humility, faith, zeal, all divinely directed and sanctified, will meet the emergency. To God be all the glory. On these views I have acted in my ministerial life, and never departed from them in any case on any account without hurt and damage to me and the work. "As thy day, so shall thy strength be," is just as true in a revival as any other trial. But this is an episode—relevant, yet away from the drift of this letter.

The Church needs a revival for the salvation of her own unregenerate members. This is true of all the churches. We all have some hard cases unconverted and unreformed; baptized sinners they are. Men of business, overcharged with the cares of this life, making haste to be rich; society women, devotees to etiquette and fashion, who would rather grieve the Spirit than to provoke unfriendly criticism; young people, gay and giddy, who have never actually renounced the pomp and vanities of the world. O beloved, there is a great work to be done *in* the Church! Judgment must begin at the house of God. What then? Must the revival halt and tarry till all these are washed and justified? Nay, verily. Alas for the world of sinners if this be so! Yet, what a letting out of the waters of life there would be if all these obstructions could be removed. The current would be strong and deep enough to float the world. But we must take things as they are, and do the most and best we can. The precious and the vile have always been strangely mixed. The wheat and the tares will grow together till the harvest. There is religion in the Church of the best kind—saints of God, holy people. Not a few, blessed be God. The number grows. Our Elijahs who are mourning and begging to die because they are left alone are all mistaken. Our God has a people upon the earth, and he counts them by the thousand, and he is adding to their number daily. I trust he will duplicate the whole census this year. At any rate, there is religion enough in the Church, if we can get it organized and at·work, to annex half the world to Christ's kingdom before next New-year's-day. I say half the world. God forgive me! Why not say all of it? Why not? Who can give a satisfactory reason? Anybody can suggest difficulties, urge improbabilities, make out a formidable case of unfavorable antecedents, of current opposition, of hoary hinderances. Yes; but is "any thing too hard for the Lord?" Difficulties are nothing to Israel's God, and they ought to be nothing to Israel's faith. Great Head of the Church, help them that believe to measure up to the height of the grand conception of a world redeemed! "The world for Christ" ought to be the motto of every Christian, the circle of his thoughts, the object of his desire, the measure of his faith, and the goal of his efforts.

In the meantime, let the Church get ready for the battle and the pæan. We cannot assemble in one place, as did the first disciples, but we may have one mind and one heart. Morning, noon, and night, from every sanctuary and closet and family altar, let the cry ring, "Thy kingdom come!" Let every preacher seek the power from on high. Let him go to his people freighted with the fullness of the blessing of the gospel of Christ. Let the heart of every church break with the longing. "Arm of the Lord, awake! Send now prosperity." Give the baptism of fire, the Pentecostal power. "Revive thy work," and let it grow and spread and endure till its line has gone through all the earth and its power to the end of the world. Let all the people say, Amen!

NUMBER SEVEN.

I DO not wish to worry your readers or to monopolize your columns. Perhaps I have written enough on one line, and yet I venture a closing letter.

I wish the Church papers had copied all my epistles; for they were intended for all the Conferences and all our people. The etiquette of the editorial code I do not well understand, and certainly do not mean to criticise or complain; but I would have been glad to have had the eye of all the churches. My sole object has been to do good—to call the attention of all the ministry and membership to the work that must be done to save our country and hasten the conversion of the world.

Tidings reach me through the press and by private letters of increased thought, anxiety, and effort almost everywhere. Indeed, revivals are in progress in many places. An unusual number of conversions have transpired at the stated services of the sanctuary. A presiding elder writes me that he had one at a way-side appointment as he passed from one quarterly meeting to another. All these things are omens of good—the herald-drops of a coming shower. The Master is walking among the golden candlesticks. The sound of his steps is heard in the streets, on the highways, and a gathering multitude are following after him. The signs are propitious, full of promise; but, brethren, the work of preparation is only begun. The way of the Lord is not ready. The mountains are not dug down, nor the valleys filled up, nor the rivers bridged. Our iniquities still separate between us and our God, and they obstruct his approach. Sins are to be confessed, deplored, forsaken—a huge mass of worldliness to be cast out. The Church must come up to a higher plane of moral living and a deeper experience of the things of the Spirit. There must be a fuller consecration, a clean-cut separation from folly and sin, a hungering and thirsting after righteousness. The burden of the Lord must come upon us till we pray "with groanings that cannot be uttered." Jesus travailed in spirit; so must we. We must not "despise the day of small and feeble things," nor yet be satisfied with partial results. When the work begins we must not halt nor relax. What God gives must be thankfully received, and made the ground of encouragement to ask for more. What he does in the way of saving sinners is proof of will and power, expressions of his heart, specimens of his handiwork. "He fainteth not, neither is weary." Work does not fatigue the Lord, nor does expenditure exhaust him. Let us test him, "prove him." Faith honors God. He loves to respond to it. The angels in heaven rejoice over "one sinner that repenteth;" so ought the Church. But let not one or a few fill the measure of our desires, or suspend our prayers and labors as though our work was done, our responsibility at an end. Let our faith be modeled after that gracious declaration of Christ: "Be it unto thee even as thou wilt." Again: "Ask what thou wilt, and it shall be done unto thee." What a charter of privilege is here! How free and broad! No limit but the resources of the Infinite, the Eternal, the Almighty. Unbelief may bar any mighty work. A timid, faltering faith may realize but little; but bold, strong, heroic faith can abolish all boundaries save the truth and power of God.

O for the faith that removes mountains, plucks up trees, and "laughs at impossibilities!" The prayer of the apostles—"Lord, increase our faith!"—teaches two great lessons: That we are not equal to our duties without more, and that certain necessary things cannot be done at all unless our faith is assimilated in kind and measure to the faith God has in himself. "Have *the* faith of God" is the marginal rendering. Lord help us to understand and measure up to the grandest possibilities of experience and achievements!

In the great work to be done the Church must come to the help of the ministry. We need the hearty, active coöperation of the laity—their sympathy, encouragement, and backing. They must be like-minded, and so naturally care for the Church and the state of the world. Private letters from various Conferences assure me of a great awakening among the people—more inquiry, more prayer, more expectation. As in nature, so in grace. Spring is at hand. The softened air, the early flowers, the swelling buds, all tell us that winter is over and gone. The luxuriant fullness of bloom and foliage must tarry yet awhile. There is an established order. Things are most beautiful and safest in their season. Nature is at work in the clouds, the atmosphere, and the soil—all preparatory. In due time verdure and growth and fruitfulness will come. So in the Church —not much visible yet, but the leaven is at work. There is hunger, longing, and supplication. God's hidden ones are upon their knees; humble hearts are pleading for the power from on high. The closet, the chamber, the field, the forest are wet with tears and vocal with prayer. Salvation is a process in individuals and in society. "The vision is for an appointed time, but it shall come, and will not tarry."

To illustrate what is going on, let me give a few extracts from a private letter. The writer is a plain country woman, away from the world's highways, with nothing in her environments to excite or inspire—shut up to her Bible, her *Advocate*, and her closet. See how she thinks, how she feels, how she prays. She thanks God that in my letters I have put into words the yearnings of her soul. She says the Lord has recently "enlarged her heart;" and she gives me her daily prayer. I give a mere synopsis, the substance. She begins with the Lord's Prayer; then she prays for the extension of the Redeemer's kingdom; for freedom from sin;. harmony with the Spirit; for her pastor and the circuit; her presiding elder and the district; the North Georgia Conference, the South Georgia, the Florida, the North Carolina, the South Carolina, the Missouri, the Arkansas, the Texas Conferences; for Mexico, China, Brazil. She mentions the missionaries by *name*. She prays for the Bishops and their work; for the Church, and for the heathen, that they may hear of Jesus and accept him. Now, all this is very simple, yet very broad and evangelical. The range shows thought, knowledge, heart, hope, faith, love. She reads the Church papers, knows what is going on, is interested, and is helping all she can. I have condensed her account very much; but I wish to add, her prayers are specific, definite—not vague and general, a tissue of words. Her heart articulates the sentences. She pleads her cause —is suing the Lord upon his own bond. Well, what of it all? Why, just this: This is one case out of many. In nooks and corners, in obscure retreats, among men and women, the work of the Lord is preparing. The simple, the babes in Christ, the ignorant if you will—who have no better sense than to believe every word that God hath spoken—are crying unto him day and night. Will the Lord not hear and come? Yea, verily; and speedily. Amen! Moreover, this case is exemplary. What she is doing all might do; as she feels and prays, so might all. And if all, what power in the pulpit, in the means of grace, among the people! I commend her intelligence, her broad views, her devout sympathies, her comprehensive prayers. She wrote to encourage me, and I tell this simple tale to stimulate and guide others. The great Head of the Church, hear her prayers and bless her example!

Let us all fall to prayer more and more. Fast on Friday before the quarterly meeting. Let every man fill his place. Crowd the prayer-meetings. Exhort one another. Put on the whole armor of God. Gird your loins. Take your staff in hand. Bind your sandals to your feet. Watch the cloud by day, the fire by night. Be ready when the Lord smites the waters of the river to go over and possess the land.

No civil reform, no change of dynasty, no revolution in government, no art, no science, no education can save us. Nothing but a heart-renewing revival out of heaven can do the work we need. O Lord, revive the Church and save the world!

NUMBER EIGHT.

For a reason which will be apparent I write another letter. If the local preachers can be actively enlisted, they might make an immense contribution to the work of general revival. As a class, they are willing coadjutors of the traveling ministry in the regular and especially in the extra services of the Church. But they can do more, and more effectually, upon another plan of operation. In the territory of some of our oldest circuits there are decayed, neglected churches that might be revived and reëstablished. There are waste places, out-of-the-way neighborhoods, in many counties where appointments might be made, Sunday-schools set up, societies organized, and whole communities brought to Christ. Within the corporate limits of our cities, on the suburbs, and near by, sometimes are large groups of people without the gospel. Local and social causes operate to bring about this state of things. Now, here are fields white to the harvest. They invite the reaper's sickle. As on a plantation the brier-patches are the richest spots and pay best for clearing, so in Church-work places that have been lying out unnoticed, overlooked, when once taken in, respond most promptly and most beautifully to care and attention. In other years, when I was a stationed preacher, I experimented on this line, and always with the best results.

Now, I respectfully suggest to my local brethren to hunt out these places, take charge of them, and go to work in the name of the Lord. Let each one select his field and deliver himself on it. Do not spread out, but concentrate. If there be material and promise, preach at the same place every Sunday. Two such appointments should be the maximum. Once a month preaching is slow work and of doubtful issue. Resolve to do, and let your plan be effective. Dearly beloved, you can do a great work. Just think of it! In our Church we have about *six* thousand local preachers. Suppose every man effectively employed outside of our regular work, what an increase of territory! How many new congregations, and how old and feeble churches would be strengthened! On this plan we might have six thousand more revivals and two or three hundred thousand more souls saved. Ponder these things, brethren. I know you desire to be useful. Get away from the fields if not exhausted by cultivation yet provided for, and go to work on new ground, or take in an old field and restore it. Let us turn Immanuel's land into a garden enriched by the river which makes glad the city of God. Men and brethren, help. Fulfill your ministry. Dig wells in the desert. Unseal fountains in the valleys. Multiply the green pastures. Fold the wandering sheep beside the still waters. "My soul breaks out in strong desire" for the coming kingdom. I long for the rushing wind, the descending fire, the Pentecostal count of souls. Let us all get ready—not by standing and waiting, but working, trusting, praying. "Fear not; behold, thy God will come, even God with a recompense. He will come and save you." Even so, come, Lord Jesus; cleanse Jerusalem, sanctify our homes, save our country.

THE END.

www.ingramcontent.com/pod-product-compliance
Lightning Source LLC
Chambersburg PA
CBHW032011220426
43664CB00006B/215